PENGUIN BOOKS
BLACK FRIDAY
THE TRUE STORY OF THE BOMBAY BOMB BLASTS

S. Hussain Zaidi is a journalist, specializing in crime reporting. He worked with the *Asian Age* and the *Indian Express* before joining *Mid-day* where he is currently a special correspondent. He is thirty-three, married, and lives in Bombay with his family.

GW00728121

black friday

THE TRUE STORY OF THE BOMBAY BOMB BLASTS

S. Hussain Zaidi

PENGUIN BOOKS

PENGUIN BOOKS

Published by the Penguin Group

Penguin Books India Pvt Ltd, 11 Community Centre, Panchsheel Park, New Delhi 110 017, India

Penguin Group (USA) Inc., 375 Hudson Street, New York, New York 10014, USA

Penguin Group (Canada), 10 Alcorn Avenue, Toronto, Ontario, Canada M4V 3B2 (a division of Pearson Penguin Canada Inc.)

Penguin Books Ltd, 80 Strand, London WC2R 0RL, England

Penguin Ireland, 25 St Stephen's Green, Dublin 2, Ireland (a division of Penguin Books Ltd)

Penguin Group (Australia), 250 Camberwell Road, Camberwell, Victoria 3124, Australia (a division of Pearson Australia Group Pty Ltd)

Penguin Group (NZ), cnr Airborne and Rosedale Road, Albany, Auckland 1310, New Zealand (a division of Pearson New Zealand Ltd)

Penguin Group (South Africa) (Pty) Ltd, 24 Sturdee Avenue, Rosebank, Johannesburg 2196, South Africa

Penguin Books Ltd, Registered Offices: 80 Strand, London WC2R 0RL, England

First published by Penguin Books India 2002

Copyright © S. Hussain Zaidi 2002

10 9 8 7 6 5 4 3

The views and opinions expressed in this book are the author's own and the facts are as reported by him which have been verified to the extent possible, and the publishers are not in any way liable for the same.

For sale in the Indian Subcontinent only

Typeset in Sabon by Mantra Virtual Services, New Delhi

Printed at Pauls Press, New Delhi

For my parents,
Ashfaq Hussain and Khatoon Jahan
Also for the little angels who brought so much joy into my life,
Kumail, Fatema, Narjis and Ammar

Contents

Acknowledgements

In early 1997 I submitted the plot of a novel to David Davidar. Mr Davidar wrote back saying that he felt I should write non-fiction first. The topics we discussed generally veered towards the Mafiosi and crime as I was a crime reporter of some experience. Then he surprised me by asking me to write a book on the bomb blasts of 1993.

Cakewalk, I thought to myself and took the plunge. I gave myself six weeks. That was when I thought as a journalist and not as a writer. And I hadn't reckoned with a full-time job as a journalist. The weeks soon turned to months, and as the seasons changed I realized that writing a book while fulfilling the many responsibilities of a Mumbai journalist was no joke.

Time, I needed time. Finally when the last chapter wound up and I sat back, I rediscovered that the world is full of generous people.

The most outstanding contribution to this book is CBI officer Raman Tyagi's. He has lived with the bomb blasts case for almost a decade now. His encyclopedic knowledge has helped me to unravel many of the mysteries of the conspiracy. Without him, this book could not have existed.

And what would I have done without the unstinted support and help of Vikram Chandra, who taught me the fine art of storytelling and kept my morale high? Vikram spared time to

x   acknowledgements

read and comment on the manuscript, and discussed the flow of the story at various levels. Thank you Vikram for making this book a reality.

I must thank my publisher David Davidar for being patient for four years. He never cracked the whip and for that I owe him a zillion thanks. My thanks also goes to my editors, Krishan Chopra, who was supportive and maintained that I could finish the book, and Sayoni Basu.

My special thanks to my *Mid-day* bosses Aakar Patel and Meenal Baghel who often gave me long rope so that I could finish the book. Meenal also helped in editing some chapters when we worked together at the *Indian Express*. I am grateful to Aakar for permission to use pictures from the *Mid-day* archives. *Mid-day* staffer Rashid Ansari was immensely helpful in locating and compiling pictures.

Thanks also to Saisuresh Sivaswamy with whom I had initiated this project. Had he not been there, I would have given up after the initial six weeks and said no to David.

My colleagues who were generous with their time and expertise were Shubha Sharma, Sunil Shivdasani of the Press Trust of India, Prafulla Marpakwar and Pranati Mehra of the *Indian Express*, Deepak Lokhande of *Mid-day*, Rehana Bastiwal of *Inquilab* and above all Sandeep Unnithan of *India Today* who made special efforts to trace some of the blasts victims and to whom I owe special thanks.

Friends who chipped in in their own way are Zia Abbas, Amit Rastogi and Ganesh Kumar.

I will always remain indebted to Shabana Hussain who was a pillar of strength throughout these four years. My grateful thanks to Paulette Roberts who looked at some of the chapters and took pains to edit them, and to Anuradha Tandon who pepped up my morale during dry spells.

And thanks to my very special woman, Velly Thevar, for everything, especially for making me realize that my approach to writing the book had to be stood on its head.

I extend my thanks to the Mumbai police force in general, and particularly to some distinguished police officers who contributed to the writing of this book. I received help from former Police Commissioner A.S. Samra, Joint Commissioner of Police (Retired) Y.C. Pawar, Commissioner of Railway Police Rakesh Maria, Deputy Inspector General Arup Patnaik, Inspector General Ulhas Joshi, Assistant Commissioner Nand Kumar Chougule, Inspector Pradeep Sharma, Assistant Police Inspector Srirang Nadgouda and many others.

I am also thankful to members of the Central Bureau of Investigation, especially Deputy Inspector General Satish Mathur of the Special Task Force, who read the manuscript at my request, to ensure it was factually correct in every detail.

The legal fraternity was also generous with its assistance. Advocates Abbas Kazmi, Niteen Pradhan, Majeed Memon, Farhana Shah and Subhash Kanse were an integral part of the this book. My special thanks to judge of the specially designated TADA court, Pramod Kode, who reassured and encouraged me. His support paved the way for the completion of the book.

All the characters and incidents in this book are real. Two names, however, have been changed. Badshah Khan is police witness no. 2 and according to the rulings of the judge who earlier presided over the case, J.N. Patel, his name should not be disclosed. It is he who selected this pseudonym. Catherine is also a pseudonym to protect the identity of the girl who spoke to Maria in the Al-Hussaini building and provided vital leads in the investigation.

I am thankful to several of the blasts accused who spoke to me on the condition of anonymity and gave me a proper perspective of the conspiracy. It is to the people who have helped and advised that the credit for what is accurate in these pages should be given. The mistakes are mine.

Author's Note

I always thought that it is easier to write non-fiction than fiction. After all, in non-fiction, you are dealing with a story that already exists, you don't have to invent the twists and turns. However, the past four years of researching and making sense of the mammoth jigsaw puzzle that is the Bombay serial blasts has shown me that there is more to it than that.

For *Black Friday* I did as much research as possible and met as many people as I could. Among my main sources were police documents, government records, confessional statements of the accused, CBI dossiers or newspaper reports of that time. The problem with the use of confessional statements as a source is that the veracity of the statement may be questioned, and it may be later stated that it was made under duress.

I have tried my best to be judicious to each character in the book, even those who tend to be seen in black and white in popular perception. I have tried to show things from their perspective as well, based on information gathered. All information is to the best of my knowledge; according to the information I have garnered in good faith and constitutes fair reporting to the best of my ability. Among the most contentious characters are Dawood Ibrahim and Tiger Memon, and here I have tried to get at the facts as far as possible. For example, though it is widely assumed that Dawood Ibrahim was responsible for the blasts, I have recorded only the evidence I have come across in the course of the investigations. As the case against Tiger Memon was much better recorded, the book reflects that.

Much of the story is culled from the case presented by the prosecution in the trial as the prime sources of information are the chargesheet in the case filed by the police and the statements of the accused. The prosecution did not intend to tell the entire story in their chargesheets; rather information was given in bits and pieces as far as was necessary for their case. More amplification was provided in some instances by the supplementary chargesheets filed by the CBI. It was left to a pen-pusher like me to make sense of those documents and narrate the story in all its drama and excitement.

This book is not a product of imagination. Where conversations have been recreated, I have tried to do this with reasonable verisimilitude given the situations and characters involved.

The manuscript has been checked for factual errors or incorrect reportage by my lawyer friends and officers from the CBI Special Task Force assigned to the bomb blasts case. However, if any mistakes remain, they are mine alone.

As a journalist I have learnt to raise questions and not to judge; that it is for the reader to decide. I have tried to follow the same principle in this book.

City Map with Bomb Sites

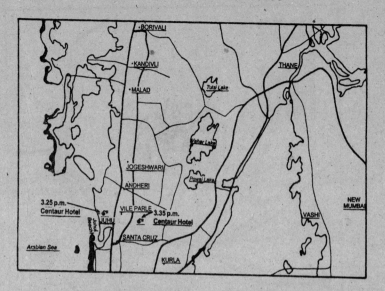

3.25 p.m.
Centaur Hotel

3.35 p.m.
Centaur Hotel

BORIVALI

KANDIVLI

MALAD

Tulsi Lake

THANE

Vehar Lake

JOGESHWARI

ANDHERI

Powai Lake

VILE PARLE

JUHU

Juhu Beach

SANTA CRUZ

Arabian Sea

KURLA

VASHI

NEW MUMBAI

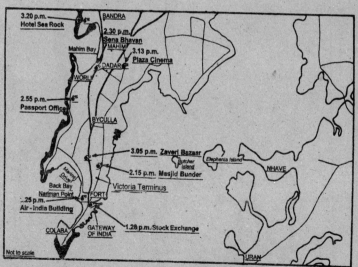

3.20 p.m.
Hotel Sea Rock

BANDRA

2.30 p.m.
Sena Bhavan

Mahim Bay

MAHIM

3.13 p.m.
Plaza Cinema

WORLI

DADAR

2.55 p.m.
Passport Office

BYCULLA

3.05 p.m. Zaveri Bazaar

Butcher Island

Elephanta Island

NHAVE

2.15 p.m. Masjid Bunder

Marine Drive

Victoria Terminus

Back Bay

Nariman Point

FORT

3.25 p.m.
Air - India Building

COLABA

GATEWAY
OF INDIA

1.28 p.m. Stock Exchange

URAN

Not to scale

Maps not to scale

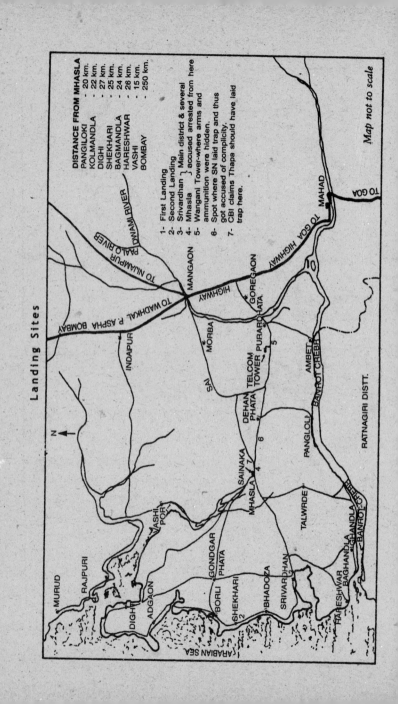

Landing Sites

DISTANCE FROM MHASLA
PANGILOKI — 20 km.
KOLMANDLA — 22 km.
DIGHI — 27 km.
SHEKHARI — 25 km.
BAGMANDLA — 24 km.
HARESHWAR — 26 km.
VASHI — 15 km.
BOMBAY — 250 km.

1- First Landing
2- Second Landing
3- Srivardhan ⎫ Main district & several
4- Mhasla ⎭ accused arrested from here
5- Wangani Tower–where arms and
   ammunition were hidden.
6- Spot where SN laid trap and thus
   got accused of complicity.
7- CBI claims Thapa should have laid
   trap here.

Map not to scale

Prologue

That the day could hold anything unusual was far from the minds of Bombay's thirteen million people when the city woke up to the start of another sweltering day on 12 March 1993. The monsoons were still three months away, but the temperature was already 32°C and the relative humidity seventy-two per cent. As office-goers rushed to work in the city's overcrowded trains, the heat was the favourite topic of conversation. Some discussed the national judo championship beginning that day for which nearly five hundred judokas had gathered.

A large percentage of the office-goers were headed for the Fort area in southern Bombay, the commercial heart of not only the city, but of the country as well. This small area, named after the British fort that once stood there, grew into the commercial hub early in the eighteenth century. Today it houses the headquarters of several banks, including the Reserve Bank of India (RBI), and large corporate houses besides the Bombay Stock Exchange (BSE), the oldest stock exchange in Asia and the largest in the country. Business worth hundreds of crores was transacted at the BSE every day.

Despite the heat, it was work as usual on Dalal Street, often called Bombay's Wall Street. The frangipani drooped visibly in the nearby St Thomas's Cathedral, but the prospect of the weekend had not yet cast its ennui over the milling crowds within the stock exchange. This Friday the trading ring on the BSE's first floor was packed with about 4,000 people. Friday was the day of *badla* trading, when residual shares are disposed of before the stock exchange shuts operations for the weekend.

At lunchtime Dalal Street, and the surrounding area, transforms itself into a food paradise, guaranteed to satisfy all stomachs and wallets. The choices range from mounds of yellow rice, dosas turning a crisp brown in the large griddle, *chaat*, heaps of noodles with white sauce, piping hot toasted sandwiches and *paav-bhaji*. At the junction of every footpath, jostling for space with pedestrians and sandwich-makers, are peanut vendors and *fruitwala bhaiyyas* with gravity-defying pyramids of fruits seldom seen in the regular market.

Trading closed at 1.30 p.m. There was a bell at 1 p.m., which signalled the last half-hour of trading and was often the cue for people not involved in trading to leave the building for lunch. A second bell would be sounded half an hour later to signal the end of trading. By this time, most of the people would have left the trading hall.

On that Friday, what was heard at 1.28 p.m. was not the shrill ring of the BSE bell but a muffled boom.

To the people milling around outside, eating lunch, the scene before them transformed suddenly from the familiar to the unimaginable. Smoke drifted out from the BSE's basement; blood-splattered survivors trickled out of the building. The Bank of Baroda branch on the ground floor was blown apart. Around them, a few of their fellow-eaters and food vendors on the roadside were also killed from the impact of the bomb.

The force of the explosion carried right up to the tenth floor, where the windowpanes shattered. Mild tremors were felt up to a radius of 300 metres, and the sound carried over the busy hum of traffic to the Victoria Terminus (VT) a kilometre away. The cheekby-jowl buildings in the densely populated area around the BSE, some of them dating back to the early half of the century, were shaken by the explosion.

Inside the BSE, the scene was chaotic. Most of the people in the basement and mezzanine had been killed. The roof of the underground car park had caved in, flattening vehicles and trapping men. The state-of-the-art EPABX system, costing Rs 1.5 crore and the lifeline of the stock exchange, had broken like a toy.

The first thought of those who survived was to get to safety. The lifts were still running and stairways were intact. The result was a stampede—several men and women were injured and crushed to death in the panic. Some people on the seventh floor used the drainage pipes to slide down.

Outside the BSE, the street was covered in a macabre mosaic of blood, limbs, glass and share application forms. The mounds of food, so attractive just minutes ago, were now splattered with the remains of people's bodies.

Twenty-six-year-old Babu Murty had heard that Bombay was the city of gold and that if he worked hard, one day he could have his own clothing store. He ran a sandwich and samosa stall outside the BSE on weekdays. On weekends, when Dalal Street was deserted, he hawked T-shirts near the Gateway of India. But despite his spirit and grit, he didn't stand a chance. He was killed almost instantly as flying shards of glass and debris pierced his body. He was rushed to the state-run Jamshed Jeejeebhoy (JJ) Hospital in Byculla but it was too late.

Four brothers of a migrant family from northern India ran a sugarcane juice stall near the BSE. The fifth brother returned shortly after the blast to find his siblings lying in a pool of blood. They did not live the short distance to the Gokuldas Tejpal (GT) Hospital, run by the city corporation.

Fifty-one-year-old Gokulchand Gupta had run a *panipuri* stall, one of the oldest in the area, for thirteen years. He and his family had moved to Bombay from Uttar Pradesh (UP) twenty-five years ago. Gupta's head was blown off. His only son, seventeen-year-old Premchand, was charred beyond recognition. Five of the hired assistants at the stall were also killed. The only one from Gupta's stall to survive was a boy called Shamsher.

Raju, an *upma* vendor from Mandya in Karnataka; Ashok Singh and Kamla Singh from UP who had a *lassi* stall; Guddu Paav-bhaji Wala, who was a big hit with stockbrokers: all migrants who had come to Bombay with hopes and dreams died in the blast.

Rita Dennis, who worked at the Graphica Printers Office close to the BSE, had decided to go down and buy the afternoon papers herself instead of sending the peon as she usually did. She didn't live to read it. She left behind two young children: Meldon, eleven, and Renita, six. It would take her husband, Matthew, years to come to terms with her death.

Ashok Dashrath Ghadge, a *vada-paav* vendor outside the BSE, was serving a customer when he felt the ground shake beneath him. That was the last thing he registered; when he came to he found himself at GT Hospital, thankful to God that he had been spared.

Twenty-two-year-old Mukesh Khatri had gone to deposit a cheque at the Bank of Baroda branch in the BSE. The queue extended outside the bank, and he was waiting there when he heard a boom that threw him on the road. 'There were pieces of glass flying all around, many were embedded in my body, and my face,' he recounted. People stamped all over him in their frenzy to run out. He finally got up, soaked in his own blood, and walked all the way to GT Hospital, more than a kilometre away. The hospital was full so they sent him to JJ Hospital. At least he lived to tell the tale.

This blast caused the death of eighty-four people; as many as 217 were injured, some severely.

Deputy Commissioner of Police (DCP) Chandrashekhar Rokade, in charge of Zone I, which came under what the police called the south region of the city, covering the area from Cuffe Parade and Colaba to Malabar Hill, Peddar Road, Dongri and Nagpada, and included the BSE, was in the Bombay High Court. He was attending the legal proceedings relating to a controversial Shiv Sena leader from Thane, Anand Dighe. When Rokade heard the distant rumble, he thought that it was caused by Shiv Sainiks assembled in strength at the court premises. But then his walkie-talkie crackled into life: 'There's been a blast in the share market.'

Police Commissioner (CP) Amarjeet Singh Samra had just begun his lunch in his anteroom at the Bombay Police Commissionerate building in the police headquarters complex near Crawford Market, the lively and centrally located vegetable and fruit market. The twenty-third police chief of Bombay since Independence, Samra had held this post for about six weeks. He was known for his flamboyance, accessibility and the sheer competence with which he did his job, and had worked with police departments and law enforcement agencies across the world.

His personal assistant, M.Y. Ramani, and liaison officer, Sub-inspector (SI) Shirish Sawant, barged in as he was eating. Sawant said, 'Sir, control has informed us that there was a blast in the share market.' Samra strode over to his desk and called his joint commissioner of police (JCP) (crime), the second in the police hierarchy, Mahesh Narayan Singh.

Singh's office was in another of the three buildings in the police headquarters complex. The stone building of the crime branch offices were known as Patherwali.

Singh too had just heard of the blast and was about to leave for the spot. Samra instructed him to keep him posted.

Though the police headquarters were within walking distance of the BSE, it took Singh twenty-five minutes to get there by car. By this time it was almost 2 p.m. Crowds had gathered in a manner that only immense calamity can summon. Singh entered the basement car park, and it required all the strength gathered from three decades of police experience not to be overcome by the scene of devastation that greeted him.

He would carry the memory of that scene to his last day: mangled cars with shattered windscreens, splotches of blood in macabre patterns on the walls and the reverberating moans of the injured. Blue-uniformed fire brigade personnel and green-clad bomb squad members were moving about with amazing agility looking for survivors.

The police at the scene had until then concentrated on keeping curious onlookers at bay. Under Singh's supervision, they started organizing rescue teams, and made arrangements to transport survivors to hospitals. A Bombay Electrict Supply and Transport (BEST) bus soon wormed its way into the narrow lane.

The city's chief fire officer, Durgadas Kulkarni, had reached the spot too, and he began to coordinate his men's work. The public joined in the rescue work. The injured and the dead were transported to the three nearby hospitals, GT Hospital, the corporation-run St George Hospital and JJ Hospital.

The hospitals, however, lacked disaster management strategies, and found it enormously difficult to cope with the sudden influx of so many grievously injured patients. The dead were dumped on the floor of the casualty ward, while those alive were propped up against the walls next to them. Faced with such an immense task, the staff had no idea where to begin.

At 2.15 p.m., a bomb went off in the middle of Bombay's largest wholesale market for grain and spice, at Narsi Natha Street in Katha Bazaar, near Masjid Bunder. This is perhaps the most congested area in the city, where trucks, handcarts and pedestrians jostle for space in the narrow streets. Two cabs, parked side by side, suddenly went up in a ball of fire.

A teenager and his father were passing by when they got caught in the explosion. The father died on the spot. The boy's lungs were shattered. A telephone booth nearby caught fire, but this was extinguished quickly.

Five people were killed in this blast, and sixteen injured. Several vehicles were damaged, as were shops and offices in the vicinity.

Rokade, whose jurisdiction also included Katha Bazaar, was still in the High Court when he heard about the second blast. He longed to be out on the streets, dealing with the situation, but he knew the matter at hand had to be resolved first.

Rokade left the courtroom for a moment and was pacing down the corridors, mulling over the two explosions, when he felt the ground under him tremble. A loud noise rent the air. An orderly rushed out of the courtroom with a message from the presiding judge that Rokade should return instantly. The proceedings were suspended. Rokade escorted the van carrying Dighe to Carnac Bunder Road, and then asked his driver to head towards the BSE.

At 2.25 p.m., a car bomb had exploded in the portico of the high-rise Air-India building, about a kilometre from the High Court. The Air-India building is near Nariman Point, south Bombay's most elite business district where major international companies, foreign banks and consulates are located. The Bank of Oman branch on the ground floor of the building, outside which the blast had occurred, was gutted. Experts were to later conclude that this was a more powerful blast than the earlier ones, the noise carrying to Ballard Pier, 2.5 kilometres away. Twenty people were killed in this blast, and eighty-seven injured. The toll was rising at frightening speed.

News of the third blast caused panic, and wild rumours began to circulate. There had been an invasion from across the seas, some insisted. Others claimed, with equal conviction, that the top brass of the Shiv Sena was being killed. Overburdened telephone lines jammed, heightening the chaos. Office workers spilled on to the streets, heading for Churchgate and VT, the city's two main railway hubs. Policemen were not immune to panic themselves. The city was on the run from itself.

Back in the Commissionerate, Samra called up Additional Commissioner of Police (Addl. CP) P.K.B. Chakraborty, and dispatched him to the Air-India building. At the BSE, Singh had by then heard of the latest blast, which he thought was the second one, as he had not heard of the Katha Bazaar explosion. He got into his car and hurried towards the site, followed by Kulkarni, the fire chief, and the bomb squad.

At 2.30 p.m., a blast shook Lucky Petrol Pump adjacent to Sena Bhavan at Dadar in the centre of the city. The Bhavan is the headquarters of the Shiv Sena, the party widely held responsible for the communal riots of the previous months. This was the only blast site where fire quickly followed the explosion, and the Mohammed Ali building next to the petrol pump was virtually brought down. A major chunk of a wall fell off onto the road.

John Thomas, an employee of New Mika Laminates near Worli, was killed. He had called his wife Sophaiya when he heard about the blast at the BSE, before he left his Worli office to deliver a cheque at Indian Oil Corporation at Sewri, to reassure her. After making the delivery, he had gone to the petrol pump to refuel his Hero Honda motorcycle before he returned to the office.

He had just crossed the petrol pump to the other side, near Sena Bhavan, an attendant said. Thomas could be identified only by the crucifix on his gold chain and his wedding ring.

The terrorist designs seemed to have failed, as Sena Bhavan was unharmed, as were Sena men. However, four people died and fifty were injured in the explosion. This blast also seemed to indicate the communal designs of the bombers. As irate Shiv Sainiks spilled on the streets, the situation looked perilously close to spinning out of control.

At 2.55 p.m., a bomb seemed to go off in a crowded double-decker BEST bus outside the regional passport office (RPO) at Worli. It was so powerful that that the five-ton bus was lifted into the air, and the upper deck blown into the hutment colony of Nehru Nagar. Residents panicked as pieces of metal and bodies rained down on them. There were no survivors on board; not even the bodies could be identified. The body of the driver was hurtled across the road into the colony. Vehicles around the bus too caught fire, and four buildings—Rupala Sadan, Ramodaya Mansion, Malkani Mahal and Manjrekar Sadan—along the road, which housed shops and an Udipi restaurant, were badly damaged. Many buildings in the area had their windowpanes shattered, including the RPO, the Brown Boweri building and Century Bhavan. On the road, a deep crater marked the spot where the bomb had exploded.

The sights were gruesome. A *paanwala*'s head was severed from his torso and deposited on the counter in front of him. The body of Neogi, manager of the Bata shop, was found sandwiched between two walls that collapsed on each other. Flying shrapnel was lodged in the stomach of Darius Khavarian, who had come from Iran to see his brother Minocher, owner of the Asian Stores and Restaurant. Sudesh Bhandari of the Blue Star Laundry died when shrapnel pierced his heart. Karim Ramodaya and his brother Rajabhai, the owners of Ramodaya Mansion, who were standing outside the Taj Cake Shop, were also killed.

Pradeep Manjrekar, the owner of Manjrekar Sadan, was using the telephone at the wine shop on the ground floor of his building when the blast occurred. 'First there was a cloud of dust, followed by thick white smoke, and then came the bang that shook the bottles in the wine shop. I saw limbs and objects flying all around, and vehicles on fire.' He said he saw at least five BEST buses and some fifteen cars burnt completely.

Raj Nath Ganjoo, the marketing manager of BASF, never stepped out of his office during working hours. But on that day, his watch had suddenly stopped working and he had been feeling uneasy about it. The bomb went off as he went out to get his watch repaired at a shop a few yards away. He was killed instantly.

Prachee Vartak and Sandhya Roy, trainee airhostesses at East West Airlines, were driving down the road in a company car. This had been Prachee's first day at work, and she was just returning from her first flight from Vishakapatnam. She was looking forward to going home to Worli and telling her parents about it. Hers had been a long battle to get the job, for her sister Aruna was already employed with East West and their company policy did not permit employing family members. The blast destroyed the car. The driver Rajan was charred beyond recognition. Prachee was rushed to the King Edward Memorial (KEM) Hospital with thirty-five per cent burns, and died after three days. Sandhya sustained only minor injuries.

Darshan Lalan, in his first year at Lala Lajpat Rai College, had gone with four friends to see the 3 p.m. show at Satyam Theatre. His friends had already crossed the road to enter the theatre when the bomb exploded. Darshan, who had stepped back to dodge a speeding taxi, was blown to bits. His friends were fine; only one suffered a minor leg injury.

This was eventually to be the deadliest of the blasts, killing 113 and injuring 227.

Back in the heart of the city the governor, P.C. Alexander, the titular head of the state administration, was informed of the blasts. The telephone lines were down, so he had to send a message to Samra through the police control room. Samra could not respond immediately. It is not known where Chief Minister Sharad Pawar, who had assumed office barely a week previously, was.

When Samra heard of the blasts at Dadar and Worli, the first thought to cross his mind was the possibility of communal violence erupting again, a horrifying prospect after the events of the previous December and January. Determined to prevent it, he ordered the police control room to relay a message to the senior officer at every police station, that every policemen should come out on to the roads. Samra firmly believed that the sight of the men in uniform not only instilled confidence in the public, but also prevented hooliganism.

After this Samra tried to contact Alexander. The only mode of communication functioning was the police wireless. But, after struggling to instruct the governor for twenty-five minutes on how to operate the system, in full hearing of the entire police network, the commissioner gave up.

At about 3.15 p.m., while Kulkarni and Singh were at the Air-India building, they heard of the Sena Bhavan and Worli blasts. The fire officer left immediately for Worli. When his car came on to the main road, Kulkarni realized that the entire city had started driving home towards the suburbs, clogging the roads. He told his driver to take the wrong side of the road, meant for traffic heading into the city, and pushed ahead with his siren blaring and emergency lights flashing. He reached Worli in fifteen minutes, perhaps a record for inner-city travel.

Rokade was informed that there had been a blast in Zaveri Bazaar, the gold market, the day's sixth blast, and the fourth in his jurisdiction. A taxi had blown up at the junction of Shaikh Memon Street and Mirza Street, at the southern end of the gold market, at 3.05 p.m., shattering windows of buildings in the area and destroying nearby vehicles. The blast was low on intensity but high on volume, and was heard at the Lokmanya Tilak (LT) Marg police station, one kilometre away.

Niwas Garge, his wife and young son were walking through Dhanji Street at the northern end of Zaveri Bazaar when the explosion occurred. Garge heard the awful bang, and the next minute all three were thrown face down. A taxi nearby caught fire, and Garge could feel his face burning too. He rolled over and struggled to his feet, looking for his wife and son. His wife was burnt badly and he could not find his son. He put her in a taxi and sent her to the hospital, while he stayed behind to look for the boy. He never found him. His wife died in the hospital.

The toll in this blast was seventeen dead and fifty-seven injured. The gold shops at the end of Mirza Street collapsed after the explosion.

As the wireless crackled with news of the blasts, Addl. CP Yadavrao Chinda Pawar, the deputy inspector general of police (DIG) of the central region, and his deputy, DCP (traffic) Rakesh Maria, who held additional charge of Zone IV, were at their common office above the Matunga police station. Bombay was divided into four regions and ten zones for police purposes. Each region was headed by an officer of the rank of DIG who was designated additional commissioner of police. The central region extended from Byculla, Worli, Dadar and Mahim to Vakola and Vile Parle.

Pawar and Maria rushed out. Since Sena Bhavan was a sensitive spot, and under his jurisdiction, Maria ordered the driver to take him there. He realized that people's mood could slowly turn from panic to anger, and the situation could explode anytime.

The crowds at Sena Bhavan had already started anti-Muslim sloganeering. Maria, taking advantage of his six feet two inches, walked up to the leader of the mob and looked down at him. 'No, it's got nothing to do with religious groups, this is part of a bigger conspiracy,' he said with great authority. He was not sure if this was true but it worked for the moment. The crowd slowly scattered. But even as it did, Maria heard on his wireless that communal riots had broken out at Mahim.

Pawar had taken the same route as Maria, but had been delayed in the traffic at Dadar Tram Terminus (TT). As his car neared the junction at the Plaza Cinema, Pawar heard a loud bang and saw people rushing away from the cinema. It was 3.13 p.m. As he got down from his car, Pawar could see that the Plaza, associated in the minds of the people with the state's legendary film star V. Shantaram, had been reduced to rubble. It was an important landmark: people crossing the Dadar bridge instinctively turned to look at the imposing façade.

Ten cinema-goers were killed and thirty-seven injured.

It took a little time for Pawar to grasp that an explosion had caused the devastation, but within minutes he was issuing orders and guiding the rescue work. Like every other Bombay policeman, he too thought of the biggest nightmare of all: communal riots. As if on cue, his wireless came alive, with news of Muslims being attacked at Mahim. Worse, there was also a report that some people had driven up in a Maruti van and lobbed grenades at Machhimar Colony, the predominantly Hindu fishermen's colony in Mahim, and sped off. The grenade attack had left three dead. Another six who were injured were being attended to. The fisherfolk had now come out on the Mahim Causeway, baying for blood. Leaving his subordinates to deal with the fall out of the blast, Pawar rushed to Machhimar Colony.

As he pulled in there, he saw the situation was almost out of control. Angry fishermen had stalled the traffic on the causeway, and were in no mood to relent. Those who had done this must pay: it was simple. Pawar was faced with a dilemma. While he was a firm believer in the efficacy of lathi charges in certain situations, he was hesitant to use it on the fishermen who after all were the victims in this attack. Then the fishermen made up his mind for him as they went on the rampage. They besieged a bus belonging to Anjuman-i-Islam, a Muslim boys' school.

He ordered a lathi charge. As the policemen cut a swathe through the crowds, the traffic started flowing once again.

As Maria headed for Machhimar Colony, he saw that a mob had surrounded a BEST bus, and was dragging out and beating up people. As he stepped out of his car and moved towards the bus, he saw an old man being beaten up. As the attackers seemed undeterred by the presence of an uniformed police officer, Maria pulled out his service revolver and fired into the air. The assailants scampered away, and Maria picked up the victim and had him sent to the Bhabha Hospital at Bandra.

It was due to the efforts of officers like Maria and Pawar that a communal riot was averted in Bombay that day. Though each member of the police force performed nobly on that and subsequent days, many going without sleep for forty-eight hours as they kept watch, Samra later wrote in a letter circulated among the police hierarchy that 'Pawar and Maria were the heroes of the day'.

After the blast at Worli, there were five more explosions, all of which took place at intervals of approximately ten minutes. The Zaveri Bazaar bomb went off at 3.05 p.m., the Plaza Cinema crumbled at 3.13 p.m., and then the dance of death continued in the suburbs. It seemed that all of Bombay had been put on a fast-burning fuse that day.

Arup Patnaik, DCP of Zone VII, in the northwest region, had had it quiet this far. But not for much longer. The northwest region extended from Bandra to Dahisar, and covered the entire western suburbs of the city. At 3.20 p.m., the seventh blast of the day was reported from the high-rise Hotel Sea Rock in Bandra, scenically located right next to the sea on one of Bombay's most popular promenades, the Bandstand boulevard. When Patnaik reached the hotel, he was stunned by what he saw. There was a gaping hole where one wing of the hotel had collapsed, and the concrete and rubble lay strewn around. By a miracle, no one was killed or injured, but the financial loss incurred by the hotel was the highest of any blast, estimated to be more than Rs 9 crore. The hotel eventually shut down.

Even as Patnaik began investigations, he was alerted by the wireless that there had been two other blasts in his jurisdiction, both in hotels—the Juhu Centaur at 3.25 p.m. and the Airport Centaur at 3.35 p.m. Shortly after that there was another message, informing him that at 3.30 p.m., miscreants had flung hand grenades over the perimeter at Sahar Airport.

Ten explosions rocked Bombay that day, taking place with almost metronomic precision at short intervals. Between 1.28 and 3.35 p.m. bombs had gone off across Bombay, the first time any city in the world was subject to serial blasts. The city was soon to spring back to its feet, but its severe lack of infrastructure to tackle a crisis of such proportions was exposed.

A city with a population of over thirteen million had only 1,500 firemen and forty-five fire engines. The fire chief, Durgadas Kulkarni, later lamented that had he had more men at his command, more lives could have been saved. The hospitals where the injured were brought were unable to cope with a crisis of this magnitude. JJ Hospital put all its five operation theatres at the disposal of the injured, but this was inadequate for the needs of the 138 people admitted. Forty-five of the victims admitted there were to die of their injuries. As many as 135 people were taken to St George Hospital, the remaining to JJ Hospital and GT Hospital. Some patients were later transferred to private hospitals.

Rumour mills worked overtime, and even government news agencies were not immune to them. Doordarshan, the sole, government-run Indian television channel, reported that the B.Y.L. Nair Hospital at Agripada was damaged in a blast, while the BBC reported that between 700 and 800 had been killed, a figure dismissed by Chief Minister Sharad Pawar. At his press briefing in the evening, Pawar put the figure at a conservative 100 killed and 500 injured. Subsequent police investigations revealed that 257 persons were either killed or went missing in the blasts while 713 were injured. Property worth Rs 27 crore was destroyed.

The worst carnage was at Worli. The maximum financial damage was at Hotel Sea Rock. At the Juhu Centaur, three people were injured; at the Airport Centaur, two hotel employees were killed and eight others injured.

At 4.30 p.m., the police wireless crackled, 'The king is coming.' That was the code for Samra. After a whirlwind visit to the BSE and the Air-India building, he was proceeding towards Century Bazaar at Worli when Doordarshan contacted him, asking him to address the public that evening over the metro network, which Samra agreed to do.

After visiting the Doordarshan studios and Century Bazaar, Samra left for the western suburbs. He used the drive to exhort his men over the police wireless to maintain peace and avoid communal incidents.

His Contessa came to a halt at the portico of the devastated Hotel Sea Rock. Accompanied by DCP Patnaik, he examined the damage to the hotel. At 10.30 p.m., as Samra was having coffee, his walkie-talkie came to life, 'Charlie Mike wants to talk to you.' The chief minister and the police commissioner had not spoken a word to each other all this while, as both were engrossed in getting the city back on its feet. They talked briefly about the situation.

Samra then left for central Bombay. Half an hour later, he got another message from the chief minister. This time Samra went to the Bandra police station to talk to Pawar on the telephone. They discussed the conspiracy behind the blasts. 'It is a proxy war,' Samra told Pawar. 'It seems to be serious bombing; plastic explosives were used and not gelatin.'

For Samra, the serial bombing was a reminder of the recent and chillingly similar car bomb blast in the basement of the World Trade Centre, New York on 26 February, less than a month earlier, and of the bomb blast in the PanAm flight over Lockerbie in 1991.

Since the riots, the army had been stationed in Bombay. That night fifty columns of the army and a hundred platoons of the police State Reserve Force (SRF) were posted on the roads. As the long and terrible day finally came to a close for most Bombayites, for senior police officers, there was still work to be done.

1

The Beginning

The explosions of 12 March had their origins in an event that had occured three months earlier in a small town 1,300 kilometres to the northeast. The Babri Masjid at Ayodhya had been a bone of contention between the Hindus and Muslims for over five hundred years, since the time when Babur's general Mir Bagi had destroyed a temple there in 1528 to build a mosque he named after his master. For many Hindus the mosque was reputed to be built at the birthplace of Rama, an avatar of Vishnu, and hence a sacred site. The antiquity of the mosque had given it similar sanctity for many Muslims.

The issue had been dormant until the 1980s when a series of events brought the dispute back into prominene. As a result, the ultra-orthodox Hindu Sangh Parivar, which comprises the Rashtriya Swayamsevak Sangh (RSS), Vishwa Hindu Parishad (VHP) and the Bharatiya Janata Party (BJP), among others, decreed that the mosque should be razed and a temple built in its place.

In 1984, the Bajrang Dal, the youth wing of the VHP, was formed with the stated intention of recruiting men for militant action to establish a Hindu nation, and for the construction of the Ram temple. International conferences were organized, and funds poured in. In 1986, a court ordered that the doors of the Babri Masjid be opened and puja permitted inside the structure. Muslims were forbidden from offering prayers. Neither the central government nor the state government questioned the decision. But this did not satisfy the Sangh Parivar, who called upon the government to transfer the property rights of the Ayodhya site so that the biggest temple in the world could be built there. Ram Janmabhoomi became a symbol of militant Hindu nationalism.

In 1990, L.K. Advani of the BJP launched a rath yatra from Somnath, the site of a Hindu temple that had been destroyed by a Muslim invader, Mahmud of Ghazni. A group of young men at Somnath offered Advani a cup of blood, signifying their readiness to achieve martyrdom. During September and October 1990, Advani travelled some 10,000 kilometres across the country, expounding on the need for militant Hinduism and leaving communal riots in his wake. On 30 October 1990, members of the Sangh Parivar stormed the Babri Masjid and raised a flag above it. Fifty people died in police firing. On 29 November 1992, a week before the demolition, Advani stated, 'The BJP is committed to constructing the temple. Court wrangling can delay and New Delhi can obstruct, but no one can deny permanently.' The rest is history—the demolition of the mosque on 6 December and the transformation of the BJP into a major constituent of the national government after the 1998 and 1999 elections.

As the news of the demolition of the Babri Masjid spread, riots began all over the country. The worst incidents took place in Bombay, Ahmedabad, Banaras and Jaipur. There was widespread violence in Maharashtra, Gujarat, Uttar Pradesh, Hyderabad, Bangalore, Bidar, and Gulbarga.

Bombay witnessed two spells of rioting, from 6 to 12 December 1992, and from 7 to 16 January 1993. According to the Srikrishna Commission Report, commissioned by the government, 900 people died (575 Muslims, 275 Hindus) and 2,036 people (1,105 Muslims, 893 Hindus) were injured in these riots. The loss to property was incalculable. Some 50,000 people were rendered homeless.

Poet Jagannath Azad wrote after the demolition of the Babri Masjid:

Ye tune Hind ki hurmat ke
aaine ko toda hai
khabar bhi hai tujhe masjid ka
gumbad todne wale.
(You have shattered the chaste soul of India,
Are you aware O ye who demolished the domes of the mosque.)

■

The postman handed the shabby rectangular packet, tied firmly with strong thread, to the servant through the large wrought-iron gate. It was the week before Christmas 1992. Earlier that week, two similar packets had been received. The address on all was rudimentary: Dawood Ibrahim Bhai, White House, Dubai, and the postmarks indicated that they had been sent from Bombay. It was a measure of Dawood's clout that even in a city like Dubai, famed for its strict compliance with regulations, he still received mail that was not correctly addressed.

Dawood Ibrahim thought he was no less powerful than the occupant of the other, rather better known, White House. His home in the plush Zumera area had become a landmark in the city since the diminutive don had shifted base there from India in 1984. Within the opulently furnished bungalow, Dawood and his five brothers—Anis, Noora, Humayun, Iqbal and Mustaqim—conducted their many businesses. The gregarious Dawood also regularly entertained friends here, ranging from sheikhs and emirs from across the United Arab Emirates (UAE) to film stars from Bombay. During the eight years that Dawood had been in Dubai, both his business and social profile had grown dramatically. In the bylanes of Pakmodia Street, Dongri, Nagpada and Dimtimkar Street in Bombay, where Dawood had first cut his teeth as a criminal, his story had assumed the proportions of a myth. He was no longer considered a criminal, but was reverently referred to as 'bhai' (literally brother but imbued with great respect).

Within the White House, the mood was mixed. On 24 December Dawood would turn forty, and this year as usual a lavish party had been planned, which would be attended by politicians from India, Pakistan and Nepal, bankers from Geneva and bureaucrats from London. Yet those close to him sensed a strange unease and reluctance. Unlike earlier years, the plans for the party seemed far from his mind.

Of course the news from India was distressing. Every day Dawood's friends and associates in Bombay sent him reports of Muslim men being butchered and women gang-raped. Along with these stories came pressure. Many in the Muslim community, especially in Bombay, thought of Dawood as a protector, and felt sorely disappointed by his apparent indifference towards the bloodshed. Reports reached the UAE of how some of his former associates in Bombay had raised slogans of '*Dawood murdabad*' (Death to Dawood) and '*Dawood bhai, hai hai*!' (Down with Dawood). And now there were also these mysterious parcels.

It had been a long way from Musafir Khana, Pakmodia Street, in southern Bombay, where Dawood and his family lived in a ten feet by ten feet room. His father, Head Constable Ibrahim Hassan Kaskar, found it hard going to support his seven sons—Dawood, Sabir, Anis, Noora, Humayun, Iqbal and Mustaqim—and three daughters—Salma, Haseena and Zainab—on his meagre salary, but at least he was grateful that he had a steady government job. From an early age, the children were aware of the need to earn. The family was from Ratnagiri district in Maharashtra's coastal belt, and the community was known as Konkani Muslims. In later years, Dawood would land his goods in the area his forefathers hailed from.

When Dawood, the eldest, was growing up in the 1960s, south Bombay's underworld king was Abdul Karim Khan, popularly called Karim Lala, a six-foot Pathan from Afghanistan, one of the many from his community who lived in Bombay and worked as moneylenders. Karim Lala's territory extended from Walkeshwar and Grant Road to Dongri and Masjid Bunder, Byculla. By the time Dawood started making his forays into the underworld, in the early 1970s, Karim Lala had retired from active work and supervised a second generation of the Pathan Mafia.

Dawood studied in a local English-medium school until Class IX. After that, the need to earn made him drop out. But both he and his brother Sabir found it hard to get a job with their meagre qualifications. The CBI dossiers on Dawood state that they gradually started stealing and extorting money from traders, hotel owners and shopkeepers in the neighbourhood. Soon, they progressed to selling smuggled goods in Mohatta Market and Manish Market, near their home. Until the early 1970s, Dawood was just another street ruffian.

The first case registered against Dawood was on 4 December 1974 when he, along with eight others, committed daylight dacoity. The gang attacked a trader, Kantilal Jain, threatened him with country-made revolvers and choppers, and robbed him of Rs 3.75 lakh. The Pydhonie police arrested Dawood and his associates. Dawood and six others were convicted by the trial court but acquitted by the High Court. This had terrible consequences for Head Constable Kaskar, whose reputation in the crime branch was forever tarnished by his son's criminal connections.

During the Emergency of 1975–77, Dawood was detained under the Maintainence of Internal Security Act (MISA), as were many people with criminal records. While in jail, he came in contact with two of the biggest gold and silver smugglers of the time, Haji Mastan and Yusuf Patel. As it happened, they were looking for someone to take over their business cabal as they were contemplating retirement. They liked the young man with his energy, determination and obvious intelligence, and decided to induct him into their business.

Once out of jail, Dawood started putting together a network to aid his smuggling operations. According to gang lore, his syndicate expanded their territory along the coast, and consequently his influence increased within the city. Karim Lala was outraged. He asked his nephew Samad Khan to teach this bunch of upstarts a lesson. Samad fired a couple of times at Dawood in the building where the latter lived, but did not succeed in hitting him. Other members of the Pathan gang, like the dreaded brothers Alamzeb and Amir Zaada, also started confronting Dawood. There were stabbings, shootouts and ambushes between the two gangs. At Pakmodia Street, they say it was destiny that Dawood survived such a deadly onslaught from the ruling gang.

Dawood was arrested under the Conservation of Foreign Exchange and Prevention of Smuggling Act (COFEPOSA) in 1979 and was lodged at the Yerawada Central Prison at Pune. He was released soon, but was arrested again in 1980 by the Dongri police.

Haji Mastan tried to intervene in the continuing gang war, but failed. In January 1981, Alamzeb and Amir Zaada followed Dawood's brother Sabir to a petrol pump near Prabhadevi and shot him dead. They also tried to kill Dawood but failed. The Zaada brothers fled to Gujarat to escape Dawood who had sworn revenge. Dawood started his hunt for them, contacting his smuggling associates in Gujarat. The search continued for over two years. In 1983, Alamzeb once again made unsuccessful bids on Dawood's life at Thane and Ahmedabad.

Meanwhile, according to official records, Dawood managed to complete another mission of revenge. He had Samad Khan followed and discovered that he was most vulnerable when he was visiting his girlfriend at Grant Road in the heart of Bombay. On 4 October 1982, as Samad Khan was getting out of the lift at the building where she lived, Dawood and six others surrounded him and opened fire. During the post mortem, thirty-two bullets were found in his body. The Pathan syndicate was cowed forever.

Dawood was again detained under COFEPOSA in 1983 and lodged at the Sabarmati Central Prison. He was released on 21 August. On 6 September, he managed to finish his mission of avenging Sabir's death.

Amir Zaada had been arrested and lodged in jail. As the jail premises were inaccessible, Dawood told the contract killer he had hired for Rs 50,000—an unemployed youth called David Pardesi—to kill Amir at the court premises. This was an unheard of fee in 1983 when the usual amount paid as *supari* (contract killing) ranged between Rs 500 and Rs 5,000. Pardesi received training in firearms at Dawood's house. On 6 September, as Amir was being escorted to court, Pardesi shot him at point-blank range. Pardesi was arrested and so was Dawood. Dawood obtained bail against a cash deposit of Rs 20,000 and was released in May 1984.

Dawood had realized that these periodic trips to jail would continue as long as he was in India. When he had been released from prison in August 1983, Laloo Jogi, a smuggling associate from Gujarat, had introduced Dawood to Haji Ashraf of Dubai, who invited Dawood to visit him and see the business prospects there. Dawood decided to follow this up. On 4 May 1984, he jumped bail and fled to Dubai.

From Dubai, Dawood systematically built his empire in Bombay. He gathered together local gangsters—Bhai Thakur of Vasai, Chhota Rajan of Tilak Nagar (northeast Bombay), Kim Bahadur Thapa of Bhandup, Sharad Shetty of Jogeshwari, Khalid Pehlwan and Chhota Shakeel—and organized them into a flourishing syndicate smuggling gold, silver, electronic goods and textiles. At that time, he avoided smuggling drugs. The D Company, as they came to be known, also collected protection money from hoteliers, builders, businessmen working in iron and steel, grain and textile industries, and the diamond merchants in Zaveri Bazaar and Panchratna. They solved disputes between businessmen for handsome premiums, known as 'matter pataana'. Their monthly income from extortion, protection and settling disputes was estimated at Rs 20 crore in 1992.

His unofficial second-in-command at Bombay at that time was Chhota Rajan, born Rajendra Sadashiv Nikhalje. Rajan had started his underworld career blackmarketing cinema tickets at Sahkar Cinema in Chembur, in the late 1970s. Gradually, he and his mentor Rajan Nair (Bada Rajan) had extended their area of influence from Chembur to Ghatkopar East in northeastern Bombay, and had achieved notoriety for their innovative use of weapons.

After Bada Rajan was killed by a gangster called Abdul Qunju under command from a rival matka king, Yashwant Jadhav, who ran a gambling business, the daring revenge that Chotta Rajan took made reigning dons like Dawood Ibrahim and Arun Gawli take notice of the youngster. As Bada Rajan had had connections with Dawood, Chhota Rajan accepted Dawood's offer

Dawood Ibrahim (right) and Chhota Rajan (Courtesy Mid-day)

to join the D-Company.

In Dubai, Dawood set up legitimate construction businesses and traded, especially in gold. His business flourished, particularly after Chhota Rajan joined him in the late 1980s, when Bombay became too dangerous for him. Dawood had offices in Nairobi, London, Singapore and Kathmandu. He soon started overshadowing the big names in smuggling in Dubai, like Haji Ashraf who had invited him there, and the Bhatti brothers from Pakistan.

There is no such thing as job security in the underworld, so Dawood consolidated his position by building up a group of trusted lieutenants whose loyalty to him was absolute, such as Chhota Shakeel and Chhota Rajan. They were responsible for the rapid growth and stability of Dawood's empire, though later their rivalry grew bitter. For example, when Rama Naik, an influential Hindu don, had a dispute with one of Dawood's associates regarding a piece of land, Chhota Rajan was assigned to take care of the problem. Rama Naik was killed in a police encounter in a hairdressing saloon in 1987.

The death of this influential don sent a chilling message that Dawood was not to be opposed. Naik's protégé Arun Gawli, who had grown up with Dawood in the Byculla Company (a group of budding gangsters in south and central Bombay) had not had any enmity with Dawood, but was enraged at Naik's death and swore revenge. Dawood tried unsuccessfully to convince Gawli that he was not behind the killing but Gawli was not convinced. His plans for revenge grew, and there were several shootouts and gang-related killings. In early 1992, Shailesh Haldankar and other members of the Gawli gang killed Ibrahim Parkar, husband of Dawood's sister Haseena, at Nagpada in south Bombay.

Dawood was deeply upset that he had failed to protect his sister. Retaliation was swift. In the early hours of 12 September that year, when Shailesh Haldankar and his colleague were in JJ Hospital, Dawood's henchmen Subhash Singh Thakur and Sunil Sawant stormed in with AK-47s and killed Haldankar. Such a killing in a major hospital stunned the city. It also exposed Dawood's nexus with politicians in Bombay and neighbouring Bhiwandi, as the car used for the operation belonged to a prominent member of the Bhiwandi municipal council.

Dawood always longed to return to Bombay, for he loved the city. Yet he knew that as soon as he returned he would be arrested. Even when his father died in 1994 or his sister Haseena was widowed, he was not able to be with his family. Life in Dubai was good—top-rank politicians, film stars and cricketers from India would go to pay homage at the White House. But his love for his native city was well known, which was why after the riots in the city, he was acutely distressed.

When the third parcel was delivered to him, Dawood and his closest associates were busy sorting out the fine print of a business deal. The room fell silent as Dawood toyed with the parcel, clearly reluctant to open it in the presence of others. The earlier ones he had received had angered and embarrassed him. He turned towards his confidant, Shakeel Babumiya Shaikh, popularly known as Chhota Shakeel because of his diminutive stature, who had moved to Dubai in 1987. With the marginalization of Chhota Rajan, Chhota Shakeel had taken his place as Dawood's right-hand man. As usual, Shakeel knew instantly what was expected of him. He gave a brief order that the room be emptied. Then he came over and took the packet from Dawood. As he tugged at the thread, the fragile box gave way, and the contents—dozens of red and green glass bangles—spilled across the oval table. Wordlessly, Dawood and Shakeel looked at the colourful pieces glinting mockingly under the light of the chandelier. Dawood's face was ashen.

There was a one-line Urdu missive with the parcel: '*Jo bhai bahen ki izzat ki hifazat na kar sake use ye tohfa mubarak* (A brother who cannot protect the chastity of his sister deserves this gift).'

The meaning was clear. Dawood was being rebuked for his inaction, for his failure to protect his community. For the proud man, this was bitter humiliation.

The trill of the phone broke the oppressive silence. Shakeel picked it up and barked, 'What?'

The speaker's voice could be heard in the silent room. He reported that Dawood's latest consignment of goods had been seized, probably by the Paksitani smuggler Dawood Jatt.

The other phone, whose number was known to barely half a dozen people, rang. Shakeel answered it and, handing the receiver to Dawood, tactfully moved away to the other end of the room.

There was a long muttered conversation.

When Dawood hung up, his demeanour had changed visibly, the earlier dejection replaced by resolution.

Shakeel remained seated quietly.

Dawood walked towards him. 'They called,' Dawood said. Shakeel had never asked and Dawood had never explained who 'they' were. It is believed that the term referred to top officials in Pakistan.

'They know about Aslam Bhatti and Dawood Jatt's attacks on us. They say that they want to land some important cargo in Bombay through our landing routes at spots near Shekhadi and Dighi. Tiger and Taufiq will handle the entire operation of landing, paying the doctors and other such things. In exchange, they will arrange total security for our business.' He paused and then continued meditatively, 'I think that this cargo will not be ordinary stuff like gold biscuits or silver ingots. It could be something meant as a retribution for the demolition of the Babri Masjid and the massacre of Muslims. I told them that if it only means using my infrastructure and nothing beyond that then I have no problem. I can seek solace in the fact that the blood of my brothers will be avenged.'

Dawood took out a cigar from his pocket and tucked it between his lips, a sign that he was feeling relieved. Shakeel lit the cigar for him. Although the don had not said it in so many words, it was clear that the cargo would be death.

2

The Conspiracy

The simmering resentment was not confined to that room in Dubai.
It spread like a forest fire. From the *kahwa-khanas* (tea joints) of
Iran to the mosques of Jordan and the *maktabs* (religious schools)
of Syria, the conversation invariably dwelt on one topic: how to
avenge the demolition of the Babri masjid in Hukumat-Al-Hind
(India).

The suggestions ranged from the sane—enforcing an oil
embargo on India—to the radical, like blowing up vital
installations. The continuing riots in India only fuelled the
determination of expatriate smugglers like Haji Ahmed, Haji
Umar and Taufiq Jaliawala, one of the most successful smugglers
of the day, as well as Pakistani smugglers like Dawood Jatt and
Aslam Bhatti, to avenge their *qaum*.

Plans were chalked out, strategies suggested and discarded
in the search for a consensus. Several bank accounts were opened
and slush funds created to fund the *tehrik-e-intequam* (movement
of revenge). Millions of dirhams and dollars secretly poured in
and many leaders in Islamic nations pledged tacit support, though
officially they would not hear of anything subversive against
India. Gradually from this haze of theories and plans, a coherent
scheme began to emerge.

As 1992 drew to a close, Taufiq joined hands with Anis
Ibrahim, Ejaz Pathan, Tiger Memon, Mohammed Dossa and

Mustafa Majnun, and began working with them. Taufiq, to the surprise of many who expected Dawood Ibrahim to play a leading role, seemed to be directing operations as the latter seemed strangely reluctant to involve himself.

As he drove his off-white Toyota down the expressway in Dubai in end December 1992, Ibrahim Mushtaq Abdul Razak Memon, called Tiger by his associates, was still smouldering as he remembered how his office had been set ablaze earlier that month during the Bombay riots. That was the first time he could remember that he had felt truly helpless. Now he was in distant UAE where a group of men had come together to plot retribution against an entire nation for the acts of a handful. As Tiger parked his car and walked towards the grey building, it seemed like the culmination of what all his life had been leading to.

Like Dawood, Tiger Memon was a Bombay boy. The Mandvi post office in Bombay stands at the junction of a Hindu area and a Muslim borough. Opposite the post office, at the corner of Mohammed Ali Road, is the Kadiya building, a rambling four-storeyed building with seventy tenements. The construction of this had been financed by the erstwhile maharaja of Gwalior some time before 1947, and it was given to the loyal masons, after whom it was named, by the maharaja. Each mason family was assigned an identical 260-square-foot room, with a kitchenette attached. Several tenants shared the common toilet on each floor. The children grew up in the common passage, a narrow veranda that faced each room, to escape from their tiny, cluttered homes.

Mushtaq was born in one such room on the third floor. The royal masons had long since gone. The residents were now predominantly Muslims. But because of the location of the house, Mushtaq grew up with access to both cultures. Until the riots of 1992, there was no Hindu-Muslim animosity, barring a few minor skirmishes. Besides, Mushtaq's father, Abdul Razak Memon, was a sportsman, and for him there was no question of harbouring communal feelings against his Hindu brothers with whom he played. Abdul Razak's small room housed not only his wife and six sons, but also the innumerable trophies and medals he had won. He excelled in all kinds of sports, especially in cricket. He once played a league match with the famed Tiger Pataudi, and from then on he was called Tiger in the neighbourhood. This was long before his second-born Mushtaq would inherit the name.

Abdul Razak was extremely conservative and religious. His youngest son was named Isa, the Arabic form of Jesus, the other five after the Old Testament prophets: Suleiman (Solomon), Ibrahim (Abraham), Ayub (Job), Yaqub (Jacob) and Yusuf (Joseph). All the boys were good sportsmen; Suleiman excelled in carrom, Yaqub in squash and badminton, and Mushtaq in cricket.

Mushtaq's grit and determination were demonstrated from an early age, especially on the cricket field. There is a story which was legendary in the neighbourhood about an innings he played in 1972, for his school, Beg Mohammed High School at Pydhonie. The team was on the ropes in a match against Anjuman-i-Islam, their traditional rival and champion of every school tournament. Beating the latter was a childhood dream of every Beg Mohammed boy, and Mushtaq, then in the ninth standard, was not going to let this opportunity pass. There was only one problem: he was the twelfth man.

Anjuman-i-Islam batted first, and notched up 142 runs. All of Beg Mohammed's six recognized batsmen were out for ninety-one runs. By this time, one of the team members had fallen ill and Mushtaq was allowed to bat. He requested the captain to allow him go in next, and the latter acceded to his request as the situation seemed hopeless.

When Mushtaq reached the crease, his team needed fifty-two runs to win. Facing him was Nazim, the most cunning fast bowler in the opposing team. Mushtaq missed his first ball, and the next four. On the last ball of the over, a full toss, he hit a six. Inspired, he started a mighty attack on the opposition bowling, though wickets at the other end continued to fall.

Mushtaq batted like a man possessed. When the team needed only seven runs to win he was hit on the nose by one of Nazim's balls, collapsed and was carried off the field. Evening was setting in and the umpires suggested a draw be declared. But, his nose swathed in a crude bandage, Mushtaq went out to bat again with only one over left to go.

He could not score off the first four balls. But as Nazim bowled the fifth, Mushtaq heaved at it with all his strength. It was another sixer.

One ball, one run. It was a slower delivery and Mushtaq missed it. Overcome with horror, he suddenly realized that he was surrounded by jubilant crowds. It had been a wide; they had got the one run needed for victory.

The family lived in Mohammed Ali Road until 1978, and then shifted to another, even smaller, tenement in northwest Bombay, in a fishermen's colony in Mahim. Abdul Razak did not hold a full-time job, and the older boys started working at an early age. While living in the Kadiya building, Suleiman had found employment as a salesman while Mushtaq worked as an apprentice clerk in the community's bank, the Memon Cooperative Bank, at their branch in Byculla.

After he started working, Mushtaq's belligerence grew. Asked by the manager of the bank to fetch tea for a visitor, Mushtaq retorted that he was not his servant. As the manager showered abuses at him, Mushtaq slapped him and the manager fell down, unconscious. Amazingly, the bank asked Mushtaq to tender an apology and resume work. But Mushtaq was adamant. 'What apology?' he asked his father. 'If they want, let the manager apologize.'

His foray into the underworld began in a very small way in the early 1980s. The family was still desperately poor. Near their house in Mahim was Makhdum Shah Baba's dargah where Sunni Muslims from all over Maharashtra came to pray for favours. It was said that those who served the saint would receive fame and fortune. The shrine was also popular with the denizens of Bombay's underworld. At this period, the main operations of the underworld were in smuggling and matka. There were frequent gang wars over territorial rights, and the seizing of one another's contraband goods.

Among the dargah's regular visitors were the smuggler brothers Mustafa Dossa, nicknamed Mustafa Majnun for his romantic proclivities, and Mohammed Dossa. They had been established in this line of work since the time of Haji Mastan, the almost legendary smuggler. They were looking for a reliable chauffeur, and somebody in the dargah suggested Mushtaq and described him as very daring. For Mushtaq, desperate for a job, this seemed a godsend.

His job involved driving the bosses around in fancy cars—Volkswagen, Mercedes and other imported brands that were yet to hit the Indian roads. Within the first month, he earned his employers' confidence and was entrusted with the job of chauffeuring their Dubai-based superiors whenever they visited Bombay. Legend has it that once Yaqub Bhatti, known as Big Boss, was proceeding towards Bandra when sirens wailed behind them. The police had been tipped off, and were hot in pursuit. Bhatti sat nervous and sweating in the back seat. 'Do something, drive faster,' he yelled at Mushtaq.

Mushtaq, however, seemed undisturbed. He adjusted his rearview mirrors for a better look at the vehicles trailing them, and answered calmly, 'Yes, sir.'

Bhatti was surprised by the youth's composure. 'Just drop me at the airport; there is a flight for Dubai leaving in another two-and-a-half hours,' he said in a beseeching tone. He added, 'If you manage to get me on that plane, I will reward you well.'

The vehicle dodged and darted past police jeeps in the western suburbs of Bombay. This area was Mushtaq's turf and he knew it like the back of his hand. Three wireless vans were pursuing the car and for two hours Mushtaq drove like a lunatic. He rammed into autorickshaws, bicycles and motorcycles, and fended off the police vans by ducking into narrow one-way lanes from the wrong direction. The pursuing police van would stop in its tracks and ask another van to go from a different route to position itself at the other end of the lane. But Mushtaq would never drive up to the end, instead he would swing into smaller lanes and *gallis*. Had the police used motorcycles, they might have intercepted him. By turning into one-way lanes at the wrong end, Mushtaq effectively cut down on the number of vehicles trailing him and finally managed to get the entire police squad off his back to reach the airport in the nick of time. Bhatti was the last passenger to board the flight.

Mushtaq abandoned the car and walked back home. The police did not know who the driver was and therefore there were no midnight knocks to bother him.

Bhatti was very happy. He immediately sent word that Mushtaq should be invited to Dubai. Mushtaq had saved him from the wrath of the Bombay police, and the prospect of rotting for years in an Indian prison, while the Bombay police drummed up cases against him at their slow pace.

In Dubai, Mushtaq got a new job. He was now a carrier, a gold carrier. His job was to ferry smuggled gold biscuits, and there was a lot of money in this kind of venture. Within a year,

Mushtaq was in charge of the smuggling operations from Bombay, much to the dismay of his previous bosses Mustafa Majnun and Mohammed Dossa, who were offended that their superior in Dubai treated a measly driver with so much deference. But nothing could stop Mushtaq's rise.

Tiger Memon

The Memon family was now rich, and in 1985 they shifted to two spacious duplex flats on the fifth and sixth floors of the seven-storey Al-Hussaini building in Mahim. Mushtaq had single-handedly lifted the family out of poverty. He paid for the education of his younger brother, Yaqub, who went on to become a chartered accountant. He also ran an office by the name of Al-Tejarath International, which was destroyed during the December riots.

The Memon community had not really been aware of Mushtaq's rise to fame. It was at his wedding that this changed. Mushtaq had been in love with a non-Memon woman, Shabana. Their wedding was solemnized at the famous Sabu Siddique Hall in south Bombay. It was a lavish event that gave the guests an inkling of the rapid rise of Mushtaq Memon. They saluted his enterprise; the means didn't matter to them. They called his father aside and told him: 'Rajjubhai, you should be proud of your son. He is the real Tiger.' Mushtaq was thus re-christened on his wedding day. He was now the Tiger.

It was this determination to succeed, to overcome the odds that had brought him this far. To the critical meeting in Dubai.

The elevator took Tiger to the second floor, to a glass-fronted office where he was guided to the meeting hall, where several known and unknown people waited in the comfortable high-backed chairs.

Tiger greeted the gathering and sat next to Taufiq Jaliawala. The other familiar faces included Shaikh Ahmed, Anis Ibrahim, Haji Umar, Mohammed Dossa, Mustafa Majnun and Sayed Arif. The room was enshrouded in a pall of smoke, giving it a funereal air, further reinforced by the sombre expressions on many faces.

Taufiq Jaliawala broke the silence. 'So have you people come to any decision?'

Nobody responded.

Enraged, Taufiq launched into a diatribe about the importance of their mission, which prompted a few suggestions.

'How about killing the BJP leader Advani and the Sena chief Bal Thackeray?' asked a man who seemed to be a Palestinian.

When others protested that this was impossible to achieve, the man retorted proudly that nothing was impossible for Palestine Liberation Organization (PLO) operatives.

'We know that Thackeray's security has several loopholes. It can be breached whenever we want to snuff his life out. Thackeray and Advani can be killed by just one handshake or one garland. That will be sufficient to dispatch them to the pit of hell.'

He was interrupted by Shaikh Ahmed. 'You are assuming that your men can get close to Thackeray and Advani. That is impossible: they will not get anywhere within several kilometres of him,' he said derisively.

'We have ways and means of doing it, and you people don't deserve to know them. But if worse comes to worst, we can always buy out one of the policemen around him and pay him fantastic sums to have the job done. Or storm their houses with a truck load of explosives, the way the Amal militia do to Christians in Lebanon.'

Tiger said, more to himself than to the gathering, 'Even if Advani and Thackeray can be killed, it will still not solve our problem. The Hindus will turn them into godlike figures and Muslims throughout India will be massacred. No. No. No. This cannot happen.'

Another Arab who had been silent so far spoke out, his voice brimming with indignation. 'Non-believers cannot cause any harm to Muslims. We will annihilate them. We will crush them. The entire Islamic world is with us. Injustice will not be tolerated any more.' He banged the table furiously as he spoke.

The only one who had the courage to interrupt him was Anis Ibrahim, Dawood Ibrahim's brother. 'Are you aware that there are sixty crore Hindus in India? Can you finish them all? Do you think the United Nations will keep quiet? What about India's mentor, Russia?'

The discussion continued, occasionally very heated, as various options were raised.

Shaikh Ahmed spoke up eventually. 'But can't we scare the Indian government and the Hindus into submission? The best thing to do will be to turn the tables on the Hindus. If we can intimidate Hindus in such a manner that in the future they will not in their wildest dreams try to subjugate the Muslims ...'

This thought seemed to appeal to all present, and heads began to bob in agreement. Taufiq clapped his hands and said it was a superb idea. But once again silence descended on the room.

Tiger spoke up. 'Bombay is the pride of India, its financial nerve centre. It is also the place where Muslims suffered the most during the riots. Why not display our might and power there? Any attack on Bombay will have international repercussions. The government will be shaken. The world leaders will be shocked.

Let us plan to take over Bombay. We can capture Mantralaya, the municipal corporation building and the airport, hold political leaders hostage and cripple the economy. We will draw international attention to the downtrodden Muslims of the country. We will ...'

Dossa, who sounded impatient and irritated, interrupted, 'But how can you do it? From where will the money come?'

'Money is no problem,' Taufiq interjected. 'But do you think it can be done successfully?'

'With proper planning the CIA has toppled governments and taken over countries. We have to only disrupt one city. I already have a network. We need to fine-tune it further and rope in some committed young people to execute the job,' Tiger said.

Suddenly the room was electrified. The glum faces lit up. The discussion grew animated.

3

The Preparations

There were two initial steps in the complex operation: first, to secure the arms and armaments and transport them to Bombay, and second, to recruit Muslim youths from Bombay and train them to carry out the bombings. It was felt that only Tiger had the leadership skills and contacts necessary to find the youths, train them, brief them and lead them throughout the mission.

He also had plenty of experience with smuggling goods to Bombay, and had a well-established network including trusted landing agents. Each landing agent has several landing spots along the coast that he and his gang have exclusive control over. Whenever smuggled goods have to be delivered into Bombay, such landing agents send their men to the high seas to off-load the goods and bring them back to shore.

One such landing agent was Dawood Phanse, also called Dawood Taklya because of his bald pate. Phanse, now in his sixties, had an unchallenged hold in the dozen or so landing points in Shekhadi and Dighi. These two coastal villages were situated in such a rocky part of the Maharashtra coast that it was difficult to believe that any landing could even take place there, yet despite that these spots were regarded as a gold mine for smugglers. Phanse had consolidated his position by forming a cartel with two other powerful agents of the region: Sharif Abdul Ghafoor Parkar, alias Dadabhai Parkar, from Sandheri village, and Rahim Abbas Karambelkar, alias Rahim Laundrywala, of Srivardhan village. Since the late 1980s the trio were involved in landing silver ingots and other goods for Dawood Ibrahim and later for Tiger.

On 15 January 1993, Phanse was summoned by Tiger.

'Some extremely important and sensitive goods are supposed to land,' Tiger told him, and asked him to personally handle the landing operations. The goods would be shipped from Dubai and would land at Mhasla.

'Who is going to ship the goods?'

'Dawood bhai.'

'How can we make sure that they are Dawood bhai's goods and not somebody else's?' Phanse asked.

Tiger was famous for his short temper and vitriolic tongue. He frowned at Phanse's tone but kept himself in check. 'These goods are approved by Dawood bhai himself.'

'We have no such intimation either from him or through his channels,' Phanse replied, unabashed. 'One needs to be careful, the times are bad in Bombay ...'

'What will convince you that the goods belong to Dawood bhai?' asked Tiger, exasperated.

'Let him phone me and tell me personally or through any such channel,' Phanse said with finality.

'What if I arrange for you to meet Dawood bhai?'

'Well, in that case you have a deal,' Phanse bobbed his bald head.

Tiger arranged for Phanse's meeting with Dawood in Dubai, and organized a visa for him. On 19 January, Phanse took the Air-India flight from Bombay to Dubai. Tiger himself met the landing agent at the airport. They drove to Hotel Delhi Durbar where Phanse was to stay.

'You will meet Dawood bhai tomorrow,' said Tiger. 'I'll

come and pick you up.'

However, on the following day, Tiger did not show up. Instead he called to say that the meeting with Dawood had been postponed by a day.

On 21 January, Tiger picked up Phanse from the hotel and took him in a taxi to the White House. Phanse was awe-struck at the sight of the huge house, the likes of which were seldom seen in Bombay. Half-smiling, Tiger said to Phanse as they entered the gates, 'This is where your Dawood bhai lives.'

Phanse could only nod. Tiger led him to a room and asked him to wait while he went out to look for Dawood. Phanse sat on the edge of the sofa and fidgeted nervously.

As the minutes ticked by, Phanse's nervousness increased. Every little sound made him jump. Suddenly he sensed movement behind him. Both Tiger and Dawood were standing in the room watching him.

'Bhai, salam alaikum, bhai,' Phanse stuttered.

'Wa alaikum as aalam. Kya haal hai, chacha (How is everything)?' asked Dawood.

'By the grace of Almighty Allah, everything is fine.'

'So what brought you here?'

Dawood's directness took Phanse by surprise.

'Nothing ... I mean, I just wanted to ... I mean, meet you ... I told Tiger bhai ... If I can talk to you, he said ... he would arrange the meeting ...'

'You don't have to explain so much. I thought you wanted some assurance that this is my operation. Be assured that this has my whole-hearted support.'

'But can I ask ... I ... just wanted to know—what will be in that cargo?'

'It will have some chemicals. Don't worry, you'll be paid handsomely for your services.'

'Chemicals?'

Dawood was taken aback and enraged because nobody ever dared to question what he said.

'Are you not aware of what the Hindus have done in India?' he said, gritting his teeth. 'Don't you think we have to take revenge for the masjid and the blood of innocent Muslims?'

'Bhai, how ... we ... how?'

'Don't worry, you do your work, we'll do our work. Tiger knows everything and has planned everything. Just give him whatever help he needs.'

That was the end of the meeting. Dawood's personal assurance was sufficient for Phanse. He returned to Bombay the following day. Dawood's rage against the infidels had influenced Phanse. He described the meeting to his partners Parkar and Laundrywala. The trio pledged support to Tiger in their assigned task of facilitating the landing of the chemicals at Mhasla-Shekhadi.

Subsequently Tiger met the three agents and informed them that the goods were supposed to land at Shekhadi at the end of the month or early the following month. They would be informed of the exact dates later. The plan seemed to be progressing smoothly.

The golden aphorism of the underworld is that anything that is known to more than two people is no longer a secret. There are hundreds of informers or *khabris* in Bombay. They straddle the two worlds of the underworld gangs and the law enforcement agencies. They secure vital information from the agencies, and just as often provide them with invaluable tip-offs, a fact that these agencies acknowledge. The customs department rewards their khabris by paying twenty per cent of the value of the seized contraband. This means a khabri can become a millionaire overnight if he can tip off the agencies of any cache of gold or contraband worth a crore of rupees. But the smugglers also have their informers within the agencies. Whenever the agencies organize a raid, such informers call up their masters and warn them, often foiling the strike. In return, the informers would be paid anything between Rs 2,000 to Rs 5,000, depending on the magnitude of the loss the smugglers would have incurred had the seizure taken place.

The Directorate of Revenue Intelligence (DRI) received specific information that between 21 and 24 January, Tiger Memon and Mohammed Dossa were likely to organize a landing of arms and explosives at Rohini and Dighi, two of the many landing spots in the Raigad area. Information about landings can seldom be more specific, as even the landing agents are frequently not aware of the date until the last moment. That is because the exact date of a landing depends on a number of factors, which include the date of the cargo leaving its port of origin, weather conditions, and the level of vigilance on the part of the Indian authorities. Thus a large part of a landing agent's work is to be constantly ready for whenever the cargo lands.

The DRI director, S.P.S. Pundir, at once alerted his deputy, V.M. Deolekar, and the superintendent of police (SP), Alibaug, T.S. Bhal, under whose jurisdiction the jetties came.

The second alert, on 25 January, came from the Intelligence Bureau (IB) who received a tip-off that some arms were likely to land in one of the nodal coastal points of Raigad sometime in the next fifteen to twenty days.

On the same day, the collector of customs, S.K. Bhardwaj, also received a tip-off. He in turn alerted the police, the navy and his own men. He telephoned his assistant collector of customs (ACC), R.K. Singh, and followed this up with a secret demi-official letter (known as a DO), stating that intelligence had been received that a large quantity of automatic weapons would be smuggled into India by the ISI (Inter-Services Intelligence) and the controlling syndicate in UAE. These weapons were likely to be landed sometime in the next fifteen to thirty days at Vasai, Dadar Penn, Srivardhan, Bankot, Ratnagiri and the southern beaches of Goa.

Bhardwaj also sent separate copies to his immediate subordinates: Additional Collector of Customs (Addl. CC) S.N. Thapa, in charge of the marine and preventive (M&P) wing of customs which had jurisdiction over the seas, and Addl. CC V.M. Deophade, who was in charge of the rummaging and intelligence (R&I) wing, whose jurisdiction was on land. In practice, the officers of two wings often trespassed on each other's territories.

26 January—Republic Day—was a holiday. Both Thapa and Deophade received the DO only on 27 January. Since the landing of contraband fell in Thapa's jurisdiction, he took serious note of the alert and informed all eight ACCs under him about it, so that they in turn could notify their subordinate officers.

Hareshwar, the small government rest house at Srivardhan, nestles in picturesque surroundings. On 29 January, ACC R.K. Singh, the first recipient of Bhardwaj's alert, checked into this guest house at 4 p.m. Singh had barely settled in when a jeep entered the compound. Customs Inspector S.S. Talawadekar and Phanse came into Singh's room. Singh and Talawadekar, law enforcement officers, were Phanse's co-conspirers.

After the meeting, Phanse, Parkar and Laundrywala gathered some forty men from the village. They hired two huge boats, owned by Harihar Khopatkar and Yashwant Boinkar, which were used for carting the contraband to shore. Normally each boat could carry up to 125 or 150 silver ingots, worth Rs 3.5 crore in the open market. However, the wages that the boatmen were paid were minuscule, despite the great risks that they had to take.

Boinkar in fact resented this so much that he had already

decided that he would help Phanse and then later squeal on him. That way he would get his money from the smugglers as well as the government reward for khabri, which he estimated should be about Rs 70 lakh, twenty per cent of the value of the ingots in his boat. He knew Phanse trusted him, and was unlikely to be suspicious.

Boinkar had come to this decision in October 1992 when Tiger had smuggled in some 700 ingots of silver and Boinkar had assisted Phanse, for what he considered were inadequate wages. The fisherman had contacted his long-time confidant, Ram of Bhardkool. The primary school teacher in Bhardkool village, Mahendra Mhatre, had a brother, Inspector L.D. Mhatre, who was a customs officer posted at Uran. Ram contacted Inspector Mhatre, who organized a meeting with his boss, Addl. CC Thapa.

In the customs department, officers of Thapa's calibre were rare. He had more than two-and-a-half decades of experience in anti-smuggling operations. Thapa met Mhatre and Ram in the first week of December 1992. Babri Masjid had yet to be demolished. In that meeting, Ram and Thapa developed a good rapport. Thapa assured a reward to Ram in return for his *pakki khabar* about future landings.

On 29 January, when Boinkar was hired for this other landing, he again got in touch with Ram who spoke to Mahendra Mhatre. Mhatre sent a message to his brother. The journey to Uran took six long hours. By the time Mhatre could inform Thapa it was 10.30 p.m. There was no way a raid could be arranged that night. The following day, 30 January, Mhatre learnt that the landing had not taken place that night. In case the landing occurred that night, Thapa made the requisite preparations for a raid.

Thapa had emphasized utmost secrecy so that Tiger would not be alerted about the raid. Tiger was reputed to have dozens of customs officers on his payroll, as did many other smugglers. Thapa also knew that should they interrupt a landing or hold up a convoy, Tiger's men would not shy away from a gun battle. That was why surprise was essential to give his men an advantage. He decided to take a group of men from Thane, a city near Bombay, as men from Bombay were adjudged to be more likely to have connections with Tiger's gang. He made several calls to his most trusted officers from that area, and gathered some twenty men. The officers were instructed to carry their guns and travel in unmarked Maruti 800s.

As a seasoned customs official, Thapa knew that all smugglers had a limited choice of roads to reach Bombay. There were only two arteries that connected the landing points near Srivardhan village to the junction of the Bombay–Goa highway, which led to Mahad and then Bombay. Since one of them, the Mhasla-Sai Morba Road, had a steep climb, Thapa surmised that Tiger would not take that route. Therefore, Thapa laid an ambush at a spot called Purarphata on the other road, which went from Mhasla to Mangaon, where there was a bridge which was so narrow that only one large vehicle could cross at a time. The road leading to the bridge snaked through thick jungle. Thapa had received information that Tiger Memon would lead two trucks in an open Commander jeep. He had decided to intercept the convoy the moment the jeep crossed the bridge. Since the trucks would be blocked on the bridge itself they would not be able to turn back.

Thapa had heard so much about Tiger's penchant for firing at customs officers that he decided to take no risks. He told his men that Tiger could easily be identified as he had a heavy beard. 'Shoot him dead. I'll take responsibility for what happens later.'

The dense bushes on both sides of the road proved good cover for the customs team. After taking their positions, the team began their long, arduous wait, in a deathly silence broken only by the call of jungle animals. They kept watch from 9 p.m. until 1.30 a.m., when there occurred an unexpected interruption.

An anonymous caller had informed the police at Mhasla that armed terrorists were hidden in the Purarphata bushes, waiting to waylay travellers. The police team reached the spot, surrounded the customs officials from all sides, and ordered the 'terrorists' to surrender.

Taken completely by surprise, the customs team sat stunned. Finally, Thapa stepped out of his Toyota and walked out to identify himself. He then called off the surveillance because he knew that in all probability Tiger would not pass that night.

The officers decided to meet again the following night. The ambush was shifted to a spot called Dehanphata, which lay between Srivardhan and Purarphata. The road there was narrow and curved so that vehicles were forced to slow down. Thapa stuck to his original plan of zeroing in on the trucks only after the jeep had moved ahead. But the bad luck of the customs officials continued. Tiger did not pass by on that night either.

During the course of that vigil, in the early hours of 1 February, Thapa received a call from his colleague Deophade, who warned him that an arms landing was likely to occur near Mhasla that night. Thapa informed ACC R.K. Singh and asked him to step up the vigilance at the landing spots of Dighi, Bankot, Mhasla and Srivardhan. He also alerted the customs control room, which sent out a coded message warning all customs officials about the impending landing.

Their quarry was as near as they could hope. When Thapa had been coordinating with Singh about stepping up vigilance, Tiger was at Hotel Vesava, Mahad. An hour after the customs alert had been sent out, Tiger received a call from a customs officer, who asked him to proceed towards Alibaug, which was also under surveillance at the time. Tiger immediately checked out and drove for over two and a half hours to Alibaug, where he checked into Hotel Big Splash at 6.45 a.m.

He asked the receptionist to dial a local number, 2050, the number of the customs control room. However, his contact ACC Singh was not there. He then called Singh's residence, and Singh asked him to call at the control room five minutes later, by which time he would be there.

During a second call from the control room, Singh asked Tiger to wait at the hotel, and assured him that he would send over his men soon. In a few minutes, Singh sent the Alibaug customs superintendent, Sayed Sultan, to meet Tiger. When Sultan went to the Big Splash, he found Tiger Memon sleeping in his suite. But he met the landing agent Parkar.

The landing did not take place on 2 February either. Tiger slept throughout the day in his suite although his men had gone to the landing spots and returned empty-handed that night. But Tiger received confirmation of the landing from Dubai on the morning of 3 February.

Between 29 January and 2 February, Tiger's landing agents had contacted various customs officials and police personnel in Srivardhan and Mhasla, and arranged for their cooperation in the landings. Laundrywala had 'fixed' the Srivardhan customs officials and a police inspector; while Phanse had sought help from the Mhasla customs officials and police officials. They were all promised a consideration, starting from Rs 1 lakh. They had advised the landing agents to bring in the goods only after 2 a.m.

On 3 February, sixteen of Tiger's men assembled at the Big Splash where Tiger had booked rooms for them. They were Javed Chikna, Anwar Theba, Badshah Khan, Shahid Qureishi, Shahnawaz Qureishi, Shaikh Ali, Shaikh Mohammed Ehtesham,

Parvez Nasir, Parvez Kelawala Qureishi, Akbar, Karimullah, Riyaz Khatri, Munna, Imtiyaz Ghavate, Yaqub Khan alias Yeba Yaqub, and Bashir Ahmed. Some were old associates and some were new men, personally handpicked by Tiger and his ace-confidant, Chikna. They were told to assemble in Tiger's suite at lunchtime, where he addressed them.

'You know what happened to our brothers during the riots in Bombay. I have requisitioned some weapons from outside so that we can settle scores with the Hindus. The cargo will arrive tonight. I must warn you that your participation in this venture has become mandatory. If any of you try to squeal to the police then I will not only eliminate that person but also his entire family.'

There was silence in the room as each man realized that the die had been cast. They were given instructions about what to do.

Tiger's group left the hotel at 4 p.m., and drove for about four hours along the breathtakingly beautiful road to Shekhadi. The village was small, merely some thirty or forty houses, predominantly Muslim with many of the villagers hailing from the Konkani community. The group was joined by a further thirty men from the village, and they all went down to the shore to wait. There were also two large trucks waiting. Tiger had a radio in his hand, and periodically he and Theba would communicate on it.

Around 11 p.m., a motorboat came to the shore. Somebody called, 'Are you people from Bombay?' After Tiger replied in the affirmative, he and a few of his men boarded the boat, and sailed towards the open sea. After about ten minutes the motorboat rendezvoused with a large red speedboat.

Tiger jumped onto the speedboat, and helped to hand some thirty or so large cartons packed in gunny bags from it to his men in the motorboat. When the motorboat was full, they returned to the shore. The whole operation had taken about twenty minutes.

The cartons were carried to a hut. After the last carton had been stashed, Chikna and Badshah Khan opened one and were dumbfounded to see huge, unwieldy guns of a kind they had not seen before. Though Chikna was Tiger's second-in-command, he was a streetside tough, and had never encountered such sophisticated weapons.

Tiger stepped inside the hut and said, '*Yeh* AK-56 *hai*.' He opened another box and removed some round objects, which he identified as hand grenades. 'If anybody tries to stop you or intercept you, remove this pin and hurl it at them,' he instructed.

Tiger handed over an AK-56 to each of his Bombay associates. They began to familiarize themselves with the guns and their various latches and switches. Tiger told some of them to go atop the cliff and keep watch. 'If you spot any policemen or customs men coming towards you, shoot those *b . . . s*,' he ordered.

The motorboat made several trips from the speedboat to the shore. Each time it carried wooden boxes and cartons, some eighty in all, packed in gunny bags. Unlike the cartons of ammunition and weapons, Tiger showed no interest in inspecting the wooden boxes. The boxes were loaded in the trucks. Tiger told some of his men to travel in the trucks. Their destination was the Wangani Telecom Tower, a deserted spot in the Raigad hills. The convoy— two trucks and four Commander jeeps led by Tiger in a Maruti van—left for Wangani Tower.

At the Tower, Badshah Khan, who had met Tiger for the first time at the Big Splash, but had already attracted the latter's attention by his obvious intelligence and keenness, supervised the unloading of the boxes and cartons from the trucks. He made an inventory of them according to the numbers written on them, and handed the list to Chikna who checked it before giving it to

Tiger. Badshah and a few others opened the cartons and unpacked the hand grenades, AK-56 rifles, magazines, automatic pistols, live rounds for pistols and detonators in them. The boxes contained a black, sticky, malleable substance, which resembled the black soap used for washing utensils. Tiger explained that this *kala sabun* was the deadliest item of all: RDX. There were at least fifty cartons of RDX, packed in corrugated boxes, each weighing at least thirty kilograms. While the other packets and boxes were unpacked, the RDX was left untouched. Some 1,500 kilograms of RDX were loaded in a tempo. The empty cartons and boxes were burnt behind the Tower.

Tiger had a tried and tested method for transporting goods. He believed that such goods should never be carried in trucks, as heavy vehicles were stopped more frequently at checkpoints than battered cars and jeeps. He had first tried this method in October 1992, when he brought in a large consignment of silver. He hired trucks to carry the ingots from Mhasla to the Tower, and from there he transferred the goods into jeeps. Each jeep had a false bottom, which could hold a large number of ingots. The jeeps would then travel to Bombay, with Tiger leading the convoy.

Meanwhile the customs officials were totally flummoxed by all the information that had been pouring in. They had been keeping vigil since 30 January and were totally exhausted by 3 February when the landings actually took place. It has never been conclusively established whether the false alerts were deliberately issued to confuse and tire out the customs officials, which they undoubtedly did, or whether there had been a genuine delay in the delivery. But whatever the reason, Tiger's mission was accomplished: the jeeps carrying the goods made it back to Bombay where they were stashed in safe hideaways in Mumbra and Byculla. Tiger travelled with the convoy, and returned to his home in Mahim.

On the morning of 7 February, Tiger gathered some of his trusted lieutenants at the Hindustan Soda Factory at Mahim, a regular meeting point. Nasir Dhakla, Farooq Pawle, Parvez Kelawala and Yeba Yaqub left with Tiger in a Commander jeep and Maruti car. At Vashi checkpoint, Theba, Munna, Karimullah, Ehtesham and Akbar joined them. Later, a third group arrived, which included Chikna and Badshah Khan. The group halted for lunch at a restaurant at the Nagothane petrol pump. Tiger also hired an open Canter tempo for transportation and asked Badshah Khan to direct the tempo to the landing spots. The convoy reached Shekhadi at night. This time the goods had already landed, and all the boxes were wrapped in gunny bags. The boxes were loaded on to the tempo and covered with grass. Then the vehicles drove to the Wangani Tower, where there were three Commander jeeps, three Maruti cars and other vehicles waiting. Except for the RDX, which was kept in the tempo, the other goods—AK-56 rifles, magazines, pistols, hand grenades, detonators, pencil detonators and wires—were distributed among the jeeps and the cars, and carried to Bombay.

The arms were all in place. All that was needed was the men to use them.

■

The challenge that now faced Tiger was how to transform his enthusiastic but untrained men into the skilled mercenaries needed to carry out the complex bombing operations. Even his trusted lieutenants had never seen AK-56s or handled RDX before. Ideally, they should have been trained for months but Tiger thought that that could be dispensed with as their opponents—Bombay security men and police—were hardly skilled or expert either. He decided that about ten days' intensive training should put his men on par with their adversaries. It was an open secret that most Bombay policemen had not fired a single round in years!

Tiger decided to send the boys in batches to Pakistan for training. They would travel to Dubai and from there sneak into Pakistan. Almost all the Indian dons at Dubai had an arrangement, called 'khancha' or 'setting', whereby they could travel to Pakistan without an official visa. Tiger planned to take advantage of this arrangement.

On 11 February, the first batch of youths left Bombay for Dubai by a Cathay Pacific flight. The seven men were Chikna, Badshah Khan, Parvez Kelawala, Salim Phansopkar who was referred to as Tainur, Salim Bazaarwala, Farooq Pawle and Zakir. At Dubai, they were met by Tiger's brother, Ayub Memon, who put them up at a flat belonging to Taher Merchant, a Dubai-based NRI. On 13 February they flew to Islamabad.

On 15 February, Firoz Amani Malik, Niyaz Ahmed and Nasim Barmare left for Dubai. They joined the first group on 17 February. On 19 February, they were joined by nine more trainees: Yeba Yaqub, Nasir Dhakla, Theba, Irfan Chougule, Shahnawaz, Abdul Akhtar, Mohammed Rafiq, Gul Mohammed Khan alias Gullu, and Bashir Khan, bringing the total number of trainees to nineteen. After an intensive course, they returned to Bombay on 4 March.

■

Badshah Khan's Story

I could look out of the windows and see the wafting clouds, below me and beside me. In the distance, I saw the fading light of the sun. I am so used to people making empty promises that I seldom get excited. However, since the time Tiger bhai came and told me, 'Badshah Khan, you and your friends are going for training to Islamabad on 13 February', I had been excited.

Tiger bhai and Ayub bhai had handed us our boarding passes at Dubai airport. We were seven young men bound by a common motive, driven by the same goal and spurred by the consuming fire of revenge. When I asked who would receive us at Islamabad airport, Tiger bhai said that we did not need to worry, arrangements had been made.

We boarded the Pakistan International Airlines (PIA) flight from Dubai. We knew PIA was notorious for its delays, bad airhostesses and pathetic service. We used to joke that roofs leaked during the monsoon and technicians used a lit match to check fuel levels inside the tank. It was nicknamed *Paleed Iblees* Airlines (Unlucky Satanic Airlines), and unfailingly lived up to its reputation!

As I was squirming in my uncomfortable seat, an airhostess passed down the aisle and grimaced when our eyes met. Suddenly the speaker, which was just above my seat, crackled into life. 'Friends, this is your captain. We are sorry to inform you that the Dubai-Islamabad flight had to be diverted to Lahore airport as one of our esteemed passengers is complaining of acute heart pain. We are afraid it is an emergency and so the flight plans have to be changed. We apologize for the inconvenience.'

The passengers reacted in whispers, a few groaned. One of the passengers who seemed to be a doctor rushed towards the cockpit. '*Paleed hai, paleed hai,*' said Javed Chikna, who was sitting behind me. Javed had a hairless face, which is why we generously bestowed the sobriquet of Chikna on him. But I differed with Chikna as I thought one must do everything possible to save a Muslim life.

After the old woman who was ill was taken off the plane at Lahore airport, we resumed the journey to Islamabad. When we touched down, it was 8.30 p.m. I stepped out on the tarmac and,

Javed Chikna

as I breathed in the cold air, felt rejuvenated. We were going to be trained to exact revenge for our martyred brothers in the riots of Bombay. I felt weighed down with the responsibility, yet strangely exhilarated. It was a new beginning, and I felt it would change my very being. At the same time, we were stressed as we did not have any visas, nor did we have any idea how we would get through immigration.

Chikna and I walked ahead, while the others followed. Tiger bhai had told Chikna about the contact person, who would identify himself as Jaafar bhai and take care of the visa and immigration formalities. As instructed, Chikna wore a white cap, which Tiger bhai had given him at Dubai airport, and carried a newspaper close to his chest. This was how Jaafar bhai was supposed to identify us.

Within a few minutes of Chikna donning the cap, a tall, gangly but dignified-looking man came up to us and asked him, 'Are you friends of Tiger?' When Chikna nodded, he introduced himself as Jaafar bhai. He gave us a brilliant smile, warmly shook hands with each of us and led us to the exit. I was surprised that no one in the airport bothered to even look at the seven of us or question us about our papers. As Jaafar bhai passed, the customs officials and policemen gave him stiff salutes. Jaafar bhai only nodded in return. We were all very impressed. I guessed that Jaafar bhai must be in some senior position in the Pakistani police, which is why the rules were waived for him and he was greeted with such respect. I wondered about Tiger bhai's connections and influence.

As soon as we stepped out of the airport, two jeeps drew up. Jaafar bhai signalled us to get in. After a short drive, we reached a bungalow, simply but tastefully done up. Jaafar bhai told us very politely that we should relax, and that dinner would be served soon.

I began wandering from one room to another. Jaafar bhai was busy talking to Chikna. He clearly considered him to be the most senior in the group. I knew that Chikna and Theba were the two closest to Tiger bhai. Chikna had been involved in several murder cases and was feared in the Mahim area. Theba too had executed many a job at Tiger bhai's behest. During my interaction with Tiger bhai, he had begun trusting me as well. He now addressed me as 'beta', according me the same affection he would his son. I had never expected to rise in the ranks so rapidly, nor to play such an important role in his designs.

Jaafar bhai brought dinner. Contrary to our expectations, the meal was spartan: mutton in thin gravy and rotis. After dinner, Jaafar bhai took away our passports and tickets. He said that during our stay in Pakistan, we should not address each other by our real names but should use assumed names. I was re-christened Nasir, Javed was Ali, Parvez was Mohammed, Zakir was called Shakir, Salim became Imran, Farooq was Faisal, and Tainur became Mujahid. Jaafar bhai left, promising to return the following morning, and we retired to sleep.

The next morning, after a disappointing breakfast, Jaafar bhai took us sightseeing. We saw the Faisal Masjid, regarded as one of the biggest mosques in Pakistan, from outside. I was shocked to see such security arrangements outside a mosque. Jaafar bhai explained that the arrangements were because the Malaysian prime minister was visiting the mosque. Jaafar bhai then took us to the City Park, which is located in a hilly region from where most of Islamabad can be seen. He now seemed like a tourist guide. At the park he told us that whenever a foreign dignitary visited Islamabad, he was requested to plant a sapling in this park, beside which a nameplate is fixed. I wanted to have a closer look at the saplings, but Jaafar bhai hurriedly took us in another direction. We had already been here for a day, but he was the only Pakistani we had spoken to!

That evening, we were told to pack our bags as we were leaving for the training camp. Again two jeeps came to pick us up. Jaafar bhai came with us. Through the darkness, I could see the jeeps leave the city limits and speed into thick jungles and mountains. The air was very cold and we were all chilled and nervous. The drive lasted over two-and-a-half hours. We must have travelled at least 150 kilometres. Jaafar bhai told us that we had to cover the remaining distance on foot. We began walking in the jungle, bushes and branches brushing us as we went forward.

After about half an hour, we reached a clearing, situated between the hills. I could see two huge rectangular tents on one side. Jaafar bhai introduced us to two tall and muscular men, who he said would be our instructors. He called them 'Babaji'. They both looked strong and stern, and wore kurtas. All of us were shivering in our sweaters and jackets, but these men did not seem to feel the cold. I had seen such characters in Hindi movies, men who were assigned the task of beating up our thin and short heroes but end up getting beaten to pulp. But these two guys looked really dangerous. They could have taken on all our screen heroes together without a wince! We were told that we should sleep now and that our training would begin the following morning.

In Bombay, I never got up before 11 a.m. But in the jungles, I was made to get up at 6 a.m. It was 15 February. That first day we were made to jog, stretch and do all kinds of exercises. In all my twenty-seven years, I had never exercised. My body was rebelling against such rigorous exertions. At the end of the three-hour session, I felt totally drained. I was so exhausted that I think I would have quit, had the goal not been so important. After all, I had vowed that I would take revenge.

The location of the camp was perfect for our requirements. There were six men to look after the camp: the two Babajis, two servants who served food and cleaned up, and two armed guards. Our meals were delivered by jeep every day at the same time. I marvelled at the excellent organization.

On 17 February three youths arrived at the camp, who had also been sent from Bombay to be trained. They introduced themselves as Akram, Aslam and Yusuf. But I thought that if we could be given false names, the same could have been done with them. I did some snooping and discovered that they were actually called Firoz Malik, Niyaz Ahmed and Nasim Barmare.

We all gathered in a tent for breakfast, after which one of the Babajis announced that he would now begin training us in handling the instruments of death. He was carrying an AK-56 rifle. When we came into the field again, we were shown automatic pistols, handguns, light machineguns and Kalashnikovs. Babaji showed us how to hold the weapon, told us about recoil and how the trigger could be pulled to distribute death wholesale. For the next two days, we did nothing but target practice. The sound of the shots reverberated throughout the jungles and the hills, and the clatter of the machineguns and blazing gun barrels filled us with respect and apprehension.

I realized why we had had to travel all the way to Pakistan for the camp. There was no other place where we could have received such training; anywhere else the booming shots and loud reports would have attracted too much attention. Such intensive

Firoz Malik

training was not possible anywhere in India, nor in Dubai or any other place I could think of. Pakistan—the one place so sensitive to the plight of Indian Muslims—was the only option.

The sound of ten machineguns spitting fire was deafening. I thought, if only I had such a gun Mohammed Ali could have never destroyed our family. We used to be a fairly prosperous family. My father had an embroidery business and owned the first floor, some 2,700 square feet, of Rippon House at Nagpada. But in 1980 Mohammed Ali produced forged papers and got us evicted by the police. My parents, two younger brothers, one younger sister and I were thrown out on the road. When my mother and sister refused to leave, the men from the Nagpada police station brutally kicked and belted them.

My father did not live long after the humiliation. I could not continue my education beyond Class VII, as I had to take care of the family. These shoulders, once so weak that they could not bear such responsibilities, were now carrying an AK-56. I was determined to help my entire community. I had failed to take revenge on one man and his stooges in uniform, but now I was ready to take revenge on the entire nation.

I was brought back to the present by Babaji's voice. A huge sheet was spread on the ground. Babaji explained how to knock down an AK-56 and how to reassemble it. He demonstrated the entire procedure and then asked us to do the same. Most of our day was spent with AK-56 rifle spares. Then we were shown light machineguns, and taught how to disassemble and reassemble these. We also did target practice with Mauser pistols and rifles.

On 19 February, nine more youths arrived in the camp. I had met all of them before. One of them, Gullu, had played an active role during the communal riots in Behrampada. The Nirmal Nagar police were looking for him and for Bashir Khan, another of the nine. Now there were nineteen of us—all Bombay boys. The large number made me proud and sure of success.

On 20 February, Tiger bhai came to the camp, along with one Ahmed sahab. Tiger bhai took lessons with us on how to throw hand grenades. We were shown two types of grenades: one which exploded after removing the pin, while the other could be activated by pulling down a thread-like cord. The instructors set up a blackboard and wrote on it, explaining with the aid of points and diagrams. Those who were literate took notes; the others tried to commit it to memory.

We learnt all kinds of exciting things. 'This may look like an ordinary pencil, but it is a detonator. We call it a pencil timer. The red pencil explodes fifteen minutes after it is activated, the white pencil after an hour, and the green pencil after two-and-a-half hours,' Babaji told us.

After lunch that day, we were shown some black soap-like lumps. I remembered that Tiger bhai had told us that it was kala sabun at the time of the landings. Babaji said, 'This is RDX—Research Developed Explosive. It was discovered after World War II, and is said to be one of the most lethal bomb-making ingredients.' He taught us how to make an RDX bomb. He attached a thirty-minute pencil timer to the bomb. We began chatting after he set it up. Suddenly an explosion rocked the jungles and mountains. The noise seemed to shatter my eardrums. The sky was raining stones and mud, and the earth beneath my feet was shaking. The black smoke from the explosion enveloped the entire area. All my companions were similarly dazed. Things seemed to be happening in slow motion: we were floating in air and time had been suspended.

I think more than ten minutes went by after the explosion before the curtain of smoke gave way and I could see and hear properly. We moved towards the spot where the bomb had been placed. The pit was many feet deep.

Babaji told us to make bombs as well. We began moulding the malleable black putty. He triggered several explosions of RDX bombs, though this time on a relatively muted scale.

The next day, 21 February, we were shown a rocket launcher. It looked so scary that we were afraid to even touch it. Babaji only explained the technicalities of the launcher, its functions and how it could be operated. But he didn't shoot it nor were we given an opportunity to do so.

Tiger bhai and Ahmed sahab were to leave that day. I think Tiger bhai had come just to observe our training, and to see whether we were participating with enthuasiasm. Before leaving, Tiger bhai told us, 'Javed, Anwar, Badshah Khan, train well. You will have to use this training in Bombay later.' We smiled in acknowledgement. I nodded, silently promising, Tiger bhai, I will not let you down. Anwar Theba, Firoz, Niyaz and Nasim left with them.

After Tiger bhai's departure, we stayed for some more days, practising what we had been taught. On the last day of our training, a pleasant breeze was blowing. We were happy that we would soon be returning to our families. 'We might not have succeeded in transforming you into a killing machine or a perfect commando but we have taught you the best way of handling weapons and explosives which will help you in your mission in Bombay. You have learnt well and I know you will live up to expectations,' Babaji told us.

The next day, 2 March, the jeeps brought us back to the bungalow where we had been housed after our arrival. There were now fifteen of us. Jaafar bhai took us sightseeing again in Islamabad. We visited the grave of Zia-ul-Haq and a picturesque picnic spot, Murree, which reminded me of Kashmir. Later, Jaafar bhai took us to the airport and escorted us to the plane for Dubai. We boarded the plane without any formal check-in. International immigration formalities were again waived for our personal convenience!

At Dubai, we took a cab to Taher Merchant's flat. Firoz, Niyaz and Nasim were there. We began teasing one another, calling ourselves commandos. Tiger bhai came to the flat and told us to assemble at a bungalow at Al-Rashidia at 8 p.m.

It was the first time that our entire group of 'trained commandos' had gathered under one roof, with Tiger bhai present among us. Gradually, the conversation veered towards the communal riots in Bombay. Dinner was served while we talked. After dinner, we all gathered in the hall. Tiger bhai seemed to be in a pensive mood. He ordered Irfan Chougule to get the Holy Quran. We all were taken by surprise because I thought that the idea behind gathering was to further discuss our strategy. I did not expect Tiger bhai to recite from the Quran.

Irfan brought the Quran reverently. The Quran is considered the most venerable and sacred object for a Muslim, dearer than one's own family, spouse and children. Tiger bhai asked Irfan to place the Quran in the centre of the table in the hall, and stood up and addressed all of us. 'Brothers, let us all place our hands on the holiest book of Allah, the most exalted, and take a solemn oath.' We were all very serious now as we gathered around the table. We all placed our hands on the book, one after another, covering the book entirely.

We repeated after Tiger bhai: 'We take an oath that we will

never disclose the secret of our mission to anybody. We will never mention our trip to Dubai and Islamabad. We will never talk about our training in firearms and explosives. Even if the police arrest us, we will never disclose the names of our associates to the police. We will maintain absolute secrecy about our plans. We will not confide in even our wives, brothers, friends and family members.'

A new enthusiasm, new earnestness had overwhelmed each of us. Tiger bhai reiterated the importance of the mission. Then the mood lightened: he distributed 200 UAE dirhams to each of us for shopping in Dubai, and instructed us to leave the bungalow in batches of four.

I left Dubai on 4 March. On the flight back, I thought how privileged I was to be an associate of Tiger bhai. I reached my house at Mahim at 5 p.m. that afternoon.

After their return the nineteen trained men were sent to scout Bombay for potential targets. Meanwhile, Tiger felt the need to recruit and train some more. He identified five other promising boys, but unlike the earlier group who could wield AK-56s with some expertise and were adept in building explosive devices, the newly recruited men had no such skills.

Thus late in the evening of Sunday, 7 March, Tiger found himself facing a dilemma. The logistics of training these new recruits in Islamabad ruled that option out. Tiger had no time to accompany them to Dubai or Islamabad, and now one of the smugglers, Ejaz Pathan, who had been involved in organizing the Dubai training, was asking for money. Tiger would have had no qualms about sidelining Pathan, except that the man might try to blackmail him or squeal to the authorities. He could no afford to jeopardize the security of the mission at this stage.

He decided he would train them near Bombay itself. This was extremely risky, and would not be as thorough as the training the first group had received, but he had no choice left in the matter. He had explored the coastal belt of Raigad extensively, and he knew that there were several deserted spots in the hills that could be used for training. He decided to escort the boys to Raigad the very same evening.

He asked Chikna to get them together. Chikna summoned the new group: Moin Qureishi, Mohammed Iqbal, Sardar Shahwali Khan, Bashir Electrician and Parvez Shaikh. He announced that they would be leaving Bombay that very night. After performing the taravih namaz, mandatory during Ramazan, they left in a jeep with Abdul Gani Turk, Tiger's driver, at the wheel.

They reached Panvel, seventy kilometres from Bombay, soon after midnight. There, Gani halted next to a shining red Maruti 1000. Tiger was standing with his back towards the car; seated inside were Anwar Theba and Yeba Yaqub. Tiger acknowledged the new arrivals and took them for tea at an Udipi hotel, where he often stopped. Afterwards, they took off again in the early hours of Monday morning.

The traffic was heavy on the National Highway (NH) 17. Near the Bombay–Goa highway, they came to a crossing. One fork led to Mahad and Alibaug, while the other, which they took, went towards Mhasla, Srivardhan, Shekhadi and Dighi. It had been a long night. By the time they reached Mhasla, they had travelled some 250 kilometres. The streets of this predominantly Muslim township were filled with youths wearing fezzes and elders with flowing beards even at this early hour of the morning. The cars pulled off the road at a roadside eatery at 5 a.m., time for sehri.

The group of ten occupied two tables and ordered kheema paratha, beef trotters, boiled eggs and cups of tea. They were joined by Tiger's aides and landing agents from the vicinity: Phanse, Parkar, Ishaq Hajwane, Hamid Dafedar and Shahnawaz Hajwane.

The first spot where they stopped was Manjiv Ghat. But as there seemed to be too many people around even at that early hour, they decided to move on. They headed towards Sandheri-Bhorghat, a small village of fourteen houses scattered over a large plateau, surrounded by lush hills. The road to Sandheri was a steep incline with several hairpin bends. The cars reached the village at 6.30 a.m. Local people were proud of the fact that a song and dance sequence for a Hindi film had once been shot there. Tiger had chosen this spot for a different kind of shooting.

The group did their fajr namaz, as dawn broke through the grey sky. They folded and put away their mats. From the boot of the Maruti 1000, three cricket stumps and green military-type bags were pulled out. Chikna set up the stumps so that chance passers-by would think they were picnickers playing cricket. From the bags, AK-56 rifles and grenades were brought out.

Tiger walked over to the edge of the cliff and instructed the five new recruits on how to hurl hand grenades. 'Look here now,' he ordered. He concentrated all his strength in his right arm as he threw a grenade into the ravine. A loud bang followed, which left a huge crater, and terrified flocks of birds flew out. A tree slowly keeled over under the impact.

Tiger handed a green grenade to Bashir and asked him to hurl into the ravine. Bashir threw it nervously. The grenade did not travel very far but landed nearby with a deafening sound. Tiger frowned; the boy was a real novice. 'Saale, kabhi cricket nahin khela kya?' he chided. 'Practice throwing small stones. Once you know how to throw, then you can move on to bombs.'

He moved on to the next trainee.

After about an hour, Tiger announced that he would teach them the basics about guns. He showed them how to handle a gun, how to hold it, how its butt should nestle in the crook of the arm, how to unlock the safety catch and depress the trigger with the index finger. He told them how to brace themselves against the recoil. He also taught them how to replace the magazine once it emptied.

Using the cricket stumps as targets, Tiger unleashed a hail of bullets. The firing practice continued for several hours. Each trainee was allowed to shoot a few rounds from an AK-56.

Fortunately for them, no vehicle came that way. Few local tribals passed by on foot, but none dared to stop: the sight of city people frolicking with guns was intimidating.

As the sun reached its peak, they were all exhausted. They had travelled all night and toiled all morning in the sun, and their exhaustion was heightened by the Ramazan prohibition on food and water. Tiger, satisfied that the youths had learnt something of the basics, announced that they would pack up and return.

Descending through the same sharp curves and bends, they drove through Mhasla and then exited towards the narrow route to Mangaon. From there, they moved onto the NH 17. Since it was afternoon, the traffic was thin. They reached the city before sundown. Moin and Iqbal were dropped at the Kalanagar junction and the rest near Mahim Dargah.

4

The Final Plan

Badshah Khan's Story

Barely a couple of hours after I reached home from Dubai, my phone rang. I reached for the receiver with a vague sense of foreboding. As I expected, it was Chikna. He summoned me to meet him near the Hindustan Soda Factory, our usual meeting place, at 9 p.m.

At the gate of the factory, I met Bashir Khan and Chikna. I was not in a very good mood. I wanted to smash Chikna's face. Perhaps he could tell. He tried to placate me. 'Badshah, actually it's Tiger bhai who wanted to meet you.'

I glared in reply.

A red Maruti 1000 pulled up. Tiger bhai rolled down the window and told us to get in. We complied without asking any questions.

We stopped briefly at Dongri, the cradle of the Muslim Mafiosi in Bombay, where men like Dawood bhai had been nurtured into dons. Then Tiger bhai drove us to the Hotel Taj Mahal at Colaba, one of the five-star hotels in the city, situated directly opposite the Gateway of India. We entered the awe-inspiring facade of the old building and Tiger led us to the coffee shop, Shamiana. It was 10.45 p.m.

We couldn't help but act awkwardly, and our conversation

was artificial and nervous. I had never imagined being at such a place. The steward came over to take our orders and of course it was Chikna who made a fool of himself. The steward politely inquired what each of us would like to have—coffee, tea, cappuccino. Before he could finish, Chikna interjected, 'Cappuccino—is it a Chinese dish?' The man smiled and explained that it is actually a kind of coffee. We all laughed out loud, drawing irritated stares from our neighbours. Only Tiger bhai was at ease, as if he was a regular here. The steaming cups arrived and we all began sipping coffee.

Finally, after half an hour of idle conversation, two men, Farooq and Mushtaq Tarani, joined us and the meeting came to life. Tiger bhai began talking animatedly about the demolition of the Babri Masjid and the communal riots in Bombay—the loss of life, the atrocities.

After a while Tiger bhai decided to take Farooq aside, and they talked privately for over twenty minutes. Then Tiger bhai came and told us that we would all conduct a reconnaissance of the spots slated as targets right away. As we left the hotel, the guard saluted us. I suppose that this was standard practice at the Taj, but it so startled me that I looked around to make sure he was saluting us, and not some wealthy guest.

We all piled into Farooq's blue Maruti 1000. He first drove us to the Bombay Municipal Corporation (BMC) building opposite VT. We simply sped by in the car, just glancing at the building. Tiger bhai told us to return for a detailed survey later. 'Badshah, it is your responsibility,' he said. Then we drove to Dalal Street and had a quick look at the old and new buildings of the share market. After that Farooq dropped us back at the Taj, and he and Tarani took their leave.

Tiger was going back to his house at Mahim and we accompanied him part of the way. He told us that one more soldier would be inducted into our army. He was called Sardar Shahwali Khan, and like us, he was eager to take revenge. Somehow, though, I didn't feel I could trust Sardar. He had not been with us during our training in Pakistan. Chikna said, however, that he would make arrangements for Sardar's training here in Bombay. Huh, I thought, that'll be a tall order.

Next day, 5 March, after Friday prayers, Bashir Khan and I went to the BMC building. I was amazed at the lax security—this is the building which houses the city administration! We entered the building without being stopped or questioned. We get our daily water supply through BMC, they run the BEST buses and corporation hospitals—inefficiently—and look after the education of our kids, though ineptly. Besides, this building also contained the offices of some of the most insidious Hindu leaders, the ones who sustained their position by spilling the blood of my helpless brothers.

I walked to the first-floor offices of the BJP and Shiv Sena. The rooms were spacious and, I realized, easily accessible. Tiger bhai's idea was to have a half-dozen trained commandos storm the building with AK-56s. Since security was minimal, I thought that the commandos would be able to reach the party offices unhindered. We'd be able to massacre the filthy bastards with bullets the way a BMC worker sprays pesticide on flies.

'Badshah bhai, *yeh to ekdum halva hai* (This is really easy)!'. Bashir echoed my feeling. Excited we abandoned the idea of scouting other locales and rushed straight to Tiger bhai to report.

I had been so engrossed in these activities that I hadn't paid any attention to my personal work for several days. So on Saturday, 6 March, I decided I needed to catch up on that and take some time off. But my holiday was not to be, for Chikna called me for a meeting that evening at a house in Hill Road, Bandra. This used to be the home of Shakil, to whom Tiger bhai had often entrusted the toughest tasks. The previous year Shakil had been killed when a team of customs officers raided his house. Tiger bhai was very shaken by his death, and now looked after Shakil's sister Mubina Aapa, whom he also called *baya* (sister).

Bashir Khan

The people gathered there that evening were Tiger bhai, Chikna, Bashir Khan, Nasim Barmare, Bashir Electrician, Parvez Kelawala, Nasir Dhakla and Firoz Malik. There were also four new faces: Salim Rahim Shaikh and Mehmood Kaloo, who had worked with Tiger bhai earlier, and Moin Qureishi and Sardar Khan, who were among the five new people Tiger had told us he was planning to induct into our group. After an initial discussion that didn't seem to lead anywhere, Tiger bhai took charge. He said that once we had decided what were the most vital spots in the city to hit, we should divide into groups and recce them. He asked us what we thought the targets should be. Suddenly I wanted to assert myself. Before anybody could say anything, I grabbed the initiative.

'Tiger bhai,' I blurted out, 'I think Sahar International Airport and the Chembur oil refinery should be targets.'

'Why?' asked Tiger bhai.

'If we can bomb even one airplane, the whole world will become aware of it,' I said. 'An explosion at the refinery will cause a huge fire. All of India will be shaken.'

'*Bahut* risky *kaam hai*,' Chikna said, peeved that I had the spotlight for a change.

Tiger bhai gave Chikna a withering look. 'Badshah, your idea is great. Why don't you find out if it's really possible?'

'Yes bhai, I will do that,' I said.

'Our goal is to shake the government,' said Tiger bhai decisively. 'Hence BMC, Mantralaya, the share bazaar, and Doordarshan should be our targets. Or, like Badshah said, the airport and refinery—it is a great idea. I think even five-star hotels should not be spared.'

'How about the Sena Bhavan at Dadar?' Sardar asked. He seemed to be a bright chap.

Tiger also seconded this idea. A short while later, we dispersed.

On 7 March, I borrowed Tiger bhai's Bajaj scooter and left with Parvez Kelawala for a recce trip to Sena Bhavan. We carefully studied the layout and decided that the petrol pump next to it would be the best place to plant a bomb. Not only would Sena Bhavan be reduced to dust, in addition the fire from the petrol pump would annihilate the surrounding area.

From there we went to the airport. I drove the scooter to a newly constructed flyover, which led to the departure area. The top of the flyover served as a lovers' lane. In the evening, couples would come and sit up there together. As I rode up the slope, I yearned for a girlfriend of my own. Just after the steep climb, next to the curve, I found a gap between the buildings. Through there I could see into the bay where they park planes. Three were just sitting there. I thought, what an uproar it will cause if we can blow up three planes!

On the way back, I told Parvez that Tiger bhai would probably want us to throw hand grenades to blow up the planes. Parvez shook with fear at this idea and said that he would rather do the job at Sena Bhavan than at the airport. After I dropped Parvez at Mahim, I picked up Nasir Dhakla and took him to the spot at the airport. I repeated the same spiel about hand grenades. It seemed to me that Nasir too was afraid.

Early that evening, Chikna again called a meeting. This time it was at Chikna's brother Babloo's house. Babloo was not there. Tiger bhai, Chikna, Bashir Khan, Salim Shaikh, Irfan Chougule, Tainur, Parvez, Nasir, Zakir Khan, Farooq Pawle, Sardar Khan and Niyaz were there. The flat was small, so some of us—Tiger bhai, Chikna, Sardar, Bashir, Tainur and I—sat inside while the others sat on the adjoining terrace.

Tiger bhai announced that the targets had been selected and finalized. 'The first targets are the Air-India building at Nariman Point; the Bharat Petroleum oil refinery at Chembur; the share market at Fort; and the gold market at Zaveri Bazaar. Then there are five five-star hotels: the Sea Rock, the two Centaurs, Oberoi Sheraton and Taj Mahal; the top film theatres: the Metro, Regal, Excelsior, Sterling and Plaza; Shiv Sena Bhavan at Dadar; the BMC building at VT; Sahar International Airport; the RPO at Worli; and Mantralaya.'

When he finished, absolute silence prevailed in the room. All of us were watching Tiger bhai although he was staring into space and not looking at anyone. The intensity in his look sent shivers down my spine. For the first time it occurred to me that Tiger was not acting alone. He was, I began to believe at that moment, discussing this plan with others. After every meeting with us—I was suddenly sure—he referred back to some unseen and unknown High Command.

'How can only a handful of people plant bombs at so many places?' I asked.

Tiger bhai took his time in replying. 'The bombing will be done in two stages. We will set time bombs at Air-India, the oil refinery, the share bazaar, the gold market, the five-star hotels, the movie houses, the passport office and Sena Bhavan. At the airport, hand grenades will be hurled to destroy airplanes. Similarly at BMC and Mantralaya, whoever is good at using a *lambiwali* (an AK-56) will storm these places and shoot down the important leaders.' Tiger bhai's eyes glowed brighter with each sentence he delivered. 'Badshah.'

Hearing Tiger bhai say my name gave me a jolt.

'Explain to everyone your analysis of the airport and BMC.'

'Yes, bhai.' I could barely speak. I suddenly developed stage fright. I cleared my throat and explained that that there was a spot on the flyover from where the parked planes could be seen. When we had been there, there were three planes in the bay. I described the absence of security at the BMC, and how one could easily enter from a small gate in a lane opposite Azad Maidan and reach the party offices on the first floor. I suggested that a car should be kept waiting downstairs and four people could go upstairs. Two would take on the Shiv Sena office and the other two would finish off the BJP leaders. The entire job could be accomplished in five minutes flat.

When I finished, everybody was looking at me with a mixture of awe, admiration and also envy.

A short while later, Tiger bhai indicated that the group discussion was over. He would now talk to people in small groups in the room while the rest waited on the terrace. Irfan Chougule, Tainur and Farooq Pawle made up the first group. Tiger spoke to them for few minutes, then they left. Then Chikna, Niyaz Ahmed, Bashir Khan and Sardar Khan were summoned. Tiger spoke to them for some time before they departed. He also spoke briefly to Salim, Parvez, Nasir and Zakir. Tiger bhai finally called me. When I stepped in, only then did I realize that he and I were alone.

'Come, beta, sit,' he said warmly. 'I have the most important task lined up for you. Because I know you are the most intelligent of them all.'

I nodded.

'You have to conduct a recce of the Chembur oil refinery. It has to be a thorough job. One proper bombing at the refinery could mean the total annihilation of Bombay's northeastern region. Thousands of kafirs can be sent to hell in one stroke.' He gazed intently at me.

I nodded again, but I could not hold Tiger bhai's gaze for long. I looked away.

'*Chalta hoon*, bhai,' I said, more as a statement than permission to leave.

'Khuda hafiz, beta,' Tiger said.

'Allah hafiz, bhai,' I said, and walked out of the room.

On 8 March, Bashir Khan and I borrowed Tiger bhai's Commander jeep. Tiger bhai was away for the day, training the new recruits. I took the wheel, Bashir sat next to me, and we drove towards the refinery. I entered the restricted area through the Dadar checkpoint. Four cops were standing there. One of them waved the jeep to a halt.

For a moment my heart skipped a beat. But then I thought, why am I nervous of men like these? I dipped a hand into the pocket of my starched kurta and fished out a ten-rupee note. As the policeman stealthily took the tenner, he gave me a sheepish grin and waved me on.

We sped along a narrow road with foliage on both sides. There was hardly any traffic, probably because it was a high security area. On my right were gigantic round tanks. As I was driving, I could only dart quick looks at them, but to my disappointment I read a hand-painted sign that said 'water'. I came to a fork in the road and took the right turn. Here there were other huge tanks. I was sure these contained oil. They might have belonged to Bharat Petroleum or perhaps Rashtriya Chemical

Fertilizer (RCF). I slowed down for a good look, and began searching for a suitable place to throw a grenade. Finally, I stopped to take a closer look, but to my disappointment realized that the tanks were too far from the road to target.

The entrance into the area where the tanks were was sealed. It was simply impossible to enter. If only we had a rocket launcher, I thought, we could take out one tank. Just one tank. Suddenly I started imagining what actually would happen if we succeeded in blowing up those tanks. What if ..., I thought to myself. And then, from somewhere inside me that I almost didn't recognize, I thought, No!

What destruction! What havoc we would bring upon the neighbourhood! How many people would die! I could not bring myself to imagine the full extent of the devastation we could cause. At that moment, I just gave up the idea of bombing the refinery. I felt so clear about this that I thought I could convince Tiger bhai as well.

I stepped on the accelerator. The jeep picked up speed and I quickly exited from the Chembur gate and drove towards Mahim.

I was engrossed in thought when Bashir said, 'Did you know about Gullu?'

I remembered Gul Mohammed Khan. I realized that he was at none of the meetings, and that I hadn't actually seen him since I returned from Dubai on 4 March. But he was only one of several who had trained with us but had not been attending the meetings.

'What about Gullu?' I asked.

'He has gone underground.'

'Why go underground even before the work has begun?' I asked incredulously.

'I heard that dresswalas were looking for him.'

We call the police dresswalas, tholes or mamus.

'You mean the Nirmal Nagar police?' I asked Bashir. I knew

that they wanted Gullu because he had stabbed several people during the riots.

'*Haan yaar, bol raha tha jama ho jaaonga*,' Bashir said. He wanted to surrender to the police.

I did not say a word and took a turn to the Western Express Highway. We sped towards the Golibar area. Gullu lived here, in the Navpada area, a labyrinth of slum alleys, in Behram Nagar, Bandra East. After visiting several roadside teashops, I finally located him in a small hutment where he was hiding.

'What the hell is going on?' I barked at him. 'I hear you want to surrender to the police.'

'You tell me: Why should my family suffer because of my wrong doings? Huh?' Gullu said. He was crying. 'They have taken my brothers and are beating them up in the police lock-up.'

I was moved. I did not know what to say. Now more than ever I had to see Tiger bhai.

I pulled up in front of the imposing Al-Hussaini building where Tiger bhai lived and went up to his apartment. Tiger bhai seemed to have just returned and looked exhausted. I told him that Gullu wanted to surrender.

I could make out that Tiger bhai was enraged, though he showed no emotion. He instantaneously made the decision. '*Thok do b... ko* (Kill him).'

'No, Tiger bhai, I will convince him.' I was not too sure I could but I thought it was worth a try.

'Take Chikna along with you—and tell him to keep his mouth shut! Remind him about my warning: If anybody spills the beans then I will not only kill him but I will finish off his entire family.'

His threats upset and confused me. How could Tiger bhai even talk about killing one of us? As I reached the foot of the stairs, I saw Tiger bhai was coming down too. He wanted to come along. On the way, we picked up Chikna. But when we reached Gullu's place, he was already gone. Our trip had been pointless. Chikna and Tiger bhai went home in the jeep, I took a cab and returned home.

The next day, 9 March, I heard that Gullu had been picked up by the police. I also found out that when Tiger bhai, Chikna and I had gone to Gullu's house, he had still been there, hiding. I wondered what would happen if Gullu squealed on our plans. He knew everything: he'd been trained in Pakistan, he was there at Dubai, and he knew that we were planning to bomb the city. What if he told the police? He could ruin everything.

Chikna, who lived nearby, came over to my house and asked me, 'Do you know that Gullu has been picked up by the police?'

I said I did.

'Tiger bhai is pissed off,' Chikna said. 'He has called an urgent meeting at Shakil's place at Bandra at 8 p.m. today.' He glared at me as if I was partly responsible for the mess. I dreaded facing Tiger bhai. It was I who had argued against killing Gullu, and now the sword was hanging over our heads.

Without looking at Chikna, I said, 'I'll meet you there.'

■

Gullu's arrest had dealt a severe blow to the plans of Tiger Memon. Many in the group feared that there would be a sweeping crackdown and all of them would be arrested. Their first instinct was to get away from the city and abandon the mission. The fear and uncertainty was so palpable that Tiger felt he could not keep them on a leash for long.

Tiger called a meeting after *iftar*, the breaking of the daily fast. Everybody was present: Chikna, Salim Shaikh, Bashir Khan, Zakir Khan, Nasir Dhakla, Parvez Kelawala, Moin Qureishi,

Mohammed Iqbal, Sardar Khan, Bashir Electrician, Mehmood Kaloo, Nasim, Badshah Khan, Anwar Theba, Irfan Chougule, Tainur, Farooq, Shahnawaz Qureshi, Abdul Akhtar and Shaikh Ali. There was also Shafi Jariwala, whom many in the group had never met before but who was an old associate of Tiger's. They were all visibly nervous, and hoping that Tiger would say something inspiring to bolster their flagging courage, or come up with a plan that would salvage the situation.

But Tiger did nothing of the sort. He merely strode in and opened a huge maroon briefcase. He brought out wads of fifty-rupee notes. He placed several wads on top of the briefcase. Everybody was awestruck at the sight so much cash. Taking everyone by surprise, Tiger gave a wad of Rs 5,000 to Chikna, another to Badshah Khan, and then one wad each to everyone in the room. They were all overwhelmed. The message was clear: if they remained steadfast in their loyalty they would get more such rewards.

Thus forestalling any murmur of protest, Tiger began to speak: 'Gullu's arrest can ruin our plans. But *Allah ki kasam*, I will not cancel my plans even if it means that I have to sacrifice my life. We can outwit the police. The cops will be expecting us to strike in a while, but like Napoleon Bonaparte we will strike earlier. So before Gullu has time to tell the police all our plans, we will put them into execution.

'Friday, 12 March, is the seventeenth day of Ramazan. It will be the day when the Holy Prophet fought the first battle of Junge-Badr against the heathens of Mecca and forced them to retreat. The auspicious date will help us achieve success.' Tiger paused for effect, looking around the room. His listeners seemed spellbound.

'Bhai, it is already Tuesday evening. How can we make preparations and execute our plans in three days?' Badshah Khan asked.

Tiger did not reply immediately. Then he said, 'I have thought out everything. What remains now is the final selection of the spots and planting of bombs. We can finalize it tomorrow and make preparations on Thursday. We will meet again tomorrow at my residence and chalk out our strategy.'

As they had all missed their *tarawih* prayers that night in order to attend the meeting, the meeting for the following day was scheduled at 10 p.m., after prayers.

They all gathered on 10 March at Tiger's luxurious apartment in the Al-Hussaini building. There was a new sense of hope and resolution. Only Nasir and Parvez Kelawala were missing from the previous evening's group. Niyaz Ahmed and Nasim Barmare who had not been there the previous evening were present, as was Chikna's brother Babloo. Among those not present but who would participate in the bombings were Imtiyaz Ghavate, Parvez Shaikh and Asgar Mukadam, who were part of Tiger's inner circle and were briefed separately.

The meeting began briskly. Tiger asked Badshah Khan, 'So, what is your report?'

'Bhai, I think the job at the refinery is not only almost impossible to carry out, but also dangerous.'

'How and why?'

Badshah Khan described the security and the distance from the road. He did not mention his fear about the destruction it would cause for he realized that if Tiger knew the magnitude of devastation, he would insist the refinery be attacked.

'Okay, let us cancel the refinery,' Tiger said reluctantly. 'I think that car bombs would be the best way of achieving our ends. We will park cars with RDX at the share bazaar, the Air-India building, Zaveri Bazaar, the grain market at Masjid Bunder, the Shiv Sena headquarters at Dadar and Plaza Cinema. Those places where car bombs cannot be exploded, we have to storm, like the BJP and Shiv Sena offices.'

'You mean only these few places will be targeted?' Chikna asked.

'The five-star hotels in the suburbs too will be hit. At the BMC, we can storm in and fire with AK-56s. At the airport, Badshah will show you from where you have to throw grenades to hit the planes. And don't forget to throw some grenades on the fishermen's colony at Mahim. Those people should also be taught a lesson for messing with me.' Tiger suddenly changed track from the practical to the rousing: 'Let this city and Advani and Thackeray remember forever what we are capable of doing in the span of a few hours.'

Badshah interjected a note of practicality: 'Bhai, can we do all this in a few hours? It is a hell of a job to unpack RDX bags, fill them in cars, attach detonators and timers and then park these cars at the locations.'

'You can start after iftar tomorrow evening. Use my flat and the car park downstairs for filling and loading explosives. The cars have all been organized. You can work throughout the night. Then, on Friday morning, you just have to drive the cars to the targets and park them there,' Tiger said.

'Yes, I think it can be done,' Anwar Theba said.

Tiger looked at Anwar, Chikna and Irfan, and then at the others and said, 'Anwar, Javed and Irfan are the best at fixing detonators and pencil timers, so they will supervise that part of the work. The rest of you should work under their direction. I will leave by the early morning flight to Dubai. After you have finished your jobs, I have also made arrangements for your escape. There might be communal riots after this. Either you can use the machineguns and ammunition that we have, or you can give them to other Muslims.'

They talked late into the night, planning details of who would carry out what part of the operation and detailing plans of escape. Finally, Tiger asked Shafi to bring out his bag, which contained wads of fifty-rupee notes. Tiger again distributed Rs 5,000 to each of the assembled men. He also gave them his Dubai telephone numbers so that they could contact him if the need arose. He designated Chikna and Theba as leaders of the mission in his absence. The group dispersed after that.

All through that long night, Tiger was on the telephone, talking to his financiers, friends and associates in Dubai, finalizing details. He went to bed only at about 10 a.m.

When he woke up, the calendar facing him said 11 March. He looked around his comfortable home, knowing that this was the last morning he was waking up there for a long, long time. He did not know whether he would ever be back. His parents, five brothers and their families as well as his wife and children had all left for Dubai on 9 March. He got up, prayed, and continued his series of telephone calls, finalizing details about the following day. He was flying out by the 4 a.m. Emirates flight on 12 March, by which time preparations for the bombing would be well under way but he would not be able to see the fruits of his labour or be there to counsel at the final moments.

Tiger sat brooding for hours, until he heard the evening call of the muezzin. It was time for iftar. His manager, Asgar Mukadam, and his driver, Abdul Gani Turk, arrived soon after and he began to make preparations for his departure.

5

The Worst Day

Like all Ramazan mornings, 12 March had begun on a sombre note. Most of the group had not slept the previous night, as they discussed their plans in precise detail and prepared the vehicles carrying the bombs. By the break of day, all the vehicles—an Ambassador, two Maruti vans, three Maruti 800s, a Commander jeep, a motorcycle and four scooters, most of which belonged to the Memon family or their friends—were loaded with RDX putty and connected with detonators in Tiger's car park. Three suitcases were also filled with explosives with timers attached to them. After that began the task of dispatching the bombs to their targets. Some of the members of the group were missing, such as Nasir Dhakla and Parvez Kelawala, who had also not been present at the last meeting with Tiger. Sardar Khan, having worked through the night, slipped away in the morning. This worried them but there was too much to be done to bother.

The first one to be sent off by Chikna was Mohammed Iqbal, who left at 8 a.m. to park one of the scooters at Dadar TT. The scooters were set up to go off if the vehicle was pushed around, and also contained pencil timers.

Dadar is one of the most crowded terminuses of the suburban railway network of Central and Western Railways. At every hour of the day, there are over ten thousand local commuters as well as hundreds of passengers for the long-distance trains that halt at the station. An explosion there could wreak havoc and potentially kill at least a couple of thousands people.

Iqbal wanted to park the scooter just outside the main exit of the station. He rode to the Swami Narayan temple, located diagonally opposite the terminus. As he searched for a suitable parking space, a stream of passengers came out from the station and began to queue up at the nearby taxi kiosk, which was supervised by a traffic policeman. Iqbal tried to park near the kiosk, but the policeman blew his whistle at him, indicating that he could not park there and that he was interrupting the flow of traffic.

The whistle and accompanying angry gesture so unnerved Iqbal that his first instinct was to abandon the scooter and flee. But he realized that would only aggravate the situation, so he nodded apologetically and rode towards Naigaon Cross Lane. He was sorely tempted to abandon the project, but quailed at the thought of telling Chikna. So finally he decided to park the scooter near the footbridge used by passengers, another densely crowded area. The first bomb was planted in the dicky of the scooter. Then he hailed a taxi and returned to Al-Hussaini.

At about 11 a.m., Parvez Shaikh, Asgar Mukadam and his cousin Shoaib Ghansare, who had been roped in to help, set off for Anwar Theba's house at Turner Road, Bandra, in a Maruti van with the three medium-sized suitcases, filled with RDX, which were meant for the hotels in the western suburbs—the Sea Rock, the Juhu Centaur and the Airport Centaur. Theba had already booked rooms in the three hotels and collected the keys for these on 11 March. They honked to alert Theba when they reached his house. Theba confirmed that they were carrying the three suitcases and then asked them upstairs. There they met Mushtaq Tarani, who had met with Tiger and some of his associates at the Taj Mahal Hotel. He was dressed in an expensive and well-cut suit, and looked every inch a businessman. He was to leave the suitcase at the Juhu Centaur.

The five set out again. Mushtaq was dropped off at Linking Road. Theba gave him the keys and the receipt for room 3078, booked in the name of Sanjeev Roy, as well as a light blue suitcase and some money. He told Mushtaq that the bomb was supposed to go off after about two-and-a-half hours. He also reminded Mushtaq to return the keys and receipt to him after depositing the suitcase. Mushtaq nodded and hailed a taxi to his destination. Parvez was dropped off further down the road.

Juhu Centaur, facing the beach, was regarded as one of the finest hotels in Bombay's western suburbs and was very popular with business travellers from all over the world. Mushtaq entered the foyer and hesitated for a moment, feeling the weight of the suitcase. He decided to go straight to the room, but had difficulty finding it, and had to seek help from the hotel staff. His broken English, he felt, would seem suspicious given his sophisticated appearance. Beads of sweat dotted his face as he followed a bellboy to his room. The bellboy went through a long introductory spiel, explaining the various facilities to him and then lingered on hopefully for a tip. When he finally left, Mushtaq immediately looked around for a place to hide the suitcase. The space between the bed and the bedside table seemed the most suitable, so he placed it there. It could not be seen unless one looked carefully. Mushtaq took one last look at the suitcase, and then left the room and strode rapidly down the corridor. He took the lift downstairs and hailed a taxi to go to Al-Hussaini. It was 11.35 a.m.

While Mushtaq was looking for his room in Juhu Centaur, Shoaib Ghansare dropped off Theba at the portico of Hotel Airport Centaur at Santacruz, located near the domestic terminal of the airport. He had booked Room 157 there in the name of

Anwar Theba

Rajkumar Saxena. His dour visage and air of being in a hurry discouraged the hotel staff from exchanging pleasantries. Room 157 was on the first floor, and Theba took the stairs, refusing to wait for the lift.

He barely managed to stop himself from breaking into a run when he saw the door of his room. As he slid the key into the door, a room service waiter who had come out from the adjoining room offered to help him with his suitcase. Theba simply glared at him and entering the room, shut the door on his face. He looked around the room, debating where to hide the suitcase, and finally opted for the wardrobe. He stood it inside and shut the door.

The moment he finished doing this, he rushed to the bathroom to relieve himself. He left the hotel in haste as well, jumping into a taxi before it had fully come to a halt. He asked the driver to take him to Mahim. The time was 11.40 a.m., and the third bomb had been planted.

The final hotel bomb was deposited by Parvez who had also dropped at Linking Road with the suitcase which he was to leave in Suite 1840 at Hotel Sea Rock, booked by Dominic D'Souza for Advani of Gorakhpur Metals. Parvez took an autorickshaw to the hotel, one of the most luxurious in the city. He asked a bellboy in the ornate lobby to show him to his room, but had difficulty keeping up with the man as he was so mesmerized by the paintings and chandeliers. He was shown to his room on the eighteenth floor.

He looked around the room wonderingly, and then at the suitcase on the bed. He slid it below the bed. Then he opened the door, peeped out and seeing the empty corridor, he walked out and closed the door. Like the others, he took a taxi back to Mahim. It was 12.05 p.m.

Some time before noon, the blue Commander jeep left Al-Hussaini and sped towards the city centre. The jeep, one of those used by Tiger for smuggling, had a huge cavity under the floorboards. This time the cavity contained some twenty-five kilograms of RDX. The driver was Abdul Gani Turk. He was supposed to park the jeep outside the RPO at Worli.

Traffic was thin, and the journey did not take too long. He reached the area shortly after noon and slowed down to find a parking space such that the explosion would cause maximum damage. But all the parking spaces near and around the office were taken. He had two alternatives: either to double-park the jeep in front of the office and run the risk of the vehicle being towed away by the traffic police, or to leave the jeep on the other side of the road, facing the RPO. There was a space in front of a wine shop in the opposite side, and he just about managed to fit the jeep into it. He locked the doors and left the jeep. The fifth bomb was in place.

The moment Gani left the jeep, he started feeling queasy. He managed to find a taxi, and headed for Bhendi Bazaar. It was 12.30 p.m.; he thought that with luck he could still attend Friday prayers in town.

When Gani was struggling for parking space for his jeep, an official-looking white Ambassador with an uniformed chauffeur, Farooq Pawle, had left Mahim for Nariman Point, the heart of the city's business district. His destination was the Air-India building. It took him some thirty-five minutes to negotiate the heavy traffic.

Finding a parking space for the Ambassador at the Air-India building proved to be easy. As the Ambassador was still considered the official car used by bureaucrats and politicians, the security guard at the building let the car through when it entered the narrow passageway beneath the huge skyscraper. Pawle drove down the passageway and parked the car outside the rear exit of the Bank of Oman on the ground floor. The sixth bomb was planted.

As he left the compound and walked down the pavement, he saw a blue Maruti 800 drive by, with Irafan Chougule at the wheel, and Tainur, dressed in an impressive three-piece suit, seated next to him.

As they drove past Mantralaya, Tainur looked at the drab building. 'If Chikna is planning to storm the BMC, then why not Mantralaya? After all, this houses bigger bastards.'

'Your wish will soon be fulfilled. Chikna plans to come after them here once he finishes those at the BMC,' Irfan replied.

The car sped towards the BSE. It was 12.50 p.m.

Outside the building, Tainur stepped out of the car and seemed to mutter instructions to his 'driver' Irfan, who nodded in reply. Irfan went down the street, looking for a place to park. Dalal Street is one of the most densely populated areas in the city, and even if Irfan had been riding a bicycle he would have found it difficult to park. They had discussed the problem of traffic when the group was planning the bombings but they had never realized that parking would be such a problem.

Irfan knew that the stock market was one of their main targets; they could not skip this. He took a U-turn and let the car crawl again towards the gate of the BSE.

Tainur, who was standing at the gate, realized that Irfan had not found a parking space. He saw a Hindustan Contessa leaving the car park in the basement of the BSE, and frantically

Tainur

waved to Irfan to bring the car in. As Irfan drove in, the security guard who had not seen Tainur waving, signalled the former to a halt. Seeing this, Tainur rushed towards the guard.

Irfan, a hot-tempered man, had already got into an argument with the guard. Coming up to them, Tainur began talking to the guard in Gujarati, the language associated with the wealthiest players on the market. Impressed, the guard allowed the car to drive into the basement car park. Irfan parked the car in bay 64, and he and Tainur quietly left the area.

Pawle reached Al-Hussaini by 1.15 p.m. and set out for his second assignment, for which he had asked Badshah Khan to accompany him. They had to park a white Maruti 800 car outside Sena Bhavan. Badshah chose to drive. When they reached their destination, Badshah wanted to park just outside the fortress-like building, but a traffic policeman threatened to challan them. As Pawle got into an argument with the policeman, Badshah suggested that they park at Lucky Petrol Pump, adjacent to Sena Bhavan, which was what he had proposed during the planning. An explosion at the petrol pump would inevitably cause havoc in Sena Bhavan.

But they ran into trouble at the petrol pump as well. The attendants told them that they could not park unless the car was going to be serviced. Pawle was getting into another altercation, when Badshah decided to drive towards the Mohammed Ali building, next to Sena Bhavan. Badshah asked Pawle to get a taxi, while he parked the car. He parked towards the far end of the petrol pump, as close as possible to Sena Bhavan, locked the car and jogged towards the taxi in which Pawle was waiting. They set off for Mahim. The eighth bomb had been set in place.

Asgar Mukadam, Tiger's business manager, was asked to accompany Shahnawaz Qureishi to park a Maruti 800 outside Plaza Cinema. Asgar was reluctant, but had to agree when Chikna insisted. He got behind the wheel sulkily.

'Where should we park?' Shahnawaz tried to strike up a conversation.

'Your call. I am here only to give you company,' Asgar replied tersely.

They were silent after that. It was past noon, and the matinee show of the Nana Patekar-Raaj Kumar film *Tiranga* had begun. There was plenty of space in the streets and lanes around the Plaza. Asgar managed to park just outside the cinema hall, within the compound, but a watchman came running and asked them to move the car.

Shahnawaz started getting aggressive, but Asgar tried to reason out with the watchman. 'We are already late for the show. If we miss out on Nana Patekar's dialogues, then what is the point in watching the movie?' There was some argument and exchange of expletive, but in the end they left the car almost touching the western wall of the building. They strolled out of the cinema premises when the watchman was not looking, and took a cab to Mahim: Shahnawaz to report to Chikna and Asgar to go home.

Mushtaq, Theba and Parvez Shaikh returned from their assignments and reported to Chikna that the hotel bombs were in place. Chikna instructed Mushtaq and Imtiyaz to take a scooter each to Dhanji Street and park them in the vicinity of Zaveri Bazaar. He told them that Shoaib Ghansare would be planting another bomb at the other end of Zaveri Bazaar, in Shaikh Memon Street. The idea was to inflict maximum damage on the gold market.

'Haan bhai, then what?' Mushtaq asked.

'You can both go underground after that,' Chikna told them in an obliging tone. Mushtaq and Imtiyaz left around 1 p.m.

When Shahnawaz reached Tiger's fifth-floor flat, it was almost 1 p.m. Chikna and Parvez were talking in muted tones. As Shahnawaz waited, Parvez ended the conversation abruptly and left with his customary 'khuda hafiz'.

Parvez was assigned the task of parking a scooter in any of the big markets in the Masjid Bunder area, in such a location that some prominent wholesalers would be affected. Riding very fast, Parvez soon reached the incredibly congested streets of Masjid Bunder. Afternoon was generally the worst time to visit this area. Looking around, he decided to make his way to Katha Bazaar, which seemed relatively easier to enter.

With much effort and argument, Parvez managed to enter the market but soon realized that he would not be able to go far in the bumper-to-bumper traffic. He switched off the engine and dragged the scooter along the pavement until he felt he could pull it no further. He could see no place where he could park, and he began to regret that he had accepted this problematic assignment.

He spotted a small public telephone booth just opposite the Matruchhaya building. The attendant had gone out for lunch and the kiosk was closed. Parvez parked the scooter next to it, took a quick look around, and rushed towards the Masjid Bunder railway station from where he planned to catch a harbour line train to Mahim. The tenth bomb was placed. It was almost 1.30 p.m. and the first bomb was about to go off.

Meanwhile, Mushtaq and Imtiyaz had set out on two scooters

for Dhanji Street, at the northern end of Zaveri Bazaar. As Mushtaq
rode over the Princess Street flyover, he could see a massive traffic
jam ahead. From the conversations of people around them, he
gathered that the bomb had exploded at the BSE. This increased
his desire to finish his assignment and get underground as soon
as possible. He rode to Dhanji Street and, locating an empty
space in front of DP Jewellers, parked the scooter there. The
people around the shop objected, but he said that he was merely
going for the Friday namaaz and would return soon. As Mushtaq
pulled his scooter onto its stand, he could see Imtiyaz parking a
short distance away.

The duo parked their scooters and walked away. The time
was 2.15 p.m. Mushtaq went back to his house at nearby
Mohammed Ali Road, while Imtiyaz left for Mahim.

Within minutes of Mushtaq and Imtiyaz entering Dhanji
Street, Shoaib Ghansare reached Shaikh Memon Street. He parked
his scooter at the junction of Shaikh Memon Street and Mirza
Street, at the southern end of Zaveri Bazaar. This was the target
where the maximum number of bombs—three—were planted,
and at both ends of the area. The thirteenth bomb was in place at
about 2.15 p.m. too. Locking the two-wheeler, Shoaib left for
home.

At Al-Hussaini, the morning frenzy was over. Chikna
summoned his remaining men. 'All that remains are the frontal
assaults. We have to throw grenades at two places: Macchimar
Colony at Mahim and the airport. And we have to storm into
two buildings: the BMC headquarters and Mantralaya.'

He assigned Iqbal and Nasim to throw the grenades at the
airport. He asked them to take a bike and gave them four grenades
each. Tainur, Moin, Zakir, Firoz, Bashir Electrician, Abdul Akhtar
and Mehmood were to take the blue Maruti van and hurl grenades
into Macchimar Colony. He and the other four—Babloo, Badshah

Khan, Shaikh Ali and Bashir Khan—would storm the BMC in the last remaining vehicle: a maroon Maruti van, and then carry on to Mantralaya.

Shortly after 2 p.m., the three vehicles left the Al-Hussaini car park. Within minutes, the second blast shook the city's grain market at Katha Bazaar, and soon after there was the blast at the Air-India building.

As Babloo drove the van down Cadell Road towards the BMC, everyone in it seemed to be in a pensive mood. They were carrying several AK-56 assault rifles, detonators and hand grenades. Badshah broke the silence once to ask if they had enough ammunition for all the BJP and Shiv Sena leaders. Chikna assured him that they did. As they drove down Prabhadevi Road, the fourth blast took place at Lucky Petrol Pump, near Sena Bhavan. It was 2.30 p.m.

Meanwhile, the blue van had halted on the road outside the Mahim fishermen's hutments, close to Al-Hussaini. Tainur brought the car to the kerb at a position where the eastern end of the hutments was within throwing distance. He kept the engine running while the other six got out, each carrying three or four grenades.

They stood some distance from each other and automatically settled into the stance of a bowler. They counted: one ... two ... three, and then began throwing the grenades one after the other. Almost before the grenades could land, they turned and scrambled to get in the van. By the time the first grenade exploded, Tainur had already turned the car and was driving away down Mahim Causeway. Later, the men separated and went their own way.

As the maroon van crossed over from Prabhadevi and was heading towards Worli, Chikna noticed that a detonator had begun blinking. He thought it would explode, killing all of them. He instinctively picked it up and passed it to Badshah Khan. All the men were paralysed with fear, and unable to think. Badshah promptly passed it over to Shaikh Ali. Shaikh lost no time but flung the detonator outside the window. The car was outside the RPO at Worli.

A loud explosion numbed their minds and senses. The van was lifted off the ground and landed again on the road with a thud, fishtailing. The rear windscreen was shattered. But the men were profoundly grateful still to be alive. They believed that if the detonator had remained in the car for a second more, they all would have died.

In a freak coincidence, it was the blue Commander jeep parked by Gani in front of the wine shop that had exploded at the very same moment as the detonator was thrown out.

Chikna and his men were so badly rattled by their brush with death that they interpreted the incident as a sign from God for them not to pursue their mission further. Chikna asked Babloo to park the van at some place, and said they would abandon the vehicle. Babloo took a right turn from the Glaxo factory and drove by the Siemens factory. Chikna indicated that this was where they should leave the van.

Babloo parked the van outside the locked gates of the Siemens factory. The men got out and he locked the car. In their shaken state, they forgot to collect the weapons in the vehicle, though it would have been hard to carry unwieldy AK-56s without attracting attention. They walked up to a taxi stand. As a precaution, they decided they would switch taxis after a point. They took two taxis to the Haji Ali junction, from where they took another two to Nagpada in south Bombay, where Chikna had decided to hide in the house of his relatives for a few hours.

As the explosions carried on at Zaveri Bazaar and the Plaza, Iqbal and Nasim were riding towards the airport on a Hero Honda motorcycle belonging to Tiger's brother, Ayub Memon.

Iqbal, riding the bike, knew that he had accepted this job because what the others were doing was much more risky. Nasim, the pillion-rider, would have to undertake the actual task of throwing the grenades.

They entered the airport and rode towards the flyover, to the point that Badshah had briefed them about. They could see bay 54. It was mid-afternoon and the airport was deserted. They looked around to check that no one was watching, and then Nasim lobbed three grenades one after the other. The moment Nasim said 'Chal bhaag', Iqbal twisted the bike's throttle and they rode down the bridge at full speed. They anticipated wailing police sirens behind them, but their fears were unfounded.

The first priority was to get rid of the motorcycle in case somebody had noted the number and informed the police. As they passed the Marol fire station, they saw fire engines go towards the airport. Iqbal took a right turn into a slum area. At the first convenient spot they parked the bike and parted ways.

That evening, while the people of Bombay were submerged in sorrow, the terrorists rejoiced in their victory. At Nagpada, Javed Chikna and his aides were in a festive mood. They had heard the reports of explosions in many parts of town and congratulated each other, Chikna especially pluming himself for coordinating the task so well. Now the escape of each and every person involved in the bombings was the most essential task. Chikna gave Rs 10,000 to each of them when they met that evening. He instructed them to leave the city as soon as possible, but to keep in touch with Tiger in Dubai.

The Bomb Detection and Disposal Squad (BDDS) in Bombay, an arm of the crime branch, was reckoned to be the best bomb

Nand Kumar Chougule
(*Courtesy* Mid-day)

handling and diffusing team in the country. It was very well equipped, and had a well-trained staff comprising three inspectors, nine SIs and fifteen constables. A talented and unconventional officer, Senior Police Inspector Nand Kumar Chougule, headed it.

Chougule was regarded as one of the finest officers in the city. He was a gentle giant, affectionately called 'Nandu' by his colleagues. He had taken charge of the BDDS in July 1991.

Though at that time he did not know much about bombs and explosives, he had since undergone intensive training with the NSG at Delhi and the 203 Bomb Disposal Company at Khadki, Pune.

At lunchtime on 12 March, it had been another unexciting day at the BDDS offices in Stone Building, behind the LT Marg police station, a stone's throw from the police headquarters. Given the specialized nature of its work, the BDDS was summoned only under exceptional circumstances. Otherwise, it was a drab existence.

Like many others that day, Chougule's lunch was interrupted. It was the police control room, announcing the explosion at the BSE.

Chougule rushed out, spewing orders: 'Load the equipment. Get the van ready. Hurry up! Call Pandhre and Zarapkar. Bring Zanjeer. Let's go!' SI Shankar Pandhre and Inspector Abhay Zarapkar were his two most trusted officers.

A flurry ensued. Officers and men began yanking on their

pale green uniform overalls, with 'Bomb Squad' emblazoned on the back. The van was loaded with the vital equipment, most of it imported, each in its own place in a specially designed cupboard. The most important among these was the Radio/Cable Control Mobile Investigation Unit (RCMIU), a radio-operated robot which went into bomb sites too dangerous for men to go; and carried bombs to safe spots for detonation. Other important pieces of equipment were the Explosive Detector Model 97 (EDM 97), which used gas chromatography to detect volatile substances and the portable Mini X-ray System which was used to study the innards of suspicious objects. Other items included Radio-Operated Wire, used to unlock bags that are suspected to contain explosives, the Deep Search Metal Detector (DSMD), which could detect a device hidden up to three feet below the ground, and the hand-held Simple Metal Detector (SMD), most commonly used to frisk passengers at airports.

The most important detector however was at the men's feet as the van left at 1.42 p.m. This was Zanjeer, a one-year-old golden Labrador who had joined the team in December 1992. He too had been trained at Pune like Chougule, but his specialization was sniffing out explosives.

Sirens blaring, jumping signals, flouting rules, the BDDS convoy of the van and two escort jeeps reached Dalal Street almost at the same time as the fire brigade. In front of the BSE, the men in green started leaping out of the van even before it had come to a complete halt.

Chougule was not prepared for what he saw. The ground was covered with scattered food, shards of glass, and puddles of blood; an eerie silence prevailed, and wounded people staggered around or lay on the ground.

The bomb squad men pitched in with the local police officers and the passers-by who had stopped to help, extricating people trapped in the debris.

One of his officers panted up to summon Chougule. 'Sir, we have located the centre of the blast. It's in the basement car park.'

The scene in the basement was even more horrific. The car park could accommodate about 200 cars, and many lay damaged and wrecked. Several cars were flattened by the two ceiling slabs that had collapsed. A mangled blue Maruti seemed to be where the explosion had happened. Thankfully the pillars had remained intact, reducing the extent of carnage and allowing the bomb squad and fire brigade to begin removing the injured. In at least six cars, the drivers were found dead behind the steering wheel. The air in the basement reeked of lead azide, a key component in explosives. The noxious gas was so strong that it was difficult to breathe.

The first thing Chougule did was to ask the officers and men to see if there was another bomb-laden vehicle in the basement. Chougule knew that terrorists around the world, including the Irish Republic Army (IRA), the Amal militia of Lebanon and the PLO, always set up bombs in such a manner that a second blast would follow the first by half an hour to forty-five minutes. The second one was intended to kill the rescue workers and the police. Zanjeer and the EDM 97 were brought in the basement and a search was initiated. Within thirty minutes, they had combed the basement but did not find any other bomb.

JCP (crime) M.N. Singh arrived. Chougule and his officers sprang to attention. Singh turned to Chougule. 'What kind of bomb was this?'

'Sir, it seems to be some kind of plastic explosive. I think it was RDX.'

'Was it a time bomb left in a bag?'

'Difficult to say anything right now, but from what I have seen, the bomb was kept in a Maruti 800.'

'A car bomb?' Singh's forehead creased.

'It could be. The amount of explosives used was much more than a few kilograms.'

'Kilograms of explosives?' Singh sounded incredulous.

'Absolutely, sir. They must have used at least forty or fifty kilograms of some high-intensity explosives,' said Chougule. 'They'd have to carry that in a car.'

Singh was still trying to absorb this information when Pandhre came running towards them. The Air-India building at Nariman Point had been bombed. By the time they received this information, twenty minutes had passed since the explosion.

Singh left immediately while Chougule, asking his team to assemble in the van, paused to give instructions to the officers from the Palton Road police station involved in rescue work. 'Tow out the vehicles in which the drivers have died. Do it very carefully. Don't try to remove the slabs manually. Call a crane for the job. Empty the basement area. Search each and every car parked in the neighbourhood. Tow away any unoccupied or suspicious looking car.'

Chougule and his team took off in the van, sirens shrieking. They emerged at Horniman Circle, opposite the Town Hall, and sped off to the Air-India building.

The scene was no different there. Fire brigade personnel had already arrived and were busy removing debris and rescuing trapped people. Chougule and his men got out of the van and fanned out in three directions. One group went towards Hotel Oberoi and began inspecting the cars parked around it, and another towards the Express Towers to check the vehicles there. The third team began removing all cars from the area. Parked or unoccupied vehicles were towed away by the traffic police.

Chougule himself investigated the mangled Ambassador car that was obviously the source of the blast. After closely scrutinizing the skeleton of the car, Chougule knelt to look at the crater below. It was at least ten feet in diameter and seven feet deep. He decided to take another look from the basement.

Chougule stepped into the office of Gulf Air, on the ground floor. The office was a pile of debris. Several bodies lay around— well-dressed executives, whose starched white shirts were dyed red with their own blood. These nightmarish scenes will haunt me forever, he thought. Hi-tech terrorism, as was practised in Lebanon, Palestine and Ireland, had finally arrived in India.

He slowly climbed down to the basement and stood looking up at the destroyed car. Pandhre and Kadam, another member of the BDDS, came to him and reported that cars had been evacuated from the whole area. Nothing suspicious or dangerous had been found in the vicinity. Chougule went out again and stood facing the Oberoi building, with Pandhre, Kadam and Zarapkar. Towards their left, there seemed to be a mass exodus of office employees. Chougule glanced at his watch. It was 3.45 p.m.

'That's a strange time to leave work,' he commented.

'Sir, they're panicking. With two blasts in the business district, they're afraid that they'll be next,' Pandhre said.

'I have never seen the fear of death in the eyes of so many people,' said Chougule, almost to himself.

The scene was both funny and tragic. People were scampering to get away from Nariman Point, where all the skyscrapers were clustered, to Churchgate, jostling for space inside BEST buses, fighting for a taxi. In normal times, Chougule would have laughed at the sight. Today, however, it seemed tragic that a bombing in the city could cause such terror.

The bomb squad conferred with M.N. Singh and concluded that least forty-five kilograms of RDX had been used in the car. Chougule was again approaching the basement, when a constable ran to him. 'Sir, there is a message which has just come in. There has been an explosion in Masjid Bunder.'

Chougule stopped in his tracks. Once again the bomb squad ran towards the van. In a couple of minutes, the van was flying towards Masjid Bunder, to yet another site of tragedy.

Apart from the BDDS of the city police, there was an independent office of the BDDS at Sahar Airport, headed by Major (Rtd.) Vasant Laxman Jadhav. This bomb squad was part of the Ministry of Civil Aviation. Jadhav was appointed the bomb squad chief after twenty-six years in the Indian army, where he had been handling explosives since 1981.

The police control room had also notified Jadhav of the blast at the BSE at 1.45 p.m., shortly after Chougule was informed. Jadhav had much more experience than Chougule or any other officer in dealing with such emergency situations.

Jadhav and his team left in their jeep and Ambassador car. As their office was at the other end of the city from the BSE, it would take them an hour to get there. As they were driving through the Mahim area, they heard about the second explosion.

At 2.55 p.m., Jadhav's jeep passed the Manish Nagar building at Worli. Suddenly, an explosion tore through the area. The two BDDS vehicles were thrown at least a foot high. Both were dented and their windscreens shattered. The team was badly shaken.

Jadhav halted the convoy to inspect the damage to their vehicles and the area. Then, in swift succession, he heard about the explosions at Masjid Bunder and at the Plaza Cinema. As he debated where to go, he heard that Sahar Airport had also been hit. That was a clear priority for Jadhav, and he and his team returned to their base.

The congestion at Masjid Bunder after the blast was such that it was nearly impossible for even the police to enter the area. The blaring sirens allowed the BDDS team to finally get into the market but they knocked down a couple of parked scooters, damaged a handcart and a bicycle. At 4 p.m., the van reached the Matruchhaya building. Though this was where the second blast had taken place, only the Pydhonie police had rushed to the scene as the rest of the force was occupied with the Air-India building and the BSE. By the time the BDDS team arrived, most of the dead and injured had been shifted to JJ Hospital.

Chougule conducted the mandatory search around the mangled scooter, which seemed to have carried the explosives, and of vehicles parked in and around Narsi Natha Street and then walked Zanjeer through. But he hesitated before declaring the area clear, because at the other two sites the bombers had aimed for destruction on a much larger scale than was seen here. He asked Pandhre to take the EDM 97 and scan the street. 'The scooter didn't carry more than twenty kilograms of explosives. We'd better be safe than sorry.'

Chougule pulled a handkerchief from his pocket and mopped his brow. The handkerchief reminded him of his wife Madhuri, who had tucked it in that morning. The thought of her had a tranquilizing effect.

'Sir, a message just came in from control,' Kadam interrupted his reverie. 'There has been another blast. At the RPO, Worli, about an hour ago.'

The van took off towards Worli. As soon as they reached Annie Beasant Road, the van ground to a halt as this main artery connecting the western suburbs to southern Bombay was clogged with bumper-to-bumper traffic. A while later, a trickle of cars started to get through, as traffic police swung into action and began diverting the vehicles. The van reached Worli only at 5 p.m.

The blast here had been the most destructive. Though about two hours had passed since the detonation, the area was still enveloped in a grey pall of smoke.

Chougule got out of the van very slowly. He walked towards the cordoned area, looking around carefully. He noticed that the explosion had thrown up a lot of dust which had settled on everything—leaves of trees, roofs of parked cars, windows of buildings. He looked at a third-floor balcony, where several long ribbons were hanging on the clothesline. He wondered why anyone would wash so many ribbons, but then it dawned on him that originally it had been a six-yard sari. He stumbled over some object. He looked down and stifled a scream—it was a woman's arm, blown off at the elbow. The red bangles on the wrist were still intact. Further on, he found a leg severed at the knee, clad in a Nike shoe and black trousers; and some distance on, a black mass he could identify as a head but so covered in blood and dust that he could not tell whether it was a man's or a woman's.

Chougule sat on his haunches and buried his face in his palms. His men surrounded him. They should have been inured to this after the three blast sites they had visited that day, but nothing had affected them so badly.

Somehow, Chougule collected himself and set to work. They moved to investigate the huge crater that had been the centre of the blast. This time the explosives seemed to have been loaded on a jeep. They brought out the EDM 97 and other detectors. Zanjeer was already sniffing around for any more explosives.

Though he kept mechanically supervising the operations, Chougule had not fully recovered from the horror and he knew that he was not thinking as clearly as he needed to. Kadam approached in brisk strides. 'Sir, the blast was so powerful that it shattered the glass for well over a mile. The Century Bazaar is badly ruined.'

Chougule nodded. 'Have you checked all the vehicles in the vicinity? Any suspicious objects?'

'We found nothing. This jeep alone would have done the job.'

Chougule saw the mangled remains of a BEST double-decker bus, now reduced to a ball of metal. Weak and dazed, he strolled aimlessly until Zarapkar and Pandhre joined him.

'Who could have done this and why?' Zarapkar asked.

'I can only think of one name,' replied Chougule. 'Dawood Ibrahim. But even he would not be capable of executing such blasts on his own.'

'You mean the LTTE (Liberation Tigers of Tamil Ealam) or PLO must have chipped in?' Pandhre said.

'It could be anybody,' Chougule said without conviction. 'It could be the JKLF (Jammu and Kashmir Liberation Front), Khalistani commandos or even the ISI. But I think Dawood has to be involved in this.'

'But Dawood is a gangster, not a terrorist ...' Zarapkar said.

'None of the blasts have taken place in Muslim areas. Dongri, Mohammed Ali Road and Pydhonie are untouched. Bombs have gone off in areas which Muslims rarely frequent in large numbers, like Nariman Point, the BSE or even Masjid Bunder.'

'But then why seek help from terrorist groups?' Kadam interjected.

'No gangster could bring in this much high-intensity explosives,' Chougule said, 'whether plastic or otherwise. This is RDX. You cannot buy this stuff in the open market. Dawood would need backing. He'd need a powerful and resourceful terrorist organization. They must have used at least eighty kilograms of explosives here.'

As Chougule spoke, the radio in Kadam's hand came to life.

A squawky voice directed the bomb squad to the Plaza Cinema at Dadar. Without a word, they took off.

This time the roads were relatively deserted as panic had driven most people home. They drove at eighty kilometres an hour, a speed unimaginable on normal days. They had started from Worli at 6.15 p.m. and were at the Plaza at 6.30 p.m.

For the BDDS team, despite the numerous sites they had visited that day, the horror struck them afresh at each one. As they finished their search of vehicles parked in the vicinity and an inspection of the location, and moved into the cinema hall itself, their radio informed them that bombs had exploded in two trains at Bandra and Dadar, and in three hotels: the Sea Rock and the two Centaurs in the western suburbs.

Chougule debated where they should go first. He also wondered whether they should divide up the team. As the team talked it over, the police control room informed them that the blasts in the trains were just rumours. Chougule heaved a sigh of relief. After finishing their work at the Plaza, they decided to go to the Sea Rock.

Pandhre was walking Zanjeer around the Plaza. Chougule, going to meet them, suddenly realized that the entire road was empty. Not a single vehicle could be seen. The sun had set only a few minutes before, but the emptiness and hush were like that before dawn.

The walkie-talkie crackled again. 'Crime asks the bomb squad to proceed to Worli. There's a suspicious Maruti van. The orders are immediate.'

Chougule abandoned their plans of going to the Sea Rock. The bomb squad headed back to Worli, to the Siemens factory.

By the time Major Jadhav returned to Sahar Airport, it was 5 p.m. The journey through the crowded roads had taken a long time. The BDDS squad and officers from the Sahar police station immediately went to bay 54 of the airport, where the hand grenades had been thrown.

There was a crater at the spot of explosion, at least a foot in diameter and three feet deep. Jadhav dug his fingers into the soil and found several small steel balls. He collected these and a handful of soil to take to his office. He would send the samples to the forensic laboratory for chemical analysis. Before he left, he instructed the police to do a *panchnama*, the official documentation of the crime scene and of the area.

Jadhav and the other officers found solace in the thought that the grenades had not damaged any aircraft, but had only hit the ground.

After passing through several diversions and detours, Chougule and his squad reached the Siemens factory at 9 p.m. The vehicle they had been called to inspect was a maroon Maruti van, which looked as if it had been recently battered. Its rear windscreen was shattered and shards of glass still dangled from it.

Chougule conferred with the officers from the Worli police station. The police constables and bomb squad men started to disperse the curious onlookers. When the crowd was pushed back to a safe distance, Chougule, Pandhre and Zarapkar went up to the van. They peered through the windows, but there was nothing immediately evident which indicated the presence of explosives. Then Chougule spotted two black bags lying on the back seat.

Chougule walked towards the driver's door and inspected the lock minutely. He had read about the instances in Ireland and Lebanon where the bomb mechanism was fitted in the lock, which detonated the moment somebody tried to open it. But it looked as though the lock was clear of any wires.

He took a long rope with a hook on one end. He slowly

tucked the hook in the handle and walked away. Some distance away, he turned and tugged gently at the rope. That way, if the bomb went off, the damage to limb and life would be minimal. The door flew open. The remaining doors were opened using the same technique.

Pandhre looked inside the car, below the seat and on the dashboard. The two rexine bags on the back seat, both about two feet in length and a foot in width, were carefully pulled out and put on the ground.

It was Zanjeer's turn now. He twitched his nose as he sniffed, lifted his face as if to exhale and then again dipped his nose towards the bag. It was as if the dog wanted to make sure. All eyes were on him. Once again Zanjeer inhaled and twitched his nose, but this time he'd made a decision. The dog looked towards Pandhre, then directly at the bag and barked three times. A hush descended on the police officers. Beyond a doubt, the bags contained explosives.

Chougule stepped towards the bag, his heart thumped wildly. In those brief moments it took to walk three steps to the bags, he thought of his wife and his son. Then he pushed those thoughts aside so that he could do his work.

He bent and unzipped the bag. He was certain that the zip was not a detonator, yet he could feel his heart beating as he waited for the loud explosion. But nothing happened.

Chougule exhaled in relief. He began to examine the contents: there were five AK-56 rifles, but none were loaded. Zarapkar moved towards the other one and unzipped it casually. He extracted two AK-56s, four hand grenades, several empty magazines and some live cartridges.

Pandhre, Zarapkar and Chougule searched the vehicle thoroughly. In the glove box, Chougule spotted a small packet containing a green rosary, used by Muslims during namaz, and a plastic bottle, half-filled with water, bearing Arabic inscriptions, which he guessed must have come from some holy spring. It seemed clear that the van and the weapons belonged to a religious Muslim. But why were they carrying weapons and why did they abandon them? .

In the dashboard were xerox copies of registration papers in the name of one Rubin Memon, as well as a yellow receipt from the Mahim Petrol Pump. Someone paid Rs 200 for petrol on 11 March. He pocketed it for further inquiry.

Chougule handed over the van, bags and guns to the Worli police officers. He and his team returned to the office, reaching after midnight. The plans to visit the western suburbs were postponed till the next morning.

'Want some dinner?' Zarapkar asked.

'Dinner?' Chougule looked dazed. 'I don't think I will ever be hungry ever again.'

He called the police control room to see if any more emergency calls had come in, but was told only his wife had called several times. He called home wearily. On the second ring, Madhuri picked up the phone.

'Hello?'

Her voice was enough to relieve all his tiredness. 'Madhu ...' Chougule was not allowed to finish.

Madhuri hurled a barrage of queries. 'Nandu? How are you? Where were you? Are you hurt? I did not have dinner. Where are you now? When are you coming home?'

He smiled. He told her that he would not be going home that night and hung up. He crossed both legs on his desk and closed his eyes. Sleep was far away but he needed it so badly that he was going to fake it.

In the midst of all the misery of that day, there were some who rejoiced. The conspirators were delighted at the stupendous success of their operation. Some called Tiger to congratulate him. They told him that his palatial mansion in Paradise was assured for he had followed the tradition of jehad. Tiger revelled in the flood of adulation. His spirits soared as he watched television reports. To celebrate, he decided to meet up with a childhood friend Shaikh Aziz Ahmed, formerly of Dongri, who now lived in Dubai. Aziz had grown up playing cricket and football with men who would later become underworld kingpins like Dawood Ibrahim and his brother Sabir. In their schooldays, he used to ridicule Tiger for his stout build and slow thinking, and bully him around. But Tiger had forgotten all that. He called Aziz and arranged to meet him at Hotel Delhi Durbar.

Tiger came in his gleaming red Ferrari, clad in a white kurta-pyjama. As they settled down in a corner of the restaurant, Tiger asked, 'Did you see the news of the blasts on BBC?'

'Who do you think did it?'

'I remember you said you were eager to take revenge for Muslim blood,' Tiger taunted. 'So what have you done?'

'Well, I wanted to...,' said Aziz weakly. He was hurt by the jibe.

The waiter had been hovering around them. They ordered food and lit up.

Then Tiger said, 'I must tell you. It was I who planned it. I assembled the boys, financed the operation, and executed it entirely on my own.'

'What?' Aziz exclaimed so loudly that people turned to stare. His half-smoked cigarette had fallen from his fingers into his glass.

Tiger smiled at his amazement. '*Mama kahani sunate rahe aur baccho ne chand chu bhi liya* (The uncle was still narrating the tale when the kids landed on the moon).'

Aziz felt a deep sense of humiliation at this tale of triumph from the person who used to be his favourite whipping boy.

As dinner was served, Aziz stared at the food, his mind working furiously. Suddenly, he found a weapon. He said, 'But you should have made better preparations. You will not be able to get away with it, you know.'

'What makes you think so?'

'The police have found a maroon van in Worli. It was filled with weapons. They said it could be an important breakthrough.' Busy with his calls, Tiger had failed to see this piece of news on the BBC.

Tiger looked crestfallen, and his face reflected pain and anger. Aziz had never seen him look like this.

'It should not have happened.' Tiger rose suddenly from his seat and strode out of the resturaunt. Aziz was too flummoxed to react.

■—◇✕✖

The control room of the home ministry in New Delhi was alerted to the first attack at the BSE at 2.37 p.m., more than an hour and nine minutes later. For information that was so closely linked to the country's security, this was an unpardonable delay. However, the union home minister, S.B. Chavan, and the minister of state for internal security, Rajesh Pilot, were both away attending a function of the Border Security Force (BSF). A runner was immediately dispatched to inform both the ministers, who rushed to their respective offices to take stock of the situation.

Chavan called a meeting at 5 p.m. in his Parliament House

office with the top brass of the IB, the Research and Analysis Wing (RAW) and the Central Forensic Science Laboratory (CFSL) to take stock of the situation. He asked a choice team of officers, including ballistics experts from the National Security Guards (NSG), to leave immediately for Bombay. Chavan himself planned to go there early the following morning. The control room of the home ministry was instructed to flash alerts to all the state capitals, alerting them to the possibility of terrorist attacks and sabotage.

Pilot had instructed his secretary that morning to reschedule all his meetings in the evening for he wanted to go home early and spend the evening with his wife. It was their wedding anniversary. But that was not to be. He tried to set up a meeting with the prime minister, P.V. Narasimha Rao. Rao was in Sikar, Rajasthan, when he received the news. When he returned to his office in Delhi at 5.30 p.m., Pilot intercepted him at the entrance and briefed him. Pilot suggested that the urgency of the situation demanded that he should leave for Bombay at once.

When Chavan heard of Pilot's plans, he too decided to leave the same evening. Rao asked them both to go together. Meanwhile, Rao's advisers reminded him of the criticism he had faced from the media and the public by delaying his visit to riot-torn Bombay after the worst riots in January. He too, they felt, should go to Bombay at the earliest opportunity.

6

The Days After

13 March dawned on the bomb-scarred city.

Many newspapers carried banner headlines. 'Black Friday' said the *Free Press Journal*, while the *Indian Express* headline was 'Blasts Rock Bombay: 250 Perish As Thirteen Blasts Rock City'. 'Bomb Blasts Rock Bombay', the *Hindustan Times* screamed, and the *Times of India* reported that '205 Die, Over 1,000 Hurt in City Blasts'. In its editorial, the *Times* harped on 'High-tech Terrorism', while the *Express* pondered over 'The Sinister Plot'. Television journalism was in its infancy so the print medium provided primary coverage and comment.

There would be no clues until 14 March, except that the guest at Hotel Sea Rock had registered as Advani. So reporters lapped up everything that Chief Minister Pawar had said the previous night and what the prime minister, the other ministers and L.K. Advani would say during their visits to the city on that day. Rao mentioned that a 'foreign hand' was involved, which had newspapers speculating about which country he meant. However, in the absence of real information, rumours raged. None of the papers agreed on the number of blasts or the numbers of those killed and injured. The BBC stated that 800 people had been killed. The real numbers would emerge only during the coming days. Many papers gave rumours as facts: one for example stated that there had also been a blast on a local train at

Nerul; another reported a blast at Madanpura, a Muslim locality.
Doordarshan reported a blast at the B.Y.L. Nair Hospital. Pawar
had to issue denials. A Gujarati paper stated that the inspiration
for the bombing had come from the film *Angaar*, starring Jackie
Shroff and Nana Patekar, where the protagonists orchestrate serial
blasts that destroy several government and other buildings. One
recurrent theme in most papers was that the blasts proved that
the Mafia had more power than the police and government
agencies.

But the piece everyone read and remembered was by Busybee,
widely regarded as the spokesman for the city, written in his
characteristic style in his 'Round and About' column in *The
Afternoon Despatch & Courier* on Monday, 15 March:

> ... No doubt, some organization will claim credit for the
> Bombay blasts ... The city has been so quickly and
> efficiently sealed that the terrorists have not had a chance
> to get out of it ... So the organization is waiting for its
> men to get to safety before making the announcement ...
> sooner or later an announcement will be made. Because
> that is the whole idea of the exercise: terrorist
> organizations require publicity for their acts ...

However, no one came forward to take responsibility. This was
unusual as after a terrorist attack, the organization responsible
announces it proudly, usually by having a spokesman call up a
major newspaper. This was especially prevalent in Europe,
America and the Middle East. This serves as a warning about
their capability. At times, for the sake of publicity, some small-
time organizations have also been known to claim hits that they
could never have executed. There are very few instances of a
terrorist group denying their involvement in an incident. But after

the 12 March bombings, there was a strange silence. The LTTE, a prime suspect, actually denied their involvement. Paris-based Lawrence Tilagar, regarded as a close associate of K. Prabhakaran and one of the chief lieutenants of the LTTE, reportedly told a Sri Lankan journalist on 14 March that their organization had nothing to do with the attacks. The denial was reported by United News of India (UNI) and reproduced in a single column in the local dailies the following day.

■

CP Samra reached his office at 9 a.m. sharp on 13 March. A pall of gloom hung over the 125-year-old police headquarter, which normally was abuzz with activity. The city of the seven islands had been ravaged without the famed Bombay police having any inkling about the diabolical plot.

Samra got busy fielding phone calls, from the chief minister Sharad Pawar, Governor Alexander, the director general of Maharashtra police, S. Ramamurthi, and several ministers from Mantralaya. Samra was also informed that the prime minister was arriving in Bombay that day. S.B. Chavan and Rajesh Pilot had already landed the previous night. The leader of the opposition and BJP stalwart, L.K. Advani, was also expected.

As commissioner of police, Samra knew that his day would go in dealing with the politicians, in the company of the chief minister, as protocol dictated that both Samra and Pawar brief the dignitaries. Apart from the fact that this would take him away from the work of investigation, what made matters worse was that given the status of his relationship with Pawar the day was bound to be stressful.

While communal frenzy had been at its peak in Bombay in December 1992 and January 1993, not a single incident of sectarian violence had been reported from the neighbouring city of Thane, where Samra was the police commissioner. This had been duly noted in the press. When Bombay's police chief Shrikant Bapat was asked to leave on 31 January, Samra had been brought in to replace him. The then chief minister, Sudhakarrao Naik, had told Samra: 'Samra sahab, you have a one-point programme: maintain peace.' Samra had

A.S. Samra (*Courtesy* Mid-day)

promised that he would restore peace and normalcy to the city within three months.

By the end of February, the campaign to replace Naik had gathered momentum. Narasimha Rao decided to send the Congress heavyweight, Defence Minister Sharad Pawar, to Bombay as chief minister.

Soon after he was sworn in, Pawar called a meeting of the city's top police officers on 6 March. Among those present were Samra, JCP Singh, Addl. CP Chakraborty and Addl. CP Hasan Ghafoor. Pawar had ignored Samra and spoken to the rest of the officers. Samra, annoyed at being sidelined, had interrupted Pawar several times and even boasted that the situation had improved since January and would not be allowed to get out of hand. Subsequently their relationship had not been cordial. Samra knew that everyone in the city would be wondering if this would hamper the investigation.

Samra himself was not too worried about this. He knew how

capable his team was. JCP Singh, who headed the crime branch, was highly regarded, as were additional commissioners Chakraborty, Ghafoor and Pawar. Cream among the lower levels included DCP Arup Patnaik, who handled Zone VII, and Rakesh Maria, DCP (traffic), who had just returned from Japan after a three-month training in traffic management and held additional charge of Zone IV.

The biggest hurdle that faced the police department was that thus far, they had no clue as to who had orchestrated the bombing. The sheer scale and meticulous planning suggested that it was the handiwork of a terrorist group, rather that the local underworld, who in the opinion of the police, lacked the expertise, infrastructure and resources for something of this magnitude. Samra could think of only a few organizations in the world that could execute such a ruthless plan. As similar bombings had occured in Beirut and Israel, he thought that Middle Eastern Islamic groups like the Hizbullah, the Fatah Revolutionary Council, the Muslim Brotherhood or Hamas could be likely suspects. However, the involvement of Kashmiri militants, the LTTE and the Punjab separatist groups could also not be entirely ruled out.

The Hizbullah was an Islamic fundamentalist group based in Iran, with fanatic members and powerful patrons. They were known to have aided Lebanon in attacks against Israel. Most notorious among such attacks was the suicide bombing of the US army base in Beirut, Lebanon, in 1983, when a truck filled with explosives had been driven into the base, killing over two hundred marines. Two minutes later, another truck had run into the nearby French barracks and killed fifty-eight people. The attacks were designed to show Israel that even their supporter, the mighty US, was powerless against them, and were partly responsible for the US withdrawal from Lebanon.

The sophistication of the bomb attack led Samra to suspect the involvement of the Hizbullah. Thousands of Iranian students lived in Bombay and Pune. It was not entirely unlikely that the terrorists may have found willing operatives amongst them.

There was also the PLO to consider, more precisely the Abu Nidal faction, also known as the Fatah Revolutionary Council (FRC) or Sabri-al-Banna, which was perhaps the most dreaded terrorist outfit in the world. They had made headlines with the bombing of a PanAm flight from Rome to New York that had crashed over Lockerbie in Scotland in 1991. This group had collaborated with terrorist organizations of Egypt, Algeria and several Middle Eastern countries. They were rumoured to have been behind the assassination of the Egyptian president Anwar Sadat in 1982 and the Algerian president Mohammed Boudiaf in 1992. The 1989 US Department of State-published *Terrorist Group Profile* claimed that this group had been active in India since 1982. They had allegedly been behind the assassination of a Kuwaiti diplomat in Delhi in June 1982 and that of the British Deputy High Commissioner in Bombay in November 1984, as well as the gun and grenade attack on the Alitalia crew at the international airport in Bombay in 1988. Like the Hizbullah and the perpetrators of the previous day's incidents, Abu Nidal also used plastic explosives.

Another terrorist organization which could have been involved was Hamas, which operated in the Israeli-occupied territories since the early 1990s, and carried out guerilla attacks on the Israeli army. However, the only problem with the theory that one of these groups had masterminded the blasts was that they would require extensive local networks which they were not known to have in Bombay.

There was also the LTTE. They had perfected a technique called 'black tigers', where they wired explosives to trucks, bowsers or lorries, and rammed the vehicles into Sri Lankan army camps. The first successful attempt was on 5 July 1987 at Nelliady in Jaffna, when over a hundred soldiers were killed. On 2 March 1991, the Sri Lankan minister of state for defence, Ranjan Wijeratne, was killed in Colombo by a car bomb carrying an estimated hundred kilograms of high-intensity explosives. Sri Lankan navy chief Clarence Fernando was killed in 1992 when his car was hit by a black tiger motorcycle bearing explosives. Therein lay the similarity with the Bombay blasts.

The LTTE had ample reason to be annoyed with India. In January 1993, a top lieutenant of the LTTE called Sathasivam Krishnakumar, alias Kittu, had reportedly entered Indian territorial waters off the Madras coast in a ship suspected of containing arms and explosives. The Indian navy had tried to establish contact with Kittu and warn him off. But instead of talking to them or surrendering, Kittu, along with his nine-member crew, committed suicide after setting up a time bomb which blew up the ship. The LTTE cadre had sworn to revenge Kittu's death. The Indian government took the threat seriously, as it had every LTTE threat since the assassination of the former prime minister, Rajiv Gandhi, at Sriperumbudur in 1991.

But Samra's gut feeling was that the bombings were related to the communal riots of December and January. This also made the involvement of Middle Eastern terrorist groups more likely. He thought that the involvement of the ISI could not be ruled out either.

It would be tragic if Islamic terrorists suddenly started getting interested in this part of the world, he thought. Perhaps it was inevitable. He thought of the history of his own religion. Prolonged subjugation of the Sikhs by the Mughal emperors had resulted in the sixth guru, Guru Hargobind Singh, revolting against the oppressive regime despite the fact that the first five gurus advocated nonviolence. The tenth guru, Guru Gobind Singh, too had rebelled against Aurangzeb. Had it been the same with the Muslims?

He swung his chair around towards his bookshelf, which held over 200 volumes. He found two thick books on Islamic literature, an English translation of the Holy Quran, a translation of *Nahjul Balagha*, and a compilation of sermons and letters of Hazrat Ali, the brother of Prophet Mohammed.

He was still immersed in his books when JCP Singh entered the office and saluted. He too had been pondering on the attacks, and suspected the involvement of the ISI. Soon Addl. CP (police administration) Chakraborty and Addl. CP (crime) Ghafoor joined them, and it turned into a high-level conference.

'It's interesting that the blasts hit three regions—south, central and northwest—while leaving the northeast untouched,' Singh observed. The northeast region included the area from Kurla to Mankhurd and Mulund.

'How should we go about the investigation?' Samra asked.

'Addl. CP Pawar is supervising the investigation into the incidents of the central region,' Chakraborty reported. 'DCP Patnaik is taking care of Zone VII in the northwest region.'

Singh did not approve of this fragmented investigation. He said, 'Even if local police stations like Worli, Dadar, Palton Road and LT Marg are handling the separate cases, the crime branch will remain in the picture. I will personally supervise the investigations.'

'That seems fine,' Samra nodded. 'Today the prime minister and Advani are coming to the city. I will be busy with them. Singh, you take charge and ensure that there is some headway. What is the status now?'

Y.C. Pawar (left) and M.N. Singh (Courtesy Mid-day)

Singh sensed the strain in his superior's voice. He said, 'Sir, we have already worked out some facts.' He took the file which his deputy, Ghafoor, had brought along. He and his team of officers had compiled it through the night of 12 March. 'At the BSE, the Air-India building and the Plaza, car bombs were used. Scooter bombs must have been used in Zaveri Bazaar and Katha Bazaar. At Worli, everything points to a car bomb too. In the three hotels, guests deposited the bombs in rooms. The person who checked in at the Sea Rock gave his name as Advani.'

Ghafoor added, 'The Worli police found an abandoned Maruti van near Siemens. The windscreens were shattered and there were two bags with seven AK-56s and some hand grenades.'

'I think the explosions at Macchimar Colony were from hand grenades,' Singh said.

'What about the airport?' Samra asked. 'Weren't grenades also used there?'

'Major Jadhav of Sahar Airport confirmed that it seems likely that they were grenades, but we cannot be sure,' Ghafoor said.

'What else?' Samra asked.

'The BDDS is reassembling the chassis of the vehicles which were used in the bombings,' said Singh. 'They're trying to establish the identity of the owners.'

'We have also detained a Sri Lankan,' said Ghafoor. 'He was picked up trying to exchange a suspiciously large amount of foreign currency. He's possibly involved with the LTTE. A Turkish national has also been detained.'

'Is there anything else?' asked Samra.

No one seemed to have anything else to add at this point.

'Then I think I should be leaving,' Samra said. 'The prime minister is due to arrive any moment. Ask your men to devote themselves to the investigation. We need to crack this case as soon as possible.'

'The officers have their orders. They're working hard,' answered Singh. 'Let's hope we make a breakthrough soon.'

'Let the DCPs form their own special teams of investigating officers—especially Patnaik and Maria.' Samra rose from his chair, and Ghafoor, Chakraborty and Singh took their leave.

Chavan and Pilot had reached Bombay on 12 March and examined the bombed sites the following day.

Rao reached Bombay on 13 March on a special Indian Air Force Boeing. His entourage included two union ministers, N.K.P. Salve and A.K. Antony. The plane landed at INS Kunjali, the naval base at Colaba.

Rao visited the BSE and the Air-India building, accompanied by Pawar. He also visited the St George Hospital and met some of the injured. Later, he addressed a packed press conference at the naval headquarters.

'We must find the connection between the hands that did this and the brain that masterminded it,' he declared. When a foreign correspondent asked whether LTTE involvement was suspected, Rao quipped, 'We investigate. You speculate.'

Meanwhile, the IB and RAW had swung into action. They established contacts with the intelligence agencies of several foreign countries, including the Federal Bureau of Investigation (FBI) at their Washington office, Israel's Mossad, Britain's Scotland Yard and Military Intelligence (MI5 and MI6), and the Interpol headquarters at Lyons, France, seeking information about various terrorist organizations.

■

The city was slowly limping back to normalcy. The visits of the politicians continued on 14 March.

L.K. Advani visited Worli and Dadar. The previous day he had categorically denied in Delhi that the blasts in Bombay were a fallout of the communal riots. Both Advani and Murli Manohar Joshi laid the blame on foreign hands.

The foreign intelligence agencies were more than helpful and responded with comprehensive lists that started coming in by 14 March. The lists demonstrated these agencies' expertise and professionalism in dealing with the problem of terrorism in their countries. They included names of men and groups in Lebanon, Pakistan, Egypt, Syria, Tunisia, Algeria, Turkey, Iran and Sri Lanka. Interpol also provided several photographs and handwriting samples. It was hoped that these would match descriptions and evidence provided by hotel staff and other eyewitnesses.

Like most others in the city, Rakesh Maria loved to spend his Sundays at home with his wife, Preeti, and son, Kunal. Especially this Sunday, after three days of running around furiously, he was hoping to spend most of the day at home. Towards evening, he planned to make rounds to Dadar police station, his office above the Matunga police station, and then to the traffic office at Worli, which had been badly neglected these past couple of days. He'd also decided to handpick some officers from the traffic division whom he'd come to know in the past few months for the team Samra had asked him to assemble. But at least he would have a leisurely lunch and a nap after that.

As lunch was announced, the phone rang. It was Inspector Shinde from the Matunga police station. He reported that a call had come in from a resident of Naigaum Cross Lane at Dadar. A suspicious-looking scooter had been parked in front of his building since Friday. Some policemen had asked around the neighbourhood, but the vehicle did not seem to belong to anybody. They suspected that it might contain explosives.

'Cordon off the area. Inform the bomb squad. I'm on my way.' There would be no lunch or nap for him.

When he arrived at Naigaum Cross Road, the scene was chaotic. The men from the Matunga police station could hardly hold back the crowd swarming to see the scooter. The two-wheeler was parked with its front tyre touching the narrow kerb, beyond which were some shops and a residential building under the footbridge. A few minutes later, the BDDS van arrived with sirens wailing.

Senior Inspector Chougule got out of the van and saluted Maria, who asked him to take over.

Chougule asked the policemen to move everybody at least fifty metres away from the scooter. He asked the police to evacuate the shops and the residential building. The scooter was registered in Maharashtra; the number plate read MH-04-261.

Rakesh Maria (*Courtesy* Mid-day)

Chougule walked Zanjeer to the scooter. The dog walked around the scooter, sniffing. Suddenly, Zanjeer jerked his head towards the front of the scooter and sniffed with renewed concentration. He leaned towards the dicky and barked several times, confirming the presence of explosives.

Chougule examined the scooter more closely. He and his team discussed how to defuse the bomb. The bomb could be rigged to go off the moment the scooter was touched. After thinking deeply, Chougule asked Maria, 'Should we ask Major Vasant Jadhav of Sahar Airport to help us?'

'I was thinking the same thing.'

Jadhav received the call at 3.20 p.m. and left for the site immediately. On reaching Dadar, he was briefed by Chougule. Jadhav instructed the crowd to be pushed back even further. The central police control room had flashed the message about the bomb, and alert crime reporters had begun to descend on the scene with camera crews.

Jadhav commenced work. He pulled out a hook with a thin nylon rope and carefully tucked the hook into the lock in the dicky of the scooter. He tugged gently at first and then with little bit of force. The lock came apart. Jadhav wiped sweat from his forehead and smiled at Chougule and Maria with relief. Chougule peered inside. Then, very softly, he touched the pencil detonator, which was surrounded by a mesh of thin wires. Jadhav gingerly examined the wires and identified the main one. In a few minutes, the bomb was defused.

The rest of the BDDS group got busy analysing the bomb. Chougule smelt and felt the black putty-like substance, and declared it to be RDX. There were more than fifteen kilograms of the deadly material. Jadhav extracted some 200 grams of the putty and gave it to Chougule for chemical analysis and examination at the CFSL.

Maria was curious why the bomb hadn't gone off when the detonator was in place.

'The bomb explodes when the striker reaches the detonator,' Jadhav explained. 'Here the passage for the movement of the striker was blocked by some RDX putty, which got into the detonator.'

Maria nodded at the explanation. Then he asked, 'When do you think the passage must have got blocked?'

'It could have happened at the time of assembly, when they were fixing the connection between the RDX and detonator. Or the RDX may have melted in the heat of the sun. But probably,' Jadhav explained in a matter-of-fact tone, 'in this case the bomb maker was just careless.'

Jadhav accepted the responsibility of disposing of the RDX.

It was 5.05 p.m. by the time the operation was over. Maria decided to go on his rounds. On a random impulse, he decided to visit Mahim police station as well.

Samra sent a wireless message to Maria, asking for a report on the scooter. Maria called him from the Mahim police station and briefed him. Then Samra said something that surprised Maria. 'Rakesh, I trust that you're giving this your best shot, but I'm under the gun here. It's been more than forty-eight hours and there's been no breakthrough.'

'I hear you, sir. We're doing our best.' As Maria hung up, his hands felt like lead. He telephoned Assistant Commisioner of Police (ACP) Bhaskar Dangle. 'I just spoke to the CP. We have to get on with the job. Have we got anything?'

'Nothing. The crime branch is still working on identifying the owners of the vehicles that carried the bombs through the chassis. I can tell you that we're barking up the wrong tree with the Sri Lankan and Turkish nationals. But that's it.'

'Okay, right, right.' Maria's mind raced. 'Check out the owner of this scooter.'

'I've already put my men on it. But don't expect much. It could be stolen.'

'Did you follow up on the papers in the Maruti van found at Worli?'

'Yeah.' Maria could hear some papers shuffling on the other end of the line. 'A Mrs Rubina Suleiman Memon, a resident of the Al-Hussaini building at Dargah Road, Mahim.'

'Dargah Road, Mahim. Call Senior Police Inspector Maneckshaw.'

N.J. Maneckshaw was the senior police inspector of the Mahim police station. He arrived soon after being summoned.

'Maneckshaw, do you know the Al-Hussaini building at Dargah Road?' Maria asked.

'It is quite close to our police station.'

'Did some Mrs Rubina Memon ever report her Maruti van stolen?'

'I don't think so.'

Maneckshaw's reply silenced Maria. He had been sure that Mrs Memon would have lodged a complaint. Then they would have to track down the car thief. After a while, Maria said, 'If this building is nearby, then let's pay Mrs Memon a visit.'

When Maria, Maneckshaw, Dangle and a few other officers

arrived at the seven-storey building, it seemed wrapped in an uneasy calm. People stared at the police team as if they had expected them to come knocking sooner or later.

Dangle stopped an old man and asked him about the Memons. 'Saheb, they stay here on the fifth floor. But I have not seen them for several days now.'

They went up to the fifth floor and located the flats belonging to the Memons. Both were locked. Inquiries with the neighbours revealed that most of the family had not been seen since Monday, though one of them was here until Thursday evening. His name was Mushtaq bhai, also called Tiger bhai.

Maria turned inquiringly towards Maneckshaw.

'Sir, Tiger Memon is a smuggler with a long criminal record.'

Maria's eyes grew round with surprise.

Further inquiries revealed that Rubina, the woman in whose name the missing car was registered, was the wife of Tiger's elder brother, Suleiman. They also found out that Tiger Memon had been there until the time of sehri, a couple of hours before sunrise, on Friday, the day of the blasts. He had seemed very busy the previous ten or fifteen days.

When was the car stolen, before Monday, or between Monday and Thursday when only Tiger was around, Maria wondered. And why had no one in the family reported the theft to the police? Tiger had been here until Friday dawn and the car was found the same afternoon. Could the Memons be connected with the bombings?

Intense concentration and hunger made Maria's temples throb. He decided to search the Memon residences.

The police broke the locks and entered the flats. They ransacked the immaculately appointed flats—opened drawers, jimmied cupboards, turned shelves and cupboards upside down—and their boots soiled the exquisite Iranian carpets that adorned the marble floors. A crowd of onlookers assembled outside the doors, down the staircase, and through the building compound. The informal police visit had turned into a raid.

One of the police officers found a scooter key in a drawer. He took it to Maria.

The key touched a chord in Maria's mind. He kept turning it in his hand and looking at it from various angles. He felt as if he'd been given a jumble of letters to fit into a crossword. Despite sifting the letters around many times, he still had many to account for. 'Dangle, why don't you take this to the Matunga police station and try to fit it into that scooter we found today?'

'Sir, do you think ...?'

'I am not sure. But at worst, it will just be a wasted trip.'

Dangle immediately took off. Maria returned to searching.

Maria had developed a rapport with some of Tiger's neighbours, not that much effort was necessary. The neighbours were more than willing to help the police. Maria was looking for information on Tiger's network.

At one point a middle-aged, bearded man said, 'Sahab, I think Tiger bhai has a manager.'

'Manager? Where does he live? What's his name?' Maria tried not to sound too eager. He fervently prayed that the manager hadn't left with his boss. As he spoke, the muezzin of the Makhdoom Shah dargah called azaan: 'Allah-o-Akbar ... Allah-o-Akbar ...'

The assembled people instantly started to leave. 'Sahab, *roza ka waqt ho gaya*,' said somebody. 'We should break our fast. Why don't you join us?'

Maria went into one of the neighbouring houses, where there was a feast of fruit, kebabs and naans laid out. He was famished. For the first time he understood how difficult it must be for Muslims during the fifteen-hour-long fast. As he talked with the neighbours, he found out the name and whereabouts of Tiger's manager.

As he was finishing his meal, an officer walked in. 'Sir, Dangle sahab has come back. He wants to talk to you.'

Maria immediately rose, offered his thanks and apologies, and stepped out to meet Dangle.

'Sir, sir, the key belongs to the scooter,' Dangle was very excited. Maria found he was barely moved, as if he had known all along that this would happen. His mind raced ahead.

'Well, Dangle, you have to do two things now. First, you will go and locate Asgar Mukadam, from the Nagnath building at Seven Bungalows, Andheri. Bring him here. Secondly, contact the Road Transport Office (RTO) and trace the owner of this scooter. Though I have a feeling that it belongs to one of the Memons, we need to check it out.'

Dangle left for Andheri immediately. Maria thought, I should call Preeti and tell her I will be late. But first, he had to call Samra and let him know that at last there had been a breakthrough. Samra was delighted at the news and asked Maria to keep him informed.

Maria instructed Maneckshaw to stay on at Al-Hussaini, and search the flats for more leads. He then left for the Mahim police station. There he went to the office of the senior police inspector, slumped in the cushioned chair and closed his eyes. The phone rang and Maria picked it up on the first ring.

'Ha-lo?' This was his characteristic way of responding. Whoever had spoken to Maria on the phone a couple of times knew right away when he answered.

'Dangle speaking, sir.'

'Haan, Dangle.'

'Sir, I found Asgar Mukadam at home.'

'Bring him to the Mahim police station.'

It was about 8.30 p.m. Maria called several of his senior

officers and brought them up to date. He also called Preeti and told her that he would be home by 10.30 p.m.

Dangle came into his office, accompanied by a short, frail youth. He had a thin moustache, nondescript eyes and looked harmless, though rather apprehensive.

'Sir, this is Asgar Mukadam. He says he's been Tiger Memon's manager for a year.'

Maria offered Mukadam a seat. 'Asgar, we want to know each and everything about Tiger Memon and your relationship with him.'

'Sir, I don't know much about him. I have been working at his office only for a year.'

'A year is quite a long period to get to know somebody.'

'I know that Tiger bhai is into smuggling. He used to deal in silver bricks. He was also into hawala business. My job was to keep accounts of his income from smuggling and hawala.'

'What was your salary?'

'I was paid Rs 4,000 every month'

'How frequently did Tiger smuggle silver?'

'In this last year, as far as I remember, he must have been involved in at least six landings.'

'Where do you people operate?'

'We used to work from his office at Nishanpada Road at Dongri.'

'Used to?'

'The office was destroyed during the communal riots in December.'

'Then what happened?'

'We were going to open another office. But then there was the second phase of riots, and that didn't happen.'

'Then how did you people work?'

'Tiger bhai used to contact me by phone or call me through

one of his men.'

'Who else did you deal with?'

'Tiger bhai's younger brothers, Ayub and Yaqub.'

'What do they do?'

'Ayub stays in Dubai most of the time and looks after Tiger bhai's meat export business. Yaqub is a chartered accountant.'

Maria continued to gently quiz Mukadam to find out more about Tiger Memon, but did not broach the subject of the bombings. By the time he finally moved to this subject, it was already well past midnight.

'What do you know about the bombings?'

'Nothing. I know nothing.'

Maria did not have to be an expert in interrogation to detect the wavering note in Mukadam's voice.

The police, it is said, resorts to 'special treatment' to make the accused talk, the term being a euphemism for physical torture. The police of course always deny such allegations. According to Mukadam, he was accorded 'special treatment'. Thin and nervous, Mukadam had already been half-broken by the mere sight of policemen at his door. After being accorded 'special treatment', from around 2.30 a.m., there was no need to ask him questions. He began talking on his own, not always coherently.

'Tiger had three hawala accounts with someone named Mulchand Shah or Chokshi. The accounts were called Hathi, Irani and Auliya. Tiger's dealings with Choksi amounted to crores of rupees at times. Tiger's smuggled silver was bought by Raju Laxmichand Jain, whom we called Raju Kodi.

'Tiger and Javed Chikna left for Dubai on 11 February. At that time, I did not know what for. But I later learnt that it was for training young men to handle arms and ammunition. Tiger had some serious plans in store for Bombay. Before leaving for Dubai, Tiger instructed me take Rs 5 lakh from Chokshi and deliver it to Dadabhai Parkar for a landing. He also asked me to keep in touch with his brother Yaqub. If Yaqub needed money, then I was to borrow it from Chokshi and give it to him.

'Yaqub asked me to take *sau peti* or a hundred lakhs from Chokshi and give it to him, which I promptly did. A couple of other times, as Yaqub instructed, I asked Chokshi to transfer funds from one account to another—once Rs 25 lakh from Hathi to Irani, and another time Rs 10 lakh to Auliya.

'The other people working with Tiger that I know of are Javed Chikna, Anwar Theba, Shafi, Abdul Gani, Imtiyaz Ghavate, Parvez Shaikh, Salim, Rafiq Madi and Mohammed Hussain.

'Towards the end of February, I began to feel uneasy about Tiger and his plans. I wanted to quit. I told Tiger that I wanted to leave because of some domestic problems. Tiger abused me and called me many names. He said I could leave only when I had settled all the accounts with him after his return.

'Tiger returned from Dubai only in the first week of March. I saw him a couple of times and he took accounts of all the dealings for February and March. On 11 March he called me home and told me that there were a few things I needed to fii ·sh before he took off for Dubai again the following morning. I went to the airport to get his boarding pass on 12 March. He came to the airport at around 4 a.m. He told me to go to Al-Hussaini and do some jobs that Anwar Theba would tell me. Then he left.

'When I returned to Al-Hussaini, I found that Chikna, Gani, Parvez, Bashir and several others were in the garage, loading cars and scooters with black chemicals and inserting aluminium pencil-like things in them ...'

It was 5 a.m. by the time this tale was finished. Maria realized that he had forgotten to call Samra. But now he was too tired. He went home, instructing Dangle to question Mukadam further and to arrange to record his confession as per the provisions of the Terrorists and Disruptive Activities Prevention Act (TADA). He realized that in looking for international terrorist organizations, the police force had totally underestimated the abilities of a local smuggler, someone he had not even heard of until this day.

Mukadam languished in police custody for days after that. The police records show Mukadam was arrested on 18 March and that DCP K.L. Bishnoi recorded his confession on 23 March. What Mukadam underwent between 14 March and 23 March is anybody's guess.

◼

The weekend was over. It was time for the city to return to work for the first time since the day of the bombings. To the delight of most Bombayites, the BSE was operational again. For the police force, however, the weekend had provided no respite.

Chougule was in at work by 9.30 a.m. on 15 March, going over files and making records of the past three days. He called Major Jadhav at the airport and discussed the recovery of the scooter at Naigaum the previous day. At 9.40 a.m., Pandhre walked in to his room and waited for him to finish his conversation, despite the fact that he was violating protocol by entering a room where a senior officer was on the phone and lingering there.

Chougule finished the call and glared at Pandhre.

'Sir, there is a call from the police control room that a suspicious scooter has been found at Dhanji Street. We have been asked to go there.'

Chougule was on his feet immediately. Dhanji Street was a stone's throw away from the BDDS office. The terrorists were encroaching on his backyard! The BDDS team rushed to the spot.

The maroon scooter was surrounded by police officers from the LT Marg police station. The area was cordoned off and a crowd was gathering. The DP Jewellers shop in front of the scooter had been evacuated.

Chougule instructed his officers and the policemen to move the public back at least fifty metres from the scooter. Zanjeer was taken around the two-wheeler. He sniffed it and at once barked to confirm the presence of explosives. As Zanjeer seemed to be indicating the dicky of the scooter, they used a hook and rope to open it carefully.

Inside were three polythene bags containing a brownish material and a blackish substance attached to a pencil timer.

Pandhre used a fishing rod and hook to separate the timer from the polythene bags. After this, the officers removed the bags from the dicky. Upon examination, it was found that the black material was RDX, while the brownish one was gelatine.

The bomb was defused in less than an hour. As Chougule straightened and stretched, feeling very relieved, Zarapkar told him that they had received information on the wireless that another suspicious scooter had been found a few yards away.

Chougule handed over the scooter and explosives to the police officers for drawing up a panchnama and other paperwork, and then walked over to the second scooter. There was no need for Zanjeer to confirm the presence of explosives for the black stains on the handle of the scooter and black fingerprints on the dials were enough evidence of the presence of RDX. The place was immediately cordoned off, and the hook-and-rope method used to open the front dicky.

Inside the dicky, Pandhre and Chougule found similar polythene bags attached to a pencil timer. The bomb was defused, and the vehicle and explosives again handed over to the officers from the LT Marg police station. It was after mid-day. The team had defused three scooter bombs in less than twenty-four hours.

The Bombay police force is divided into two branches: the main branch—police station postings, crime—and the side branch—welfare, special departments, traffic. The traffic department is generally considered the least prestigeous.

However, to all other departments' chagrin, it was the traffic department which had managed to provide the first breakthrough in this important case. Maria had not only gained the trust of all his superiors, including Samra, but he had virtually been granted a carte blanche to handle the case as he chose.

Maria had been asked to form an investigative team. The men he selected were largely drawn from those he interacted with every day, primarily from the traffic department and also officers from Mahim and Worli: Dinesh Kadam, Subhash Varpe, Jolly Verghese, Dhananjay Daund, Virendra Vani, Naval Driver, Abhay Shastri, Kirdant, Subhash Gunjal and Deedar Singh. SI Srirang Nadgouda was Maria's personal assistant, hence automatically an integral part of the team. Maria was known to inspire loyalty among his juniors, and this team became a closely-knit unit.

DCP Arup Patnaik of Zone VII also formed his own special team. The third special team was headed by CP Samra, and comprised three veterans from the IPS—Sukhdev Puri, Gyanchand Verma and Ambalal Verma—whose brief was to look into specific aspects of the bombings such as the financial records of Tiger Memon's firm, Al-Taj International, and the bombings at the three hotels.

On reaching home after interrogating Mukadam, Maria took a brief nap and a hot shower. He called Samra and JCP Singh, and briefed them about the arrest and the information they had gathered. Singh said he would visit the Mahim police station to discuss the case further.

On his way to the Mahim police station, Maria decided to stop over at Al-Hussaini, to see if he could gather some more information to question Mukadam about.

The art of interrogation is like a game of chess, where good players always anticipate their opponent's next move and have their counter-move ready. Others say, an interrogator should employ the warfare tactics of Gideon. According to the Old Testament, Gideon's army was weaker than his adversaries, but when he attacked them he raised such a hue and cry that they were fooled into thinking that his army was much stronger than theirs. Thus Gideon had managed to rout his rivals. Similarly, an interrogator should always have information from other sources, however meagre, and use it on the person being questioned to con him into thinking that the interrogator knows a lot more than he actually does, so that he will not dare to lie.

On reaching Al-Hussaini, Maria walked towards the building, at the entrance of which two policemen were on guard. Having spent so many hours there on Sunday, Maria was already a familiar face to the residents.

As he waited for the lift, Maria saw a teenaged girl. She looked intelligent and eager. He felt that she wanted to say something but was scared to do so. So he called her over and asked her name.

'My name is Catherine.'

The lift was waiting for Maria but he gestured to the liftman to proceed without him.

'Do you live in this building, Catherine?'

'Yes, sir.'

'Do you know Tiger Memon?'

'Yes, sir. He is a bearded, stout man, not very tall, and always seems to be angry. The kids were afraid of him. Once when my friend Babloo's tennis ball hit the windscreen of his car, he slapped Babloo so hard that he cried for a long time after that. Since then we were always afraid of him and never played near his cars.'

'Are you scared of him even when he is not around?'

'No sir, it is not that.'

'Then?' Maria smiled reassuringly.

'Sir, the thing is, we had seen a lot of activity the last few days in the building. There were many known and unknown men coming to his house, and driving in and out of the compound in his cars.'

'And ... ?'

'On Thursday evening, there were huge flashlights in the garage and all those friends of Tiger uncle were filling cars and scooters with a black substance. My friend Raju tried to go near them, but one of the men yelled at him and told us to go home. But we all kept looking at them from a distance. Late at night, when my family and I were watching television, we could hear them talking loudly and laughing among themselves. I think they must have been there throughout the night because when I was going to school in the morning, some of them were still there.'

Mukadam had made a passing mention of the events of that night, but the young girl's details were a revelation. As Catherine was relating the story, some other residents of the building also joined in with more details. Maria decided to confront Mukadam with the new information.

Mahim was a nondescript and dingy police station, and now suddenly this was where all the action was happening. Maria barged into the cabin of Maneckshaw, the senior police inspector. Maria's team of officers was already present in the police station. Maria instructed Nadgouda: 'Get Mukadam here, we need to talk to him.'

He hardly recognized the man who was brought in: swollen

face, dark circles around the sunken eyes, dishevelled hair and dirty rumpled clothes. Maria reflected that in other circumstances he would have felt pity for Mukadam. Mukadam was told to sit in front of Maria's chair.

Maria looked straight into his eyes and said, 'Look, we know what all you people did throughout the night in the garage of Tiger Memon and who all were there with you in it. We also have their names.' Maria glanced at his diary where he had been making notes while waiting for Mukadam, as if reading the names. 'I want more from you now.'

'Sahab, I have told you everything I knew. I have not lied or hidden anything from you.'

'Shut up, you have not told me everything. You did not tell me how and why it all originated. Was your Tiger Memon alone on this or did Dawood Ibrahim or other gangs back him? Did you tell me who planted the car bombs at the various spots in Bombay? Tell me everything now or I will hand you over to my officers again.'

Naked fear could be seen in Mukadam's eyes; his lips were parched and his throat dry. 'Sahab, I ... I will tell you ... whatever ... you ask me,' he said in between sobs.

'Let us begin with the addresses of Tiger's close associates.' Maria turned towards Nadgouda. 'Nad, get the addresses. I want each and every one of them here by the evening. Understand?'

Mukadam began listing Tiger's associates and their addresses, which the police team took down, occasionally asking questions and seeking directions to the places mentioned. This session was interrupted when an officer came in to inform Maria that Addl. CP Pawar and JCP Singh had arrived. Maria asked his team to leave in search of the people on the list, while he went to meet the officers and update them.

For the next few days, the Mahim police station was a flurry

of activity. People were brought in, questioned, yelled at and led
out. The police station became Maria's second home where he
worked, ate and slept, going home only to bathe and change.

The advantage of operating from the Mahim police station
was that it had a spacious four-storeyed lock-up, containing over
sixty-four detention cells with room for 300 detainees, located
just behind the police station. Within a few days, the lock-up was
crowded as the suspects were picked up and detained there.

The arrests were meticulously planned so that the arrest of
one suspect did not alert the others. Almost all were carried out
late at night, after long stakeouts outside the houses of the suspects.
Imtiyaz Ghavate was picked up from Navpada in Bandra west,
Abdul Gani Turk and Mushtaq Tarani from Dongri, and Parvez
Shaikh from the railway quarters at Andheri.

Apart from the people whom Mukadam had said were actually
involved in the bombing, the police also began picking up those
people who were neither involved nor were aware of the
conspiracy, but had got sucked into the case due to association
with the wrong people.

Such people included the owners of the scooters seized from
Dadar and Zaveri Bazaar. After making intensive inquiries,
Maria's team had traced them to Asghar Ali Masalawala, who
had purchased them from Sayed Farid. However, as both knew
and trusted each other, there were no documents for these
transactions. They both knew Tiger Memon, and stated that they
had lent these scooters to him without knowing what purpose
they would be used for. The police arrested them, charging them
with abetting terrorist acts.

According to many of those arrested, the police used third-
degree methods on them, despite their admitting to their role in
the blasts and disclosing the whereabouts of their associates. They
were made to sign confessional statements, which was sufficient

evidence to indict them in court under TADA.

Within a short span of time, the police had picked up hundreds of suspects. There was panic among the Muslim community, especially those with any association with Tiger. By 21 March, over a dozen suspects had been booked under TADA.

7

On the Run

Tiger had known that his men would be confused and scared after the attack, as only then would they realize the magnitude of what they had got into. Therefore, on the night of 11 March, he had specifically told them to leave the city and go elsewhere, as they would not be safe if they stayed on. They were to return to Bombay only after things had returned to normal and the police had stopped looking for the people involved. He had also assured them that if they required any help, they should contact him at his Dubai number.

Tiger had reiterated to Chikna the need for all the men to leave Bombay immediately. Chikna had given each of them Rs 10,000 for this purpose at Nagpada after the bombings, on the night of 12 March. Most of the men had planned to leave that very night, or the following day.

Badshah Khan decided to go to his native village, Rampur in UP. Chikna gave him an additional Rs 5,000 and told him to maintain contact with Tiger in Dubai.

Badshah told his mother that he would be gone for a few days and took off to Delhi with Bashir Khan. They boarded the Frontier Mail from Borivali station. On reaching Delhi, they wandered aimlessly for a while and finally went to the dargah of Hazrat Nizamuddin, a much-loved Sufi saint. People from all parts of the country flock to this shrine, and the two men thought it would be easy to get lost in the milling crowd of devotees. They decided to spend the night there.

However, despite the crowds, Badshah felt as if all eyes were on him. He asked Bashir to call Tiger at Dubai from a telephone booth and see if he had any advice. It was just past midnight in Delhi, about 10.30 p.m. in Dubai. Tiger picked up the phone on the first ring. When Bashir told him that he and Badshah were in Delhi, he was furious.

'What the hell are you doing in Delhi?' he yelled. 'You're supposed to go underground. There's no difference between Delhi and Bombay. Get out of there before the police hound you out. Go—fast. Call me from wherever you both end up.'

Tiger's venom unsettled Bashir. He and Badshah decided to leave for Rampur by truck that night. They reached the following morning and went to Badshah's family home. As Bashir was still rattled by Tiger's anger, he asked Badshah to call Tiger that night.

Tiger was relieved to know they were in Rampur. He told them to make their way to Jaipur, from where he would try to get them over to Dubai, or at least across the border to Pakistan. From Jaipur, they were to go to Tonk, where they were asked to meet Salim Khan Durrani, also known as Salim Tonk. The same evening, Badshah and Bashir boarded a bus to Jaipur.

The man they were to meet, Durrani, was a scion of an illustrious family. His father was a judge at the session courts. His brothers had fought in the wars with China and Pakistan. Durrani's uncles included much-decorated police superintendents and a collector of the erstwhile province of Bombay and Sindh, who had received the Victoria Cross.

Durrani had been asked by his friend Aziz Ahmed of Bombay to put up some friends for a while. When Badshah and Bashir reached Durrani's palatial home in Tonk, Javed Chikna, his brother Babloo, Yeba Yaqub, his wife and a friend, Murad Khan, were already there.

After a brief discussion on what was happening in Bombay, Tiger's associates decided to part. Yaqub gave Rs 10,000 to Badshah and offered him and Bashir a lift to Jaipur in his Tata mobile van. They accepted.

Badshah Khan was disappointed in Jaipur. He had heard that it was the pink city, but it was far from rosy. Yaqub took Badshah and Bashir to meet Anwar Theba and Shafi, who had come straight to Jaipur from Bombay. They too had been promised a new life in Dubai by Tiger, and they were excited at the prospect. Badshah thought that he would be better off there than anywhere in India. That made him think of his passport, which had not been returned after their trip to Islamabad. He asked Anwar if he knew where it was.

Anwar guffawed at the question. 'It has been destroyed.'

Badshah was outraged. How could they destroy such a vital document without even asking him? 'It was my passport! Who were you to destroy it?'

'Not just your passport, we destroyed everybody's. Tiger insisted. He made some other arrangements,' Anwar changed his tone to placate Badshah.

Badshah was still seething, but he knew that Anwar must be speaking the truth as he had invoked Tiger's name. Anwar asked him to get moving as there were too many of them in Jaipur, but to stay in touch with Tiger about crossing the border.

After a few days, Badshah and Bashir left for Rampur again. Badshah felt more comfortable there. They tried to contact Tiger for further instructions, but did not manage to get through for more than a week. They moved constantly. They visited Kanpur and Gorakhpur. They were thoroughly confused and directionless, the lack of leadership and support beginning to take its toll.

Badshah thought about surrendering to the police. Bashir fiercely opposed it. Their frequent arguments strained their friendship, and they grew bitter and sarcastic with each other. Finally, they decided to part ways. Badshah returned to Rampur while Bashir stayed on in Gorakhpur.

Back in Rampur, Badshah called Tiger again. This time he got through, but only to receive a message that Tiger should not be contacted at that number any more but on a mobile. Badshah, slightly taken aback, called the new number. As usual, Tiger was nice to him. Badshah asked for money. Tiger said money would be no problem but that he would have to come to Delhi to collect it. Badshah agreed and promised to call him once he reached Delhi.

Nasir Dhakla had been nervous about the entire operation since Javed Chikna roped him into Tiger's gang for the first landing. Unlike the other young men who had trained with him in Islamabad, Nasir never experienced their excitement and enthusiasm. He was a family man, with a secure matka business, and he did not want to get into the risky business of revenge. However, Tiger had stated before the first landing that there was no way to drop out of the operation, and so Nasir had stayed on. Though he had participated in many meetings and recces, he had stayed away from the final meetings on 10 March.

While Chikna and the others drove in and out of Al-Hussaini with their loaded vehicles on 12 March, Nasir and Parvez Kelawala had hidden in an empty classroom of a nearby Marathi school from where they could get a clear view of the Al-Hussaini compound. They had watched the activity all day and finally, when towards late afternoon it petered out, they had gone home.

Late in the evening his wife Rehana woke him from his nap. She said that the entire city was in chaos, bombs were going off everywhere. Nasir was relieved he had not been involved, but he continued feeling very uneasy. He lay low for a day, but on 14 March he heard that Tiger's flats had been raided. Fearing that the noose would tighten around anyone known to have any association with Tiger, he contacted Parvez, and they decided to leave the city together.

On 15 March, they left for Ahmedabad by train and arrived the following morning. Ahmedabad was like Bombay in several respects, and they felt somewhat secure in the many Muslim pockets and shrines scattered throughout the city. As they had not attended the last meeting with Tiger, they had received only Rs 5,000 each, and they felt the absence of cash as they looked around for a place to stay. They sought shelter in the shrine of Hazrat Shah Alam. However, it was crowded to capacity, so after a couple of days they left for Ajmer.

The dargah of Khwaja Moinuddin Chhisti or Gharib Nawaz, perhaps the most important Sufi saint in the country, is in Ajmer. The shrine, one of the most sacred spots in the country for a Muslim, was the reason they had selected Ajmer as their destination. However, on reaching there, they realized that they could not stay at the dargah because it was too crowded. They were forced to rent a room in Hayat Manzil, just opposite the dargah. They gave false names and addresses. When they ran out of money after a few days, Parvez went to his native village in UP and Nasir returned to Bombay.

Nasir found his house in Bharat Nagar padlocked. He went to his in-laws' home, where he found his wife and children. His father-in-law, Ghulam Dastagir, told him the police were looking for him. Nasir decided to leave again. He went to Dongri and met Karimullah, one of Tiger's associates who had participated in the landings. Karimullah gave him Rs 700 and told him to leave the city immediately. Alone and frightened, Nasir resolved to flee once more.

Yeba Yaqub

As panic spread through the underworld with the arrest of some of Tiger's aides—Asgar Mukadam, Abdul Gani and Imtiyaz Ghavate—Yeba Yaqub, who had returned to Bombay from Tonk, was increasingly stressed. He was still sitting on unused stocks of RDX and gelatin. Only a fraction of the quantities landed had been used. Yaqub knew that if any of the boys squealed to the police, he'd be doomed for life.

When Tiger had begun assembling his group, Yaqub, swept by a wave of enthusiasm, had pledged his support, though he had not known precisely how he could help. However, in his careful planning, Tiger had taken into account Yaqub's strengths and assets. His brother, Majid Khan, was a builder, and owned a successful construction company, MK Builders. Yaqub himself had several warehouses and godowns in and around Bombay where Tiger could safely store his RDX. Tiger had chosen the warehouses in New Bombay and Thane.

More than eight tons of RDX had been landed at Shekhadi and Dighi on 3 and 7 February, about three-quarters of it on the latter day. Tiger had divided the RDX into two, and entrusted Chikna and Yeba Yaqub with half the total quantity each. Yaqub had stashed his share in about a hundred jute bags, each containing about forty kilograms of RDX, in his brother's godown at the Maharashtra Industrial Development Corporation (MIDC) sheds in New Bombay.

Yaqub had been satisfied that he had made his contribution

to the holy war. But with all those inconvenient arrests and tales of Maria's ruthlessness, he was losing peace of mind. He resolved to shift the RDX from his brother's godown to another location. At least, in case the RDX was discovered, his brother would not be involved. The only difficulty was finding a place large enough for all those bags, which was also close enough to the present storage so that they would not attract attention during transportation. He decided to store the RDX in Mumbra and Kashimira, close to New Bombay, in warehouses belonging to his builder-friends Shahid Gehlot and Mohammed Jindran.

Despite its proximity to Bombay, real-estate prices were very low in the predominantly Muslim township of Mumbra. Shahid and Amin Gehlot were small-time builders who worked in the township and had constructed several buildings there, including one called Mobin Nagar in Kausa village at Mumbra.

On 17 March, Yaqub drove to Mumbra to meet them at their offices. He asked them for an empty ground-floor room to store some important goods. He did not disclose the nature of the goods. The Gehlots knew Yaqub well, and they had no reason to turn him down, especially as they weren't using the space at that time. They also knew he would return the favour some day. They agreed, but said that they had only one room free. This room, in the Mobin Nagar building, measured barely 500 square feet.

Yaqub summoned masons and bricked up the only window in the room, so that no one could accidentally look in. That evening, he hired a tempo and three labourers to move thirty-two bags of RDX to the new location. There were also ten bags of gelatine stored there. Yaqub had also bought about fifty jute bags of dried Bombay duck, which he stacked on top of the RDX. The rest he would store in Jindran's shed in Kashimira early the following day. By this time Mukadam and others had mentioned his name to the police, and he knew it was time for him to go underground.

Kashimira is one of the most picturesque areas of Thane, with lush greenery, rolling hills, clean air and wide creeks. It is a favourite weekend spot for Bombay's wealthy, many of whom have farmhouses and cottages in the area. There are also many small workshops, factories and warehouses there.

Builder Noor Mohammed Khan and his partner Jindran owned the 2,000-square-foot Godown 150, near Nagla Bunder creek, in Kashimira, which they used to store their materials. Khan's business had been struggling until he had joined hands with Jindran, whose shrewd business tactics had made both of them prosperous. Although Khan did not approve of Jindran's unethical activities, which often bordered on the illegal, or some of his more shady buddies, like Yeba Yaqub, he held his peace.

On the afternoon of 19 March, as Khan walked into the shed, he noticed that there were about seventy jute bags neatly piled up at one side. He asked the Gurkha watchman, Pratap Bahadur, 'Yeh kya hai?'

'They are Jindran sahab's,' Bahadur replied.

Khan was surprised. There wasn't any construction work in progress that required more materials. Nor had Jindran mentioned that there was anything he was planning to store there. Khan cut open one of the bags and stuck his hand in. He found a black sticky substance that had no smell. He had no idea what the stuff was; it certainly wasn't anything he recognized from construction. He thought, this must be something Jindran is planning to use to cut costs.

Khan decided to find out what the substance was. He sent Bahadur to summon Abdul Rashid, who had a chemical-processing unit adjacent to his own warehouse.

Rashid took some of the blackish substance and rubbed it on his hands, then on a stone, but failed to identify it. He took a chunk back to his lab and conducted various tests, but still found nothing conclusive. Finally, Rashid tried to burn it. The instant he put a match to it, the chunk flared up and emitted a lot of smoke and a strong odour.

Rashid rushed to Khan's shed. 'Noor bhai, this chemical seems to be something suspicious. Where did you get it?'

'Jindran has stored this here without telling me. What should I do?'

'Noor bhai, let's get rid of it. Let's dump it in the nearest creek. But we have to do it very carefully. We have to keep the dresswalas from finding out.'

'We can't do it ourselves. This stuff weighs a ton. Who's going to help us?'

'I know a guy, Munna. He's very daring. He'll do this, but we'll have to pay him.'

'No problem. I'll pay anything to get rid of this.'

Rashid organized a meeting at his Marol residence with Noor Khan, Jindran and Munna. Jindran, duly rebuked by his partner, explained that he had stored it because he owed Yaqub a favour. He could not manage to locate Yaqub who had gone underground, otherwise he would have asked him to remove the sacks himself.

Through sheer coincidence, Munna had already worked with Tiger and had helped in the landings. He saw this as an opportunity to make up for some of the money he could have earned had he participated in the bombings. Jindran and Khan were obviously desperate, so Munna demanded Rs 5 lakh. The deal was struck.

Munna scouted the Nagla Bunder creek area for a deserted spot. He hired a dump truck and seven labourers. On the night of

23 March, they loaded up the truck and drove to the Kapur Bawdi area of Nagla Bunder. The work was done in less than three hours.

8

The Investigation Continues

It was 23 March.

Soon after the recovery of the scooters, Chougule decided to look into past recoveries of bombs or explosives in the city. He had tried to find out how many times terrorists had targeted the city, and was amazed to find that there were no consolidated records. So he had requested the office of each zonal DCP to pass on the information for their zone. Now piles of files, papers and registers littered his desk.

Inspector Zarapkar, who shared the office with him, was busy disposing of the seized RDX and sending samples for analysis to the forensic laboratory at Kalina.

The phone rang. Zarapkar picked it up. As he listened, his expression became grim. He said that the BDDS would be there immediately, and hung up. He said to Chougule, 'Sir, control room said that some suspicious looking suitcases were found on a staircase of Imani Manzil at Zaveri Bazaar.'

This time the BDDS team did not take the van or the equipment, only the invaluable Zanjeer. Zaveri Bazaar was right behind the BDDS office, and the quickest way to get there was on foot. When they reached the spot, the policemen from the LT Marg police station were already there, shepherding people away from Imani Manzil.

Just inside the entrance, at the foot of the staircase, were two suitcases. Chougule signalled to the officers to evacuate the residents and shopkeepers from the area. Zanjeer, who seemed to be enjoying being in the limelight, was guided to the suitcases. He sniffed the suitcases once, then he walked around a bit as if making sure. He again went to them and sniffed, taking longer this time. Then he made a strange sound and barked briefly, as if he was only half certain.

To Chougule and his men it seemed clear that the suitcases contained something in addition to explosives, otherwise Zanjeer wouldn't have taken so long to decide. Pandhre tucked a hook in the handle of one of the suitcases and very carefully dragged it out into the open. This operation took more than twenty minutes. Once the first suitcase was out in the open, Kadam pulled out the second one with the equal caution. Once both were out, Pandhre and Kadam opened them.

One contained five AK-56 rifles and the other contained four AK-56s and several magazines. Pandhre and Kadam examined the rifles and Chougule the magazines. They did not contain a single bullet. When Chougule went over to discuss the find with Inspector Shivaji Sawant of the LT Marg police station, Sawant told him that he had been informed that there was an unclaimed handcart with about ten similar suitcases near the Siddhi Vinayak temple in Ganesh Lane, a five-minute walk away.

Chougule handed over the suitcases and AK-56s to Sawant for making a panchnama, and went off to Ganesh Lane.

Near the Siddhi Vinayak temple, Chougule found the handcart. It was a strange sight: thirteen suitcases of different colours—grey, maroon, blue and green—piled on top of each other on a handcart parked in the middle of nowhere. They were too many to be a tourist's, Chougule thought. Nor did the cart seem like something that would be used to transport suitcases from a warehouse to a showroom.

Zanjeer sniffed at the handcart and barked instantly.

The police evacuated everyone within fifty metres. Once again, with extreme care and caution, the officers offloaded the suitcases from the cart. Chougule, Zarapkar, Kadam and Pandhre opened them one by one.

They were full of green hand grenades marked 'Arges 69'. Each suitcase contained a minimum of fifteen to twenty grenades, about 200 in all. Chougule thought of the grenades they had found in the Maruti van at Worli on 12 March. They had the same markings. One case also contained three AK-56 rifles, some empty magazines and dozens of pencil timers. Another had five pistols of .9 mm calibre and five .308 cartridges. The weapons were handed over to the LT Marg policemen.

Chougule lapsed into thought. Now that the police were turning on the heat, someone had decided to throw away the evidence before the cops landed at his doorstep.

DCP (Zone VII) Arup Patnaik had always wanted to be a tough police officer. A short, stout, dour-faced man, Patnaik had been a bank officer. But it was only when he joined the Indian Police Service (IPS) in 1979 that he was finally happy. He believed that the police should play a proactive role and tackle problems head-on.

Patnaik's first posting as DCP in Bombay was in March 1991. He decided it was essential for him to familiarize himself with the topography of the city to do his job well. His first tour was memorable. His guide was SI Prakash Mane. They set out from the police headquarters at Crawford Market.

The first area they entered was the Muslim pocket in the Chakala area, Bhendi Bazaar and Mohammed Ali Road. Mane

Arup Patnaik
(*Courtesy* Mid-day)

launhed into his description.

'Sir, this is Mohammed Ali Road. It is connected to Dongri. This is the area of Dawood Ibrahim. Although he is in Dubai now, his word is law in this area and even beyond.'

Patnaik looked at Mane in the front seat wide-eyed and nodded. Mane drove towards JJ Hospital crossroad, in the direction of the Byculla flyover. He continued, 'Now her Dawood Ibrahim's turf end and Arun Gawli's begins Gawli used to be a mill worker Today he is the only Hindu do who has stood up to the challenge of the Muslim Mafia.'

They drove towards Byculla, over the bridge, and Mane spok again.

'Sir, here ends the territory of Arun Gawli. From here it Amar Naik's territory. Naik was a vegetable vendor at Dada market but then he formed a gang of his own and became big He continued on the subject of the activities of the different gang and the traditional rivalry between the Naik and Gawli gang By this time, they were past Dadar and were turning in towar Sena Bhavan.

'Sir, this is the headquarters of the Shiv Sena party. The ar till Shivaji Park is their stronghold. You know, sir, there is weird analogy here. The way Gawli is the only gangster to ha challenged the might of Dawood, Shiv Sena is the only party take on the might of the Congress,' Mane said, a tinge admiration in his voice.

Patnaik stayed quiet, though he was seething inside. The Ambassador was passing through Mahim. 'Sir, this area belongs to smugglers. Some of the most notorious live here.' He did not mention names.

Patnaik decided to lambast his guide if he persisted with this kind of introduction to the city. As the car was about to cross into Bandra, Mane started again. 'Sir, now once again we will enter the area of Dawood and his terrible brother, Anis.'

Patnaik couldn't contain himself any more. 'Mane, you say this area belongs to Dawood, that area belongs to Gawli, the other to Amar Naik. Do we exist in this city at all or not? Do gangsters rule this city? And you tell me that happily! Nonsense, absolute bullshit! Change your attitude. Try to make this entire city the police's, not the gangsters'.'

During the communal riots, Patnaik had amply demonstrated his belief that the city should belong to the police. During the first round of riots in December 1992, there was a fierce clash in Koldongri, Andheri. Patnaik had jumped right into the middle of the flying bottles and sticks. The constables and SIs accompanying him were so inspired by his brave act that they too swooped down upon the marauding rioters. The day was saved by police daredevilry. That evening, looking tired and battered, his once-crisp uniform much stained, Patnaik stood on a handcart and announced to the crowds through a loudspeaker: '*Aap log ek baat samajh lena. Is shahar mein goonda raj nahin chalega.* And let all hooligans understand that whatever they do, they will fall short miserably of the power of the police. I will personally flush out each and every bhai in this area and show that we, the police, are the only bhais of the people and not these goondas.' When he finished and jumped down from the cart, there was silence. During the January riots, the area between Bandra and Andheri in his jurisdiction remained largely peaceful while the rest of the city burnt.

The police top brass was impressed, as was the home department. Patnaik, along with another officer who had also performed in an exemplary manner during the riots, was lauded in a ceremony in the crowded Police Club hall in early March, and a cash reward of Rs 10 lakh was announced by Sharad Pawar, who had just become the chief minister.

Now there was trouble in his area again, with the bombing of the three hotels. Like Rakesh Maria, Patnaik had also formed a special team of officers comprising among others Ambadas Pote, Iqbal Shaikh and Sohail Buddha.

During his years as DCP Zone VII, Patnaik had developed several contacts among underworld operatives in his area, who had often given him important leads in various cases. One of his contacts was Yeba Yaqub. He got in touch with him to find out about the blasts. Yaqub had given him a few names whom Patnaik had pursued.

But sometimes informers deliberately give the police names of people against whom they have a personal grouse. Among the names Yaqub had given were a few people he had a grudge against. After a few days Patnaik had come to realize he had been misinformed.

On 20 March, Rakesh Maria's team allegedly picked up Yaqub's brother Majid Khan of MK Builders from his Bandra residence and kept him in the Mahim police lock-up. Their records did not show that he had been arrested. His 'detention' would put pressure on Yaqub, who had been on the run since Asgar Mukadam, Imtiyaz Ghavate and those arrested had disclosed his name as someone involved in the conspiracy. But it is said that after two days of constant interrogation, Majid still did not provide them with Yaqub's whereabouts. In desperation, the police allegedly picked up Majid Khan's wife, Nafeesa.

When Yaqub heard of this, he felt desperately worried and guilty for he knew he was responsible. On 24 March, he called up Patnaik. 'Sahab, Majid and Nafeesa are not involved in the bomb blasts. Why were they picked up?'

'I did not pick them up, nor are they in my custody,' replied Patnaik.

'Sahab, please get them released. I have heard that they are being tortured because the police suspect that I am involved.'

'So why don't you show up and clear the misunderstanding? That way you can save them.'

'Sahab, if I show up they will frame me as well, and not release Nafeesa and Majid.'

'I cannot help it.'

Desperate, Yaqub called Patnaik again the following day. 'Sahab, please do something, I heard that Majid and Nafeesa are both in bad shape.'

'The police lock-up is not meant to keep people in good shape.'

'Sahab, *please* do something.'

'As I had told you earlier, they are not in my custody. There is nothing I can do! There is no point in calling unless you have any important information to share.'

Yaqub thought of turning himself in. But he knew it would not serve any purpose. Should he try to negotiate with the police and seek the release of his kin in exchange of information about the RDX? This would be tantamount to a betrayal but the need to save his brother and sister-in-law was more pressing than adhering to his principles.

He called up Patnaik again. 'Sahab, can my brother be released in exchange for hundred per cent pucca information?'

'I can talk to my superiors but I cannot guarantee anything.'

'Sahab, my information is absolutely accurate. But I want release of my brother and his wife.'

'There is no deal. I can only try.'

Patnaik lived in Sagar Tarang, one of several plush multi-storeyed buildings in Worli, overlooking the sea. Several IPS officers, some in the Bombay police, lived in that building. As he was finishing his daily quota of newspapers early the following day, 26 March, the phone rang.

'Sahab, *main* Yaqub Khan *bol raha hoon*.'

'*Haan, haan, kya khabar* ...?'

'Sahab, I have called to give you important information ... It is about the RDX ... but you will release my brother.'

'Look Yaqub, your name has been mentioned in the bomb blast case because of your connection with Tiger Memon. You ...'

'It is all a pack of lies,' Yaqub interjected. 'I don't know why but Maria sahab wants to fix us up. My family is being framed and now even my name is being unnecessarily dragged in.' His tone was vehement.

'Well, what is the information?'

'Sahab, my brother ...'

'I will try ... now will you go ahead?'

'Sahab, Tiger Memon had stored some RDX bags at a place in Mumbra, Thane.'

'Mumbra—where in Mumbra?' Patnaik knew the area only vaguely.

'It is in the ground floor room of Mobin Nagar, near Amrut Nagar. It is in a room in the C-wing of the house.'

Patnaik began jotting down the details. 'Is it hundred per cent confirmed that the RDX is there or are you taking us for a ride again?'

'Sahab, after you seize the kala sabun, will you let my brother go?'

'We will see. Call me tomorrow.'

The information was so specific that Patnaik thought it could be true. He called JCP Singh, who lived upstairs in the same building. 'Sir, good morning. Patnaik speaking.'

'Yes, Arup?'

'Sir, I just received the information that a huge stock of RDX is hidden at a place in Mumbra.'

'Is the information correct?'

'Sir, I have full details of the hideout.'

'Fine ... let us organize a raid right now. I will inform the CP and will accompany you to Mumbra. Let us leave at the earliest.'

'Fine, sir.'

A police raid party was organized, the bomb squad alerted and told to assemble at Sagar Tarang. By 10 a.m., Singh and Patnaik, accompanied by the BDDS squad, including Chougule, and several officers, left for Mumbra in a convoy of police jeeps, Ambassadors, Gypsies and unmarked cars. They drove along the Eastern Express Highway and within half an hour, crossed over from the Mulund checkpoint into Thane city. As the cars passed the Mumbra station, Muslims of all ages were preparing for their Friday prayers at the nearby Rizvi Baug mosque.

Singh and Patnaik were in the same car. Singh said, 'We have had several incidents of Dawood's gang members taking shelter in Mumbra. In a way, it has become a haven for criminals from the D-Company.' Patnaik nodded. He was reminded of SI Mane's words: 'Sir, this is the area of Dawood Ibrahim.'

The convoy halted at Amrut Nagar junction on the Bombay–Pune highway. A local police officer came and informed them that the blue building nearby was called Mobin Nagar. The area surrounding the building was cordoned off. Inevitably, a curious crowd of onlookers had begun to gather.

The police party went straight to the ground floor section of

C-wing. After quizzing the residents, Patnaik zeroed in on the only room that was locked. The lock was broken and the group entered the room. There was a strong stench of fish. There were jute bags stacked on top of each other in several layers. From the foul odour, Patnaik thought Yaqub had taken him for a ride again.

The policemen ripped open several bags, only to find dried fish. Disappointment was evident on everyone's face. After five layers of bags had been examined, the police team started showing signs of weariness and impatience.

Frustration welled up within Patnaik as he thought of the futility of the trip, and he sought relief in kicking a bag near his foot. The bag yielded to form a cavity in the shape of his shoe. Dried fish would not yield like that. Surprised, Patnaik bent down and felt the bag. The substance inside felt like putty. He called out, 'Chougule, Chougule, come here. Can you make out what this is?'

The bag was opened, and there was a brownish malleable putty inside. Some other bags were found which felt similar, and on opening they were full of either a brownish or blackish substance. Chougule brought in Zanjeer to sniff the bags. He barked almost immediately, signalling that the materials were explosive.

In all, thirty-two bags containing RDX and ten containing gelatine were found. Subsequently it was established that the bags contained 1,034 kg of RDX and 574 kg of gelatin. Some of the bags had numbers on them, and each was marked with a distinctive blue circle. This was the first major RDX haul by the Bombay police.

The police sealed the room. A search was launched for the Gehlot brothers. Amin and Shahid Gehlot were shocked to hear about the RDX in their building. They claimed that they did not know what the contents of the bags were, that Yaqub had asked merely for room to store them without giving any explanations. They were taken into custody by the crime branch officers. CP Samra was informed about the seizure.

It was evening when the police team was through. By this time, the press had got wind of the story and had begun converging at the spot. A huge crowd had also gathered on the Bombay–Pune highway, resulting in a traffic jam. The RDX was loaded into a separate van and handed over to the BDDS for disposal.

■

It was Tuesday, 30 March, and the sun was shining brightly. Balchandra Kamdi and Babu Salian, from Nagla village, had gone to the nearby creek with their friends Pravin Khudade, his brother Baban, and Anant and Krishan Saravne. They were all in their early twenties, and this was their favourite spot for fishing and swimming.

As Baban jumped into the water, his feet touched something that wasn't the rock or sand usually found on the river bed. He dived under to have a look. It was a large lump of blackish substance that felt like clay.

Baban called Pravin to take a look. Pravin was equally stumped. The other boys also came over to have a look. The lump seemed to have fallen out of a torn sack. Balchandra was fishing a little distance away. Seeing his friends gathered together, he threw the net aside and ran over to them.

Pravin and Baban showed the lump to him. Balchandra exclaimed for he too had caught some of that substance in his net.

The boys discussed what it could be. Finally Balchandra, the oldest, said, 'I think it is brown sugar.'

'If the police find out that we've laid our hands on brown

sugar then we're in for it. We should throw it away,' said Baban.

Babu Salian butted in. 'Don't be foolish. This stuff has our fingerprints on it. Let's burn it.'

Everyone thought this a good idea. They gathered some paper and tried to set the lump on fire. It lit up at once and billowed smoke. The thick black plumes scared the boys and they scampered away to the safety of their village.

The whole incident might have been forgotten but for an alert police constable, Shyam Phutane. Phutane was posted at the Kalamboli police station, near Panvel. He went to Owale, the village next to Nagla, on 1 April for some personal work. He overheard Balchandra and Babu talking about drug smugglers who were stashing their wares in the creeks of Nagla Bunder. Initially, Phutane thought the boys were trying to play a joke on him. Then he confronted the young men.

The two boys feigned ignorance until they realized that Phutane meant business and that he could book them under the Drugs Act. They told him about the black and brown cakes they had found on the bed of Nagla creek. Phutane took them to the creek and asked them to show him the mysterious cakes. Balchandra dived in and brought up a lump. After a close scrutiny, Phutane remembered the descriptions of RDX he had read in the papers after the raid in Mumbra the previous week.

Phutane called up his superior, ACP M.C. Naik of Panvel division. Naik came over and the material was carried over to the Kapur Bawdi police station. It was about midnight. Naik decided to call the Thane CP, Basavraj Akashi. Akashi in turn summoned Addl. CP Shankar Zarekar to identify the find. Zarekar had participated in the Mumbra haul, where he had seen RDX, and he identified Phutane's find to be the same substance. JCP Singh of Bombay police was informed.

Singh asked the area to be cordoned off and asked the BDDS

to come over to Thane. It was the early hours of 2 April. The police located Dr Vishwas Sapatnekar, who ran a deep-sea diving club, and asked him to provide them with divers. An area with a radius of about a kilometre around the spot where the boys had found the lump was marked out. The divers from Sapatnekar's team and local youths from Owale and Nagla launched a search of the creek bed.

The operation lasted all night and well into the day. The divers had to struggle with the darkness and the high tide. After an exhausting search, they located two large pits, about ten feet apart, within which sacks were concealed. The pits had been dug deep into the creek, to a depth of about twenty-five feet. They recovered fifteen sacks from one pit and thirty-five from the other. The sacks had been dumped in such a manner that it would have been possible to retrieve them in the future. Eight bags had drifted outside the pits.

In all, fifty-eight sacks were recovered. Thirty-eight of them contained RDX and twenty contained gelatine. The total weight estimated to be over 2,380 kilograms. After the bags were brought ashore and lined up, Singh noticed that they bore serial numbers, beginning with 302 and going up to 554. Each bag was also printed with the distinctive blue circle that had been found on the bags recovered from Mobin Nagar, Mumbra. Later on checking, it was found that the serial numbers on the bags recovered from Mumbra also had numbers which fell within the same range as the numbers on this lot.

■

Maria's team continued their relentless investigations with many nocturnal visits, raids, summons and arrests. Bhendi Bazaar, Mohammed Ali Road, Pydhonie, Two Tanks and Nagpada were traditionally Muslim strongholds, and it was in such areas that such raids happened the most.

The community went into a state of shock from March to May, when the police finally eased up. Young men who were not remotely connected with the blasts trembled at the sight of the police. The elders rarely stepped out of their houses after sundown. The lock-ups in the crime branch and the Mahim police station were crowded with prisoners, including hundreds who were in no way associated with Tiger Memon. Their relatives waited anxiously outside.

To make matters worse, many of those arrested did not have recourse to proper legal aid. Faced with a surge in the demand for their services, some lawyers often did not represent their clients adequately or refused to help until paid exorbitant fees. As a result, many of the accused had to spend more time behind bars than was necessary.

The *Times of India* was the first newspaper to highlight the plight of the Muslim detainees, but this report appeared only on 22 April 1993:

> While the police have arrested about eighty-eight people ... sources estimate that at least three times that number have been picked up ... and lodged in the Mahim police station lock-up ... Many claimed that though they were held for periods longer than two weeks, they were never charged.

The Bombay edition of the *Sunday Observer* reported on 13 June, 'When media attention focused on the unlawful detention, the police quietly released some 300 detainees ...' But the subject was not closed. Carol Andrade wrote on 25 June in the *Metropolis*,

... enormous sums of money changed hands ... as the jails filled up with a motley crowd that was usually guilty of nothing more than being 'the friend of a friend' and, therefore, the enemy of the state and the local policeman.

A year later, the subject was still being discussed:

The Bombay police seemed to have taken the line that anybody with a Muslim name has prima facie involvement in the blasts. There have been indiscriminate arrests, Muslims have been beaten, abused and humiliated as the police have violated every one of their fundamental rights.

—*Sunday* magazine, 3 July 1994

Newspaper reports also revealed that no records had been made of the detainees, so that when relatives came looking for them, the police could deny that they were in the lock-up. Generally, a person is supposed to be produced in front of a magistrate within twenty-four hours of his arrest. But under TADA, this was not mandatory. Sometimes the date of arrest was shown to be weeks after the person was detained, sometimes it was not recorded at all. Many of those who were released said they would bear the scars of those weeks forever.

Rakesh Rajkumar Khurana, thirty-five, the owner of a restaurant in Bandra, was a successful and happy man. He was picked up simply because he was supposed to be close to Pilloo Khan, who was wrongly suspected of involvement in the blasts. Khurana managed to secure his release through the Bombay High Court. The order was passed on 10 April. As there was some documentation to be completed, he was to be released in a couple of days.

On the night of 11 April in the Mahim lock-up, Khurana saw some drunken policemen barging into his neighbouring cell, which held three men and two women. They were Sayed Abdul Rehman, his wife, Noor Khan, and his daughter, and Baba Musa Chouhan. The policemen started savagely manhandling the women; the men was powerless to protest.

Among the policemen in the cell was one who seemed to be an officer. He looked at Khurana in the next cell and said, 'Khurana, if you do not reveal Pilloo Khan's whereabouts by tomorrow then I will drag your wife here and ask my men to treat her just as badly.'

When Khurana was released on 14 April, he went home to his wife Neeru, three-year-old son and two-year-old daughter. That night, as his family was sleeping, he pulled out his .32-bore revolver, which he had bought for self-defence but never used. He shot his wife and children. He later put the bodies in his car and drove down to a deserted lane in Juhu where he shot himself.

The city was shocked. The police did their best to play down the incident. In a press conference on 15 April, CP Samra said that Khurana 'had not been arrested but only interrogated. We never suspected that he had close links with Pilloo Khan. We only wanted to try to get a clue about the notorious drug baron's whereabouts' (*Times of India*, 16 April 1993). In a follow-up story by Naresh Fernandes (*Times of India*, 22 April 1993) Samra is quoted as saying that Khurana 'must have had a guilty conscience otherwise he would not have taken such a drastic step.'

The situation in Raigad was similar to that in Bombay. After Asgar Mukadam, Abdul Gani and others had confessed in the third week of March about the landings of the RDX in the area, the attention of the police turned to the three villages of Srivardhan, Mhasla and Mahad. Some 400 people, an overwhelming majority of whom were Muslim, were locked up and interrogated. The SP, Alibaug, T.S. Bhal, deputy superintendent of police (DSP), Chandrashekhar Daithankar, and Inspector S.A. Patil of Srivardhan directed operations.

At least some of the people arrested in Bombay—Mukadam, Imtiyaz Ghavate, Abdul Gani and Parvez Shaikh—had been closely connected with the planning and implementation of the blasts. In Raigad, however, very few of the people picked up had any connections with Tiger Memon. The few who had helped with the landings were porters, loaders and boatmen, who had no idea of the goods they were transporting or to what end they would be put. They had earned just minimal wages for their work, as for any other job. Many of them could not even say RDX, but said Iodex instead. There was little that they could reveal. Those who had been part of the larger conspiracy—the landing agents, customs and police officers—managed to get away.

As Olga Tellis wrote in her column in the weekly *Sunday Observer* on 19 June, 'the police have indeed tended to preen themselves on the completion of their task when, in actual fact, what they have accomplished is the arrest of a bunch of coolies.' Human rights activist P.A. Sebastian observed in the same issue:

> They picked up a broom maker who apparently loaded RDX. Maybe the man was paid Rs 100 instead of Rs 50 to load the box, how was he to know what he was loading? ... in Thane and Ratnagiri, which have several quarries ... the police have arrested people who had licences to deal with explosives.

The Haspatel clan lived in Walavati village, two kilometres from Srivardhan. Their nightmare began when some rocket-like objects were recovered from a lake near the village. Acting on a tip-off, the Srivardhan police raided the house of Iqbal Haspatel on 13 April. During the search, they came across some 'missiles' kept in a showcase. The police dismantled all the furniture and domestic appliances in their zeal to recover the entire cache of weapons. They decided that the missiles were actually rocket launchers used by the Afghan Mujahideen and arrested the entire Haspatel family. Those hauled to the police station included Iqbal Haspatel, his wife, sister, daughter, daughter-in-law, sons Mobin and Nadeem, besides six other villagers from whose house the police had discovered some sophisticated knives.

Bhal wanted this recovery properly publicized and issued an official press release. According to the *Times of India* (14 April 1993):

Another arms haul was reported from Walavati area of Srivardhan late yesterday evening. Twenty-five projectiles and seventeen pipe bombs and ammunition were recovered from the creek. Combing operations were going on ... In nearby Murud, five bombs were recovered, the Raigad police reported.

It was also reported that the military experts had identified the projectiles to be highly deadly missiles and that a further report was awaited.

Between 13 and 20 April, the Haspatel family was detained. According to Aparna Borkar of the *Indian Express*, 'A police team allegedly stripped and beat Mobin and Iqbal with belts and rods, burnt them with cigarette butts, gave electric shocks for two weeks and illegally detained two women of the family.'

On 20 April it was discovered that the 'launchers' were spindles destined for the Solapur textile mills, and had been dumped nearby when a truck overturned at Mahad in 1986. Some children had brought them home to Walavati. They had been thrown into the lake because the villagers feared that the police would accuse them of stealing them. 'A police complaint with the Mahad police registering the incident and confirmation from the Solapur textile mill where the spindles were headed, corroborated the facts,' reported the *Indian Express*.

The growing pressure from the human rights groups and the realization of the error regarding the 'missiles' compelled Bhal to release the Haspatels. The reports in the press attracted the attention of National Human Rights Commission (NHRC), which launched a probe into the alleged atrocities. The judicial magistrate of Srivardhan court, M.M. Sakarkar, registered a criminal case against Bhal and ten of his officers, including Daithankar, Patil and Chavan. The case is still on at the Alibaug sessions court.

While the men arrested in Raigad did not know the details of the conspiracy, they could give the police the names of those who had hired them for the landings. The three people who were instantly named as the leaders of the landing operations on 3 and 7 February as soon as the arrests began in the latter half of March were Dadabhai Parkar, Dawood Phanse and Rahim Laundrywala. It was also learnt that Phanse had been to Dubai on 25 January and had received specific instructions from Dawood Ibrahim to help Tiger Memon to land some 'chemicals'.

Bhal was however reluctant to arrest Parkar, Phanse and Laundrywala without more clinching evidence. The Bombay police had alerted Bhal about the role of the three landing agents by the second week of March. But despite receiving verification from the Raigad detainees, Bhal did not take action, a fact that was highlighted in the national media.

Finally, the Bombay police decided to act on their own. A police team from the Worli police station, led by Senior Police

Inspector H.B. Pawar, swooped down on the landing agents and arrested them towards the end of March.

At the end of March for the Bombay police, the landing agent Dadabhai Parkar's statement to DIG P.K. Jain was an education on the finer points of smuggling.

'I and my partners, Dawood Phanse and Rahim Laundrywala, have been active in smuggling for the last five years. We have worked for Tiger Memon for the last year and a half, and helped in six landings. Four of these were of silver ingots, and the last two were of arms and explosives.

'For each landing we had to pay customs, the DRI and police officials to ensure that the goods could be unloaded unhindered and transported to the city. We also had to hire men to offload the goods. Each silver ingot weighs about thirty kilograms. For every ingot we earned Rs 7,000. The four consignments of silver we had were for 135 ingots, 143 ingots, 210 ingots and sixty-five ingots. For us, the more ingots the better—because for each landing we have to pay a fixed sum of money to the customs, DRI and police. So if there are more ingots, our profits are more, because the costs are fixed. Which is why when Tiger organized the landing of only sixty-five ingots we had quite an altercation with him ...'

Parkar went on to detail how much each customs and police officer had to be bribed. The amounts ranged from the thousands to several lakhs, and involved officials from the police, customs and even the DRI.

Rahim Laundrywala and Dawood Phanse were also interrogated, and their statements corroborated Parkar's list of the corrupt customs, DRI and police officers who had helped Tiger.

The Anti-Corruption Bureau of the CBI was alerted, and it was decided to raid the houses of the officials who had been named by the landing agents. The CBI officers raided their homes in Thane, Alibaug and Malad among other places. However, the raids yielded nothing.

Addl. CC Thapa was outraged at hearing that his officers had colluded with the smugglers and suspended three of them.

9

Enter Bollywood

Among the detainees at the Mahim lock-up, SI Virendra Vani was the most feared policeman. He was a national-level boxer, and was nicknamed Arnold Schwarzenegger for his build was truly fearsome.

On 11 April, Vani entered one of the cells and glanced at the twenty-odd men huddled there. One of the men seemed to be in slightly better shape than the rest, and Vani decided that he was to be his target. This was Ibrahim Chauhan, also known as Baba Chauhan.

'Sahab, *chhod do*, sahab. I have said everything I know,' Chauhan said in a pleading manner.

But Vani was relentless. 'I want the complete story. How you and your friends did it, and who all were involved. *Samjha, b...?* Or else ...'

'Sahab, I am a builder and businessman. I went to Dubai with my brother-in-law. We were having lunch at Hotel Delhi Durbar when I met Anis Ibrahim and Abu Salem. I was told that Anis was the brother of Dawood Ibrahim, and Salem was his close friend. It turned out that like me Salem lives in Andheri. We became friends and met several times in Dubai. When I returned to Bombay, we kept in touch.

'On 15 January, Salem came to my office and said that Anis bhai had some work for me. In a little while, Anis called and asked me if I had any garage space available. I said no, but I promised I'd try to find some. Then Salem took me to the office of Magnum Videos at Santacruz. There I met Samir Hingora ...'

'Who is this fucking Samir Hingora? The one of Samir-Hanif fame? Why are you trying to implicate him?' Vani growled.

Chauhan could barely speak. 'Sahab, *sach bol raha hun* (I am telling the truth). It is the same Samir, and not just Samir but Hanif Kadawala is also involved. They both know Salem and also Anis Ibrahim. Once when I was with them, they both spoke to Anis Ibrahim on an overseas call for such a long time that Hanif ended up paying a bill of Rs 1,300.'

∎

Samir Hingora and Hanif Kadawala were film producers, and partners in a company called Magnum Videos. Their films included the Sanjay Dutt-Madhuri Dixit starrer *Sanam*. This was not the first time that they had been named in the context of a criminal nexus. They were said to organize shows in Dubai for Dawood Ibrahim, for which they would ferry well-known film personalities. Maria decided to follow up on Chauhan's story. He sent off two police teams to get the producers. Until they returned, he took over the interrogation of Chauhan.

The unmarked police Maruti car halted outside Guru Nanak Park, near Turner Road, Bandra. It was 11.25 p.m. A dog barked somewhere.

SI Nadgouda rang the bell of Kadawala's plush apartment. A woman opened the door.

'Hanif Kadawala hai?' Nadgouda asked.

'*Haan hai*, who are you?'

'I am a police officer.'

'*Kya kaam hai?*'

'Call him, I say,' Nadgouda glared. The woman retreated. The door opened again. It was a stout man of medium height

Hanif Kadawala
(*Courtesy* Mid-day)

with a moustache. 'I am Hanif Kadawala.'

'Maria sahab has called you to the Mahim police station.'

'What nonsense? What have I done?' Kadawala said in a tone of righteous indignation.

'Mr Kadawala, I think you should reserve your anger for my boss, Mr Rakesh Maria, as he has sent us here. You can ask him the reason.'

After a short argument, Kadawala got into the waiting Maruti car.

'At least now will you tell me why I am being harassed in this manner?' Kadawala asked Nadgouda in a more subdued tone.

'For your involvement in the bomb blasts and having connections with Dawood Ibrahim.'

'This is absurd, I am innocent. I am not involved in the bomb blasts. As for Dawood Ibrahim, I don't know him from Adam.' The belligerence was returning.

'Look, you are wasting your energy on us. Why don't you just shut up? If you are innocent you will be let off.'

According to Nadgouda, Kadawala offered him five petis to let him off (a peti was a lakh in Bombay slang), which he refused.

After a while, Kadawala spoke up again. 'Your police always goes after small fry like me and let off influential people.'

'What do you mean?'

'I mean if you are really serious, then why don't you arrest Sanjay?'

'Sanjay, who Sanjay?' Nadgouda was surprised that Kadawala had started revealing information rather than arguing. And that too, with no prompting.

'Sanjay Dutt.'

'Sanjay Dutt ... who?' Nadgouda wanted to make sure.

'Come on sahab, you don't know Sanjay Dutt, the film star, the son of the member of Parliament (MP), Sunil Dutt?'

It was shortly after 11 p.m., normally there would be much more traffic. But tonight even the traffic on the road seemed to have fallen silent not to disturb the tension in the room.

Maria continued the interrogation of the trembling Ibrahim Chauhan. His tone was quiet but steely. 'Chauhan, you have a choice of either talking to me here now or talking to Vani in the lock-up.'

Chauhan looked up at Maria and sobbed, 'Sahab, I will tell you everything ...' His voice was raspy. He asked for some water, which Maria asked an orderly to get. Chauhan gulped down the water and continued to sob.

Maria waited, a trifle impatiently. Realizing that, Chauhan began speaking. 'Sahab, you know Samir and Hanif are close to Anis Ibrahim. They had spoken to Anis in Dubai over the phone ... they are involved ...'

'I know that already. Tell me how they are involved.'

'Anis had instructed me and Abu Salem to deliver some guitars and tennis balls to Sanju Baba's house at Bandra. Which I had done faithfully and apart from that I did nothing.'

Maria was yet to be fluent in the jargon of the Mafia, though he understood a fair amount. Guitar and tennis balls were not part of his vocabulary.

'What are guitars and tennis balls?'

'Sahab, a guitar is an AK-56 rifle, we also call it lambiwali, the long one, because it is larger than a handgun. Tennis balls are hand grenades.'

Maria suppressed a smile at the ingenious coding. 'Who is this Sanju Baba?'

'Sanju Baba is the film star, Sanjay Dutt.'

Maria had been sprawled in his chair. At this, he sat up and his eyes widened with shock and disbelief. 'What are you saying? Sanjay Dutt and Anis Ibrahim. How the hell does Sanjay come in the picture?'

'Sahab, Sunil Dutt had done a lot of relief work for Muslims after the riots of December and January. Sanju Baba too had chipped in. As a result, the Shiv Sena guys had been threatening him. Sanju had requested Anis bhai for some guns to defend himself and his family against the Shiv Sena …'

Chauhan continued, but Maria's mind was elsewhere as he pondered on the consequences of this revelation. It was only when Nadgouda entered that he snapped back to his immediate surroundings.

'Sir, we have brought Hanif Kadawala. He says that Sanjay Dutt, the film star, is involved …' Nadgouda began.

Maria interrupted, 'Bring him in.'

Kadawala swaggered in. There was an air of disdain about him, but he greeted Maria pleasantly. Maria ignored his greeting. 'Are you Hanif Kadawala?'

'Yes, sir, I am.'

'What is your profession?'

'Sir, my partner, Samir Hingora, and I produce films and purchase official rights for videos. Our firm is called Magnum Videos.'

'How many films do you hold the video rights for? How many films have you produced?'

talking to Anis Ibrahim over the phone and asking for the delivery of arms and ammunition. Samir also told me how he was compelled by Anis ...'

Suddenly Maria signalled Kadawala to be quiet. He signalled his officers to bring in Hingora.

Hingora was in his late thirties, much younger than his partner was. He had a thick moustache and his hair was parted down the middle. He seemed to be in a state of shock, but he recovered somewhat on seeing Kadawala. Maria ordered that Kadawala be taken out. He wanted to interrogate them separately, match their statements and confront them if there were any discrepancies. After a few preliminaries, Maria straightaway came to the subject of Sanjay Dutt. Hingora spoke without much prompting.

'On 15 January, Abu Salem and Baba Chauhan came to my office and told me that Anis bhai had asked me to help them to deliver arms to Sanjay Dutt. I told them that it was not possible. After a few minutes, Anis himself called and ordered me to do it. Hanif and I were reluctant, but finally we had to agree. Salem, Chauhan and I went to Ajanta, Sunil Dutt's bungalow. Sanjay was talking to Anis on the phone and was eager to know when he would get the arms. He hugged Salem and shook hands with us. When Sanjay asked about weapons, Salem boasted that he could deliver them that very day. Sanjay told him to bring them at 7 a.m. the following day.

'On 16 January, all three of us went to Ajanta. I went in my car and the other two in a blue Maruti van. There were two constables—security cover for Sunil Dutt. Sanjay asked them to go away for a while. He instructed his driver Mohammed to remove a couple of the cars from his garage, so that Chauhan could drive the van inside the garage. Chauhan asked for a spanner and a screwdriver, and he and Salem prised open the lid of the secret cavity in the floor of the van. Salem asked for a bag and a

'We hold the video rights for over 500 films. We have produce five films, and there is one—*Sanam*, with Sanjay Dutt as the hero—which is currently under production.'

'Sanjay Dutt ... well ... Is it true that you people have an underworld syndicate in which you, Samir, Abu Salem, Baba Chauhan and Sanjay Dutt are members and Anis Ibrahim is your boss?'

Kadawala's face turned ashen as this question took him by surprise. He regained his composure with visible effort. 'Sir, there is no such syndicate, and Anis Ibrahim is not our boss. He has nothing to do with our business though he tries to interfere. My partner, Samir, introduced me to him when we were in Dubai. Anis Ibrahim has interfered in our business several times, for example he fixed a high price for the rights of Feroz Khan's film *Yalgaar*. I don't like the man.'

'If you don't like him and he has nothing to do with your business, then how come you obeyed him and delivered arms and ammunition for him?'

'Sahab, we were forced. I opposed it strongly. But we knew that if we refused, we could get killed.'

'Cut the crap. Tell me the entire incident in detail. Just remember, if you do not tell us the truth you will pay for it ...'

Kadawala sighed and seemed to be making a very unpleasant decision. As he began to speak, there was an interruption. The police party that had gone to fetch Samir Hingora had returned. Maria asked them to wait and waved at Kadawala to continue.

'We had erected a huge set of a carnival at Film City in January for shooting *Sanam*. But in the first week of the shooting itself, the riots broke out again and we had to abandon it. During the riots, the entire film fraternity used to assemble at Sunil Dutt's bungalow, Ajanta, at Pali Hill for relief work.

'It was during one of these relief meetings that I heard Sanjay large cloth, which Sanjay got. Salem asked Sanjay how many weapons he wanted. Sanjay asked how many he had with him. Salem said that he had nine AK-56s and eighty hand grenades. I peeped into the cavity—it was amazing how many weapons were crammed in there.

'Sanjay asked Salem to give him three AK-56s and twenty-five hand grenades. Salem put the hand grenades in the bag Sanjay had brought and wrapped the rifles in the bedsheets. Sanjay asked Salem to keep the rifles in his Fiat, and to keep the bag in my car. I protested but Sanjay persuaded me, saying that he would remove the bag in a couple of days. He asked me to leave the car at his house.

'I had to take my children to school, so I rushed home. Later I told Hanif everything. Then, on 18 January, Sanjay went to Hanif's house and returned the car and the keys to him. Hanif said Sanjay had told him that he had kept only one rifle and returned the rest. The other two guns and grenades were kept in my car, and were picked up by Manzoor Sayed, who Salem had sent to collect them.

'Then we all forgot about the entire episode. We were just glad it was over. Sahab, I swear by God that I know nothing beyond this.' His eyes were pleading.

When Maria cross-questioned Kadawala, his statements matched Hingora's, with hardly any discrepancies. He asked his officers to record the statements of the two men. It was almost dawn. He decided to stretch out in his chair for a couple of hours. As soon as it was morning, he would call JCP Singh and CP Samra.

CP Samra was very concerned that the evidence seized, such as the cartons of RDX and Arges 69 hand grenades, should be sent for proper examination not only to the CFSL but also to the international agencies. As the grenades were of Austrian origin, they were sent to Austria for investigation.

He was proud of the work that the Bombay police were doing, and vociferously turned down many pleas from politicians to turn over the investigation to the CBI.

Since the beginning of the police investigations, Samra had been holding press briefings at 4 p.m. every day to report on the progress. There were often more than sixty reporters, from both local and national newspapers, though the numbers diminished as time went by. Samra believed that meeting the press ensured transparency and that people had the right to know how the case was progressing. However, these briefings caused resentment among some politicians.

On 12 April, Samra announced at the briefing that the police investigation had taken a new turn. He said that the police suspected that some film industry people too were involved in the blasts, and this would be closely looked into.

The reporters sniffed a major story. There was an immediate clamour for names. Some reporters had heard that Samir-Hanif's names were amongst the list of remand applications—police requests for the custody of an arrested person—from the metropolitan magistrate in the city's Esplanade court. Someone asked for confirmation that they had been arrested. Samra gave a sheepish grin and admitted that Samir Hingora and Hanif Kadawala had been detained for questioning. The next question brought a stupefied silence in the room. 'Is Sanjay Dutt also involved with Samir–Hanif?'

Samra had not expected this question. 'We don't know. We are yet to investigate his role.'

A frail-looking girl asked, 'Are you saying that Sanjay Dutt has been framed by the producers and that he is actually innocent?'

Samra did not want to talk further about this so he merely

said, 'Sanjay may be innocent, maybe not. We are yet to investigate it fully.' He announced the end of the press conference for the day.

On 13 April, all the papers carried headlines about the involvement of people from the film industry, especially Sanjay Dutt, in the blasts. Some reporters had begun investigating other film stars who were known to be close to the Dawood Ibrahim syndicate. The weeklies and fortnightlies began planning their cover stories around the criminal nexus of the Bollywood moguls. People commented that even before investigations, Samra had called Sanjay 'innocent'. Columnists noted the friendly relations between Sunil Dutt and Samra, and of Sunil Dutt's close connections with the Congress leadership. There were rumours that Sunil Dutt had pulled strings, so that Prime Minister Rao had personally instructed Samra to be lenient with Sanjay.

Samra's phone had been ringing constantly since the news broke. Callers included Chavan and Pawar, as well as many others who were simply curious, and tired of the calls he asked his personal assistant to take them. But in the late morning, there was one call he took. It was Sanjay Dutt calling from Mauritius.

'Sir, Sanjay speaking. I heard that you said in a press conference that I am involved in the bomb blasts.'

'Samir Hingora and Hanif Kadawala mentioned your name which is why we said we need to verify it.'

'Right now I am shooting in Mauritius. If you want I can cancel my shooting and return immediately.'

'No son, finish your work and return whenever you were scheduled to. There is no hurry.'

'Sir, I really mean it. I can come right away if you want me to.'

'As I said, we can make verifications whenever you return.'

'Thank you very much, sir.'

That afternoon, at the press briefing, Samra informed the media that Sanjay had called him and offered to return immediately to aid the investigation. Samra said that he had assured him that there was no hurry.

Sanjay also called the Bombay office of UNI, and issued a denial about his involvement. Some newspapers carried this on 14 April. Over the following days, some newspapers also carried lurid accounts of how three truckload of arms and ammunition had been parked in the compound of Ajanta, and how close Sanjay's links were with Anis Ibrahim.

The pristine beaches of Mauritius, Bollywood's favourite locale for the moment, failed to soothe Sanjay Dutt as these increasingly distorted accounts appeared. Sanjay was then at the peak of his career. He was unable to concentrate on the climactic scenes of *Aatish*. The Indian media had begun speculating about whether Sanjay would ever return, or whether he would go to Dubai instead. Sanjay called Samra again to reassure him that he would be returning to Bombay, but did not mention a date.

Despite the fact that Sanjay was in constant touch with Samra, the Bombay police force got swept away by the media frenzy and began monitoring the passenger lists of the Air Mauritius flights to Bombay. There were only two flights a week. They found out that Sanjay had a seat booked for 19 April.

Samra was aware that this focus on Sanjay, whose involvement at the moment seemed peripheral, was taking attention away from Tiger Memon and the masterminds behind the blasts. But the police seemed to have lost track of that, excited at this exposé of perhaps the top cinema hero of the time. Various people in the police force wanted Sanjay arrested, though they knew that Sunil Dutt, with his political connections and his reputation for unimpeachable integrity, would raise hell if the arrest was unjustified.

Y.C. Pawar and Maria were assigned the task of arresting him. The flight was scheduled to arrive at 3 a.m. on 19 April. The scene at the Sahar international airport was grim, with some 200 policemen swarming around the arrival lounge.

Sanjay Dutt was a person whom everyone sympathized with. He was the son of Nargis and Sunil Dutt, one of the most respected and loved couples in the film industry. His mother had died when he was young. Sanjay had become a drug addict and only after painstaking efforts and treatment in a clinic in the US could he be rehabilitated. His wife Richa Sharma was ill and had been hospitalized in the US for a long time. Despite his impeccable pedigree, Sanjay's career in films was full of ups and downs. He had been criticized for sometimes doing films without applying his mind to the character. He was also notorious for his impulsiveness and quick temper, which often landed him in unpleasant situations. However, the masses adored him, and in 1993, he seemed to have established himself as Bollywood's most promising star. But there was an undeniably child-like quality to him. As Sunil Dutt would explain to journalists, 'He may be a grown man, but thinks like a child. Years of drug abuse have eaten into his grey cells.'

In the early hours of 19 April, Sanjay strode rapidly through the immigration area of Sahar Airport, his shoulder-length hair dishevelled. As he stepped out of the green channel, gun-toting commandos and uniformed police officers thronged him. It seemed like a scene from one of the action films he specialized in.

An officer walked up to him and said, 'Mr Sanjay Dutt, you have to come with us.'

'Why? What have I done?' Sanjay protested mildly, though he knew that it would be to no avail.

'We cannot answer the question. We have to take you to the

police headquarters.'

Sanjay did not say a single word after that. He was escorted out of the airport through a private door, hemmed in by police personnel from all sides, and whisked away to the Unit VII office of the crime branch at Bandra. The operation was so swift that the group managed to avoid the waiting lensmen and reporters.

Later the media made a huge fuss on using such excessive force to arrest one person, who had not tried to escape arrest though he could have had he wanted to.

At 11 a.m., Sanjay was driven to the police headquarters complex at Crawford Market, to the office of the crime branch. There, media persons and curious onlookers, including police personnel from other departments, who had heard of Sanjay's arrest, had gathered to catch a glimpse of him.

Sanjay was taken to meet JCP Singh and Maria. Initially, Sanjay simply denied that he had any association with Anis Ibrahim or that he had bought any weapons from him.

Maria picked up the phone and issued some inaudible commands. Within a few minutes, two men were ushered in. Both seemed to be in bad shape, dishevelled and haggard. With a sudden jolt Sanjay realized that they were Samir Hingora and Hanif Kadawala.

Sanjay's resistance crumbled and he broke into sobs. After a while, he admitted that he had acquired an AK-56 through Samir and Hanif.

'I have liked guns since my childhood. I have three licensed firearms: a .270 rifle of Bruno make, a .375 Magnum double-barrelled rifle and a .12 bore double-barrelled gun. I normally use these for hunting. I used to hunt with my friend Yusuf Nulwala.

'My first brush with the underworld was in December 1991 when I visited Dubai with the unit of *Yalgaar*. A fellow actor introduced me to Dawood Ibrahim and his brother, Anis. I had of course heard of them before, but I had not met them or spoken with them.

'Anis seemed to develop a liking for me and began visiting me regularly on the sets. Dawood Ibrahim also hosted a dinner for the entire unit at his bungalow, the White House, which I attended along with everyone else from the unit. At that party, I met several other dons and syndicate leaders like Iqbal Mirchi, Sharad Shetty and Chhota Rajan. I was also introduced to a man called Qayyum, who is a member of the Dawood gang. We returned to India soon after that.

'In September 1992, Qayyum met me at RK Studio. He offered to sell me a sophisticated .9-mm pistol for Rs 40,000, which I liked and instantly bought.

'After the riots of December 1992, my father was branded pro-Muslim and assaulted by furious mobs. We began receiving threatening calls from Hindu fundamentalists claiming that they would kill my father and rape my sisters. I was very upset and tense. When I sought help from the police, they were not cooperative.

'Finally, I decided I had to do something. I acquired an AK-56 through Samir and Hanif, who had come with one Abu Salem. They wanted to give me three rifles and also hand grenades. But I kept only one gun and ammunition and returned the rest. I wrapped the weapon and ammunition in a black bedsheet and hid it in my room on the second floor of the bungalow.

'After the riots were over, I contacted Samir and Hanif and asked them to take away the gun. Although they agreed to take it back, they never got around to doing it. The gun was bothering me as I knew that keeping an AK-56 is not right. When I realized that they had no intention of taking back the gun, I refused to give them dates for their film *Sanam* which was in production. We had several altercations on the issue.

'I also thought of informing the police about the rifle. But I was afraid that it would tarnish my father's reputation and affect his political career.

'I heard of the blasts when I was in Jaipur, shooting for the film *Jai Vikranta*. On 2 April, I left for Mauritius to finish the shooting of *Aatish*. On 13 April, friends in Bombay told me that Samir and Hanif had been arrested and that my name was being mentioned. I was appalled. My fears had come true.

'My father also heard the news. He called me on 13 April and asked me if I had an AK-56. I lied to him and assured him that it was not true. I called up Yusuf Nulwala on 14 April and asked him to destroy the weapons that were in my room.'

The room was silent after Sanjay finished. It was mid-afternoon by then. A police team was sent to Nulwala's house to bring him over.

When Nulwala arrived, he completed the story. After Sanjay called him, he had gone promptly to Sanjay's room and located the black bundle, inside which he found the AK-56, two magazines, 250 rounds of ammunition and a pistol. Nulwala had brought along his toolkit, which contained a hacksaw. He cut the AK-56 to pieces. But he realized that this was not enough. He needed to melt the pieces.

Nulwala contacted his and Sanjay's friend Kersi Adajenia, a Parsi businessman in his sixties who had a steel fabrication business. Adajenia agreed to help. Nulwala and Adajenia went to the godown behind the latter's house where they tried to melt the pieces of the rifle with a gas cutter. But it did not melt fully. The task of melting the AK-56 was completely exhausting for Adajenia. He started having breathing problems because of the strong odour and thick smoke. One eighteen-inch rod and a spring of the AK-56 still remained to be melted when the two friends decided to abandon the effort for the day.

Nulwala had given the pistol to Adajenia and instructed him to melt that as well later. He had collected the melted down pieces of the AK-56, made them into a packet, and thrown it in the sea at Marine Drive.

Sanjay had called Nulwala again on 15 April to check if the weapons had been destroyed. Nulwala had assured him that the work was done. Nulwala had then called Adajenia to inquire about the pistol. Adajenia had told him that he had taken care of everything. However, as he was still feeling unwell from the previous day's work, he had decided to melt the pistol later when he had recovered fully.

Soon after, Adajenia had to go to Calcutta for some business. He had left the pistol with his friend Russi Mulla who in turn had given it to a friend, Ajay Marwah. Marwah still had the weapon.

After hearing the whole story, Samra gave permission for the arrest of Sanjay Dutt under TADA and not the Arms Act, as had been expected. Sanjay was lodged in a third-floor cell of the lock-up in the crime branch, to await further interrogation. The police also arrested Nulwala, Adajenia, Mulla and Marwah. The rod and spring of the AK-56 were recovered from Adajenia's godown, and the pistol from Marwah's house.

The day dawned dark and dismal for Sanjay Dutt. It was 20 April. Time seemed to stand still and the four walls of his cell drew closer in.

A constable had delivered a cup of tea and bread but Sanjay could not eat. He was too worried about what the future held for him.

At 9 a.m., two crime branch officials entered his cell and summoned him down to JCP Singh's office. Singh informed him that he was going to be taken to court and put in custody, after which the police would continue their investigation.

Sanjay was taken to the specially designated TADA court in the City Civil and Sessions Court premises in a jeep, accompanied by four officers. The jeep was preceded by an Ambassador and followed by a Gypsy.

As the car stopped at the VSNL traffic junction, Sanjay could see a massive protest march. For a moment, he hoped that these people were his supporters, protesting his arrest. But he was sure that was not it.

He was produced in front of Judge Jai Narayan Patel, who remanded him to police custody until 3 May.

As the days went by, Sanjay's family rallied strongly around him. His father Sunil Dutt, sister Namrata and brother-in-law Kumar Gaurav were there each day to visit Samra and Singh. As he was escorted each day from the lock-up to the interrogation room, his family would be waiting to catch a glimpse of him; his father would walk up and say a few words. Kumar Gaurav especially did everything possible to ensure that his ordeal was as short and painless as possible.

The news of Sanjay's arrest swept away everything else from the front pages. Fundamentalist organizations immediately dubbed him a terrorist and traitor, and slogans censuring Sanjay were raised at meetings. The Akhil Bhartiya Vidyarthi Parishad (ABVP), the student wing of the BJP, surrounded the Maratha Mandir theatre near Bombay Central station and stopped the showing of *Kshatriya*, which starred Sanjay. Gradually, his other films were also withdrawn from the theatres. Effigies of Sanjay were burnt, and the Shiv Sena mouthpiece *Saamna* vilified him. Members of the film industry did not publicly rally to his support either.

For the film industry, it was a time of crisis, though this was not the first time that its members were at the centre of legal controversies. Bollywood had long been the target of law enforcement agencies. Early in the 1960s, Dilip Kumar's house had been raided over and over again, and he had been accused of being a Pakistani spy. He was interrogated for days and threatened with arrest. All this happened based on the flimsy evidence provided by an youth who had been arrested and claimed that he was a spy for Pakistan and that Dilip Kumar was his associate. Finally, Dilip Kumar appealed to Prime Minister Nehru, and only then did the smear campaign come to a halt. This entire experience was unforgettably humiliating for the thespian whose belief in Indian secularism was shaken to the core. Also shattering was the fact that none of his colleagues from the film world had publicly stood behind him.

Amitabh Bachchan was embroiled in controversy several times, especially during the Bofors scandal during 1985-86. It was his friendship with Prime Minister Rajiv Gandhi that allowed him to remain unscathed for a while. But when V.P. Singh became the prime minister, Bachchan was hounded by virtually every government department from intelligence and revenue to excise and income tax. Amitabh waged a valiant battle against the agencies until he was proved innocent of the charges. During this entire episode, the film industry did not publicly rally to his support.

But Sanjay Dutt's case was different. Whereas both Amitabh and Dilip Kumar had been victims as individuals, in Sanjay's case it seemed that the whole industry was under threat. Samir and Hanif were believed by many to have underworld connections, and Sanjay's association with them was in itself damning. Also, professionally, many film stars and producers had met underworld leaders. Now it seemed that the noose was tightening around everyone. The list of names of people who were somehow connected to Dawood Ibrahim seemed to be growing daily.

Though Dawood Ibrahim and the underworld's links with

Bollywood were always talked about, this time the police seemed determined to follow up the rumours and investigate the nature of the connection. People within the police department allegedly leaked names of renowned producers and film personalities to the media, saying that they were close to Dawood. The list compiled by the crime branch allegedly had some eighty names.

Part of the reason why such links existed was that film-making involved large sums of money. Frequently the only way to get loans was from the underworld, as banks and other legitimate loan-giving institutions were often reluctant to finance films. It provided the dons with a means of laundering black money, so they too were willing. They also demanded certain other benefits, such as shows with film stars staged specifically for their entertainment. There were also whispers of sexual exploitation. Anis Ibrahim's name was often mentioned in this context. Another Ibrahim brother, Noora, aspired to be a poet. It is said that several of his poems and ghazals had been used in films under a pseudonym.

Some members of the film industry allegedly tried to utilize their connections with politicians, including Sharad Pawar, and people in power in the central government to stop this line of investigation. There were also rumours of money changing hands. Whatever the cause, there were no more immediate arrests.

Rajesh Pilot, the union minister of state for home affairs, wanted to expose the nexus between the film industry and the underworld. Whatever his reason—some commentators believed it was the close relationship Pawar had with people in the film industry—Pilot was desirous of involving the central government in the investigations, through an agency like the CBI.

April and May were difficult for Pawar. Both Parliament and the state legislative assembly were in session. Pawar was still a member of Parliament, and yet to be elected to the state legislature. In both places, it was not only members of the Opposition but also his detractors within his own party posing increasingly embarrassing questions. Dharamchand Choradia of the BJP asked Pawar in the state assembly why charges were not pressed against all the people who were named in the confessions of Kadawala, Hingora and Sanjay. Pawar responded promptly that the suspect who had revealed the name of Sanjay Dutt had also named a Shiv Sena leader. Charges had not been levelled against him either.

In the second week of his detention, Sanjay was shifted to the Thane Central Prison where most undertrials were lodged. He had been remanded in custody until 3 May, but the police requested an extension of another fourteen days in order to gather more evidence. This was granted.

The days seemed interminable to Sanjay. He began to chain-smoke. Some things had improved though. He was being brought food from home. His father had promised that the best lawyers would be found to defend him. However, the whole period seemed nightmarish.

The media had a heyday at his expense. Some newspapers denounced him as a traitor, some complained about the five-star treatment he was allegedly receiving. The Shiv Sena was especially vindictive in its campaign against Sanjay.

As there seemed to be no further arrests from the film industry, its members gradually rallied around Sunil Dutt. Subhash Ghai, Shatrughan Sinha, Raj Babbar, Mahesh Bhatt and others organized morchas to protest Sanjay's continuing detention, and also approached the media, politicians and police to try to assist Sanjay. Many protested that Sanjay should be charged under the Arms Act, rather than the harsher TADA. They pointed out that both his parents were loyal citizens and that his father was an

MP who had tried to do much good for his constituents.

There were films worth Rs 70 crore, including *Amaanat* and *Mahanta*, for which Sanjay was shooting, and now work on these had halted. Their directors and producers were very worried about the losses that mounted with each day of filming lost.

The posters for Subhash Ghai's movie *Khalnayak*, starring Sanjay, which was soon to be released had a huge blow-up of Sanjay, handcuffed, proclaiming '*Ha, main hoon khalnayak* (Yes, I am a villain)!' Some people took these posters as a public message. In the film, Sanjay played a freedom fighter's son who turns traitor. People accused Ghai of cashing in on the tragedy, though Ghai protested that it was an unfortunate coincidence.

Sunil Dutt filed an appeal on 5 May before a two-judge bench in the High Court, which led to Sanjay's release on bail against the custody order of the specially designated TADA judge, Patel.

Fifteen days spent in police custody seemed akin to a lifetime to Sanjay. When he finally reached home there was a small crowd gathered outside. There were chants of 'Welcome, Sanju baba', 'Baba, we are with you', and 'We love you, Sanju'. Friends garlanded and hugged him, and admirers threw petals from a distance. It seemed like a welcome to a war hero, and Sanjay enjoyed it. Though he was frequently away from home for much longer periods, this time homecoming was special.

Sanjay was required to be present at the court every Monday, and as he had been granted interim bail he could not leave the city without prior permission from the courts.

After a few days spent sleeping, Sanjay decided to catch up on work. Many of his films were incomplete, including big-budget ones like Mahesh Bhatt's *Gumraah*, Afzal Khan's *Mahanta*, and Ramesh Sippy's *Aatish* which he had been shooting for in Mauritius prior to his arrest. There were a couple of others that required only a few days' work to complete, such as Sajid Nadiadwala's *Andolan*.

An unprecedented sympathy wave for Sanjay ensured that Subhash Ghai's *Khalnayak* became a huge hit. Initially the character played by Sanjay was killed in the end but Ghai allegedly changed the climax to suit the mood of the masses. Sanjay was shown to turn over a new leaf and pledge to surrender to the law. Later Ghai explained that he had shot three endings for his film, which was what he usually did, and used what he thought suited the film best.

Ironically, Sanjay's market value started soaring after his arrest and subsequent release. Producers wanted to capitalize on his popularity. His house was once again buzzing with activity. However, there had been a price to pay. Prior to his arrest he had been very close to actress Madhuri Dixit; now, however, she had publicly denied all connection with him.

Sanjay plunged into work, becoming uncharacteristically punctual and regular for his shootings and other commitments. Thus life continued, until the trial started the following January.

After Sanjay Dutt's arrest, people began to wonder about the involvement of film stars and politicians in the blasts. Consequently there rose a clamour for the involvement of the CBI in the investigations.

On 21 April, at Samra's daily press briefings, a journalist asked him whether he thought the CBI would do a better job of the investigations than the police were doing. Samra, who rarely got angry, frowned and replied that the police force was better equipped as they had more local expertise. He had worked in the CBI, and he did not consider the organization to be capable of doing as good a job of investigating the bomb blasts as the police force.

The demand spread from the Maharashtra assembly to the Lok Sabha that the politician–underworld nexus should be probed. Those politicians who are close to the gangsters should be unmasked. On 21 April, the opposition parties in the Lok Sabha, mainly the BJP and the Communist parties, demanded that the investigation into the blasts should be handed over to the CBI.

In early May, Pilot wrote to Narasimha Rao, informing him that party workers sensed a serious nexus between the underworld, some politicians, businessmen and bureaucrats, and that a CBI probe would prove that the government was not shielding anyone, no matter how highly placed they were.

The Maharashtra assembly was also fiercely discussing this alleged nexus, and the opposition leader Gopinath Munde repeatedly insinuated that Pawar had links with Dawood Ibrahim. The press went to town with this allegation.

Pawar had stated over and over again that the Bombay police were doing a commendable job. He had cited the example of the bombing of the World Trade Centre, New York, earlier that year where investigators had taken two months to identify the culprits. The Bombay police had managed to find the culprits within forty-eight hours.

On 10 May, Pawar wrote to the prime minister stating that he had no objection to the CBI handling the investigations. However, he also mentioned his apprehensions that this might lead to some unwanted delays. Pressure mounted on the prime minister as MPs petitioned for CBI involvement.

The union home ministry also formed a high-level team to trace the links of politicians, bureaucrats, film personalities and other influential people with the underworld. This team comprised union home secretary N.N. Vohra, IB director A.N. Vaidya, CBI director S.K. Dutta, the RAW secretary J.S. Bedi, the Central

Board for Customs and Excise chairman Mrs Govind Raj and Rajesh Pilot. At their first meeting on 15 July, they were directed to submit their report within three months. This was the first time that such a specialist team had been formed to probe a high-level nexus.

At the end of May it was announced that the case would be handed over to the CBI. CP Samra reacted sharply. At his daily press briefing the day after the announcement was made, he stated that his men had worked day in and day out and that they had made very good progress. Despite the announcement, actual CBI involvement in the case did not start until after the chargesheet was filed.

10

Prize Catches

DIG Ulhas Joshi of Thane range was much irked. He could not tolerate the fact that the Bombay police had made over thirty arrests from the area under his jurisdiction. There is an axiom in police circles that one is only as good as one's last case. Joshi did not want to be left out of what seemed to be the case of the decade.

Joshi had learned during the course of the investigations that Addl. CC Thapa was suspected of having connived with his colleagues—Singh, Sultan, Talawadekar and others—who had been implicated for collusion with Tiger Memon's men. Thapa, after receiving information, had laid a trap in the wrong place, and Tiger and his men had carried the RDX and the guns by the other route.

Thapa was a very senior official of the customs department, the second in the customs hierarchy in the state and at that time senior to JCP Singh, the chief of the crime branch. He was a central government employee. Joshi knew that to take any action against Thapa, he would have to take the help of the director general of police (DGP), S. Ramamurthy, and Samra.

On 22 April, Joshi sought permission to raid Thapa's house. Ramamurthy and Samra were both aware that Thapa had powerful connections, and that there could be many repercussions of a raid. At the same time, they realized that Joshi's reasons for demanding this were adequate.

Ramamurthy suggested that Joshi organize the raid the following day, as it was already late in the evening. Joshi replied that that might be too late. He suggested they carry out the raid the same evening.

It was 11 p.m. by the time Joshi and his team reached Thapa's eighth-floor apartment at Hyderabad Estate, Peddar Road, in south Bombay. Though Thapa expressed outrage and indignation, he did not seem to be surprised. The raid took a couple of hours, the police party showing scant respect for Thapa's senior post. But Joshi had to return empty-handed.

Joshi realized that Thapa must have somehow got wind of the raid, and this made him all the more determined to arrest him. The following day he began scouting around for people in the customs department who could provide him with information about Thapa. He talked to ACC R.K. Singh and other junior officers who had been suspended by Thapa after the landing agents had named them as being on their payroll. Their statements and other circumstantial evidence that pointed to Thapa's complicity in the landings provided Joshi with enough material to secure permission for Thapa's arrest.

Thapa was charged with complicity in landing arms. Though he had received an alert from S.K. Bhardwaj, the collector of customs, dated 25 January, he had not taken sufficient precautionary measures, it was alleged. Customs inspector L.D. Mahtre of Uran had informed Thapa that there was likely to be a landing at Shekhadi, and therefore a watch should be maintained at the Sai Morba–Goregaon junction, the main exit point from the Mhasla-Srivardhan area. Thapa had reportedly not informed the officers of Alibaug division, in whose jurisdiction Shekhadi was. Instead, he had laid a trap at Purarphata on Mhasla-

Goregaon Road on 30 January. Later, the chargesheet also mentioned that Thapa had left the site of *nakabandi* at Dehanphata for some time. The team had given up the vigil after 2 February, though there had been so many warnings about the landing.

The most damning allegation against Thapa was about 2 February, the day before the first landing. Addl. CC V.M. Deophade had informed Thapa that a landing was likely to take place near Mhasla and the consignment belonged to Tiger Memon. Thapa had allegedly sent a misleading wireless message that something had happened at Bankot, which was on an entirely different route from Mhasla and thus diverted the customs officials.

Thapa was also accused of suppressing information that the consignment that had landed on 3 February contained chemicals, not silver as was usual.

The furore over Thapa's arrest eclipsed that which had arisen when Sanjay Dutt had been arrested. Sanjay had always been notorious for his wayward lifestyle, whereas Thapa had seemed the epitome of respectability.

Despite all the controversy, Thapa remained stoic. He remained in prison until 5 April 1994.

■

In accordance with Tiger's instructions, Badshah Khan reached Delhi on 20 April. He checked in at a hotel in Karol Bagh, under the name of Nasir Khan. The next day, he telephoned Tiger to let him know his whereabouts. Within a couple of hours, he received a thick bundle of notes, Rs 10,000 in all, and instructions to go to Calcutta.

Badshah left for Calcutta, where he stayed at Hotel Nataraj

near Howrah Station. He called himself Nasir Shaikh. Once again
he called Tiger in Dubai. Tiger told him that he would have a
visitor soon and Badshah should accompany him wherever he
was going. But no one turned up, and after a few days Badshah
tried to call Tiger again. This time, he could not get through.
After a few days, Badshah shifted to the nearby Hotel Meghdoot.
He tried contacting Tiger repeatedly, but his efforts proved vain.
He decided to return to his village, Rampur, via Delhi.

Badshah was confused and lonely. His link with Tiger was
severed and he had no idea what his next step should be. With
each rapidly passing day, his anxiety increased. He was in touch
with his family and friends in Bombay, and followed newspaper
reports, and he was well informed about the developments in the
investigation. He was sure he would never be found, because no
one knew about his whereabouts except his family and a few
close friends.

But on 10 May, a police team from Bombay, led by Inspector
Mahabole, picked him up from Rampur. He did not feel shocked
or alarmed at his arrest; he realized that within himself he had
thought it was inevitable. He was brought back to Bombay by
train. The police records, however, showed that he was arrested
in Bombay, not in Rampur.

Day and night had no meaning for Rakesh Maria any more, it
had all blended into one continual feeling of stress. Though early
breakthroughs had been made, since then nothing much had
happened. Many of the key people—like Javed Chikna, Anwar
Theba, Yeba Yaqub and Badshah Khan—remained elusive. When
he heard the news of Badshah's arrest, he felt a great sense of
relief. Finally, things could get moving again.

Maria had asked that Badshah Khan be brought to the Mahim
police station on 12 May at 9 a.m. When he reached there, he

heard that Badshah had already arrived and asked for him to be brought in.

Maria sank into his chair and began fiddling with the paperweight on the desk. Inspector Mahabole escorted his charge in. Maria saw a sallow youth in his late twenties, dressed in a once-white kurta-pyjama, with a haggard face and a straggly beard. Oddly though, Maria instinctively liked him. He asked him to sit down.

'I think you are well aware of the consequences of your actions on 12 March. You must have also realized that one cannot run away from the long arm of the law. The world may look large to a fugitive but it is always small for a policeman.'

'Sahab, I was hardly involved ... I ...'

'Shut up ...' Maria interjected brusquely. 'Don't you dare lie to me! This file here is full of statements that clearly show the extent of your involvement in the blasts—Asgar Mukadam, Imtiyaz, Mushtaq, Shoaib and several others. It is better if you start talking or we know how to make a stone statue sing.'

Badshah Khan looked at Maria with despair in his eyes. The last two days had been shattering for him. He used to be a daredevil, and unperturbed by authority. But all that had changed now.

He began to talk. He started from the communal riots, the destruction of Tiger Memon's office, the killing of Muslims, and the rape of their women. He spoke of the community's desire for revenge, and out of that desire, the gradual evolution of a plan.

'Tiger Memon was the only person brave enough to come forward. He began garnering support and manpower for his mission. He picked his people carefully, those whom he knew and trusted and wanted to work with. Javed Chikna, Anwar Theba, Imtiyaz and Yeba Yaqub were his men and through them he got more trusted people. Thus he built up a team of people ready to take revenge, ready to give up our lives for the holy war.

'Tiger had sent some twenty people to Pakistan for training. I was one of them. We were trained in handling AK-56s, grenades and imported pistols. But the most important part of our training was making bombs. We were taught how to connect the RDX putty to pencil detonators.'

As he listened, Maria was again amazed at how these youths were brainwashed into agreeing to sacrifice their lives for a cause which had no direct benefits for them. This was not crime for money; they saw it as a larger, nobler cause.

Badshah Khan finished, 'Allah helped us and we emerged victorious in our battle against the disbelievers.' There was a smile on his face.

Maria walked to the window behind his chair. He stood there for a while, and then went over to Badshah. 'No, you are wrong. Allah is not biased in favour of Muslims. He always helps those who are righteous and believers of the truth. This time he helped us.'

Badshah broke in, 'No. Impossible. How can you say that? Allah helped us. We managed to kill hundreds. We avenged the blood of innocent Muslims.'

'Nonsense ... Allah will never help in the killing of innocent helpless people. After all, He is their God as well, and does not discriminate ... And that day I think Allah helped Hindus more than he helped Muslims.' Maria was yelling at the top of his voice, while a part of his mind wondered how he could substantiate this statement. He continued, 'You had to abandon that Maruti van because Allah wanted to help us and not you. That van gave us our first breakthrough. It was with the help of Allah that we managed to arrest over a hundred people in less than two months. If Allah was on your side then we would not have been able to arrest anybody, we would not have had any clues.' His conviction grew with each sentence.

Badshah Khan was silenced.

Suddenly, Maria was exhausted. He called an orderly and asked him to escort Badshah Khan to his cell.

11

The Other Teams

There are many Salims in the Bombay underworld, so many that they have to have nicknames to distinguish themselves. Usually the nicknames are related to their area of specialization, appearance or residence. Thus, Salim Passport could make multiple passports, Salim Tempo was formerly a tempo driver, Salim Talwar had once famously used that weapon for booth capturing in Dongri for a Congress candidate, and Salim Mazgaon and Salim Dongri came from Mazgaon and Dongri respectively. As Salim Bismillah Khan lived in Kurla, he was known as Salim Kurla.

Salim Kurla was one of those accused in the blasts case who had no qualms about informing the police about his former colleagues and fellow conspirators in order to save himself. He was picked up in mid-April, and after that he had been summoned to the Mahim police station repeatedly and questioned. Kurla and his family sought solace in the fact that at least he was a free man. He alleged that he had to pay the police large sums of money to maintain his freedom, but soon they demanded that he tell them about the whereabouts of some other suspects.

Kurla was the son of a criminal lawyer, Bismillah Usman Khan. He had dropped out from Class X at a local English-medium school at Deolali, Nashik. After Bismillah Khan died in 1978, the family was forced to sell off their house at Mazgaon and move to downmarket Kurla in the eastern suburbs. Salim

Salim Kurla

started anxiously seeking a job. He was forced to borrow frequently from his father's friend Jaffar Khan, whom Salim called Jaffar chacha. Jaffar was a partner of Noora Ibrahim, the brother of Dawood Ibrahim, in Suhail Tours and Travels at Nagpada, which specialized in recruitment and export of manpower to the Gulf countries. Jaffar offered Salim a job in this firm.

As soon as Salim joined the agency, he realized that the real business was *hafta wasuli*, the Marathi term for weekly protection money collected from businesses in the locality. Noora Ibrahim took full advantage of his connections with Dawood.

Kurla soon became an expert and earned accolades from Noora. In 1989, when Noora had to flee from Bombay to join his brothers Dawood and Anis in Dubai, Kurla virtually took over the running of the extortion network.

Tired of working for Noora, Kurla started his own extortion business in 1990. As a front for the business, he also started a film production company, Shabnam Art International. The firm was registered with Indian Motion Pictures Producers Association (IMPPA) and operated from a posh office at Oshiwara, Andheri. Within a couple of years, business prospered. Kurla started travelling to the UAE frequently. He enjoyed the hospitality of Noora Ibrahim, and was introduced to Dawood and Anis Ibrahim.

After the communal riots, Anis Ibrahim sought Kurla's services. In the second week of January, he telephoned Kurla at his office, where the latter was talking to some of his most trusted assistants—Hanif Shaikh, Mohammed Sayeed, Raees, Yasin Shaikh Ibrahim and Usman Man Khan. Anis inquired if Kurla wanted to avenge the blood of Muslims. When Kurla replied in the affirmative, Anis asked him to find some youths who were willing to become terrorists. Kurla recommended his assistants, and Anis spoke to each of them personally. They were asked to keep their passports ready, as they would have to meet Anis at Dubai.

Anis Ibrahim

On 22 January, Kurla, accompanied by Hanif, Sayeed, Usman and Yasin, boarded the Air-India flight 739 to Dubai. Their visas were sponsored by Noora. Anis Ibrahim and his lieutenant, Abdul Qayyum, received them. Kurla was parted from his companions, who were taken to the White House for discussion, after which they left for Islamabad for two weeks of intensive training. Kurla returned to Bombay on 26 January.

Anis offered Kurla two guns towards the end of February. Kurla was reluctant to collect the weapons. But Yasin and Raees, who were in the office and overheard his conversation with Anis, were keen to do so. Raees collected the guns from Ibrahim Chauhan and hid them at a safe place.

But Kurla and his men could not take part in later events. Kurla had been demanding money from a Gujarati businessman, who lodged a complaint with the crime branch. The crime branch laid a trap for Kurla on 3 March, and arrested him and his men. They were remanded into custody until 17 March. Soon after, Kurla was released on bail.

When Baba Chauhan was interrogated, apart from Sanjay Dutt, he had also named Salim Kurla as someone to whom Anis Ibrahim had delivered guns. Subsequently, the Mahim police had picked up Kurla and grilled him. Kurla stated that it was his men, not him, who had collected the weapons, which was corroborated by Chauhan's statement. The Mahim police kept him in custody for a few days, but then allowed him to go after—as Kurla later claimed in the TADA court, leading the judge to institute an enquiry into the matter—he paid them Rs 90,000.

Allegedly, the demands did not stop with that one sum. In April and May, Kurla reportedly had to pay several times, the total amounting to several lakhs of rupees, to preserve his freedom.

He was also being asked to provide information. The police wanted to arrest those who had gone on training to Pakistan. His assistants had fled after Kurla's arrest and divided up into groups, but they had stayed in touch with him. Towards the end of May, the police stated that unless Kurla provided them with their whereabouts within a week, he would be taken back into custody.

As the days passed and he waited at his office for one of his men to call, he grew increasingly nervous. He tried tracing them to Delhi, Indore, Bangalore and Hyderabad, but to no avail. Finally, on the afternoon of the fifth day, the phone rang, a long-distance call. Kurla picked it up gently, as if afraid that the line might get disconnected. It was Usman.

'Have you people gone back to your mother's womb that you could not call all this time? I was worried that, God forbid, you were caught by dresswalas. Where are you?'

'Bhai, we are at Vadodara, Hotel Tulsi, Room 204. We plan to be here for a week and after that we may move.'

'That is a good idea. You should not stay at the same place for more than a week. You never know when the police will get wind of your location.'

'Can you send us some money?'

'I will send you Rs 5,000. Keep in touch and let me know if you change your location.'

'Okay bhai, khuda hafiz.'

Kurla heaved a sigh of relief. He had been given a direct number to the Mahim police station, to contact the officer he was dealing with.

'Sahab, I finally got a call from Usman. They are in Room 204 of Hotel Tulsi at Vadodara.'

'You are not lying to us, are you?'

'No, sahab, how can I dare to do that?' He said later that he had asked for some of his money back but was told that that was not possible and that if he even referred to the money, the consequences would be fatal.

Kurla hung up. He had expected that he would get back at least half the amount. He and his wife packed their bags and left the city the same evening. They had no destination in mind, they just wanted to be far from the clutches of the Bombay police.

A crack team of officers, comprising SIs Virendra Vani, Dinesh Kadam, Srirang Nadgouda, Ganpat Kirdant and E.D. Jadhav and Assistant Police Inspector S.D. Angadi, was sent to arrest the men from Hotel Tulsi. They reached Vadodara on 24 May and, on making discreet inquiries from the hotel management, found out that Room 204 was occupied by three youths called Mohammed Sayeed, Usman Man Khan and Raees.

The team roped in additional men from the local Vadodara police. The hotel compound was cordoned off and surrounded by policemen in plain clothes. Special attention was paid to the corridor of the second floor and the area below the window of Room 204. Around 5 a.m., Vani knocked on the door. There was no response. Vani knocked again, but there was still no sound inside the room. The police team wondered briefly whether the hotel staff had alerted the occupants. Then Vani punched heavily on the door.

'Who is that?' somebody called from inside.

'Sahab, tea,' Vani spoke politely.

'Tea! We don't want tea at this time. Get lost!'

'Open the door. This is the police,' Vani roared.

The group outside the door could hear the scrambling sounds within, and muffled voices as if the men were whispering to one another. But the door remained shut. Vani pushed it open without too much difficulty.

Several things happened simultaneously. The police party barged inside with their revolvers drawn. Sayeed tried to push past Kadam to the door but was overpowered. Raees did not resist but Usman jumped out of the window, falling down after he landed but otherwise unhurt.

The men outside did not see him jump, but they heard the thud when he landed. It was still dark and they strained to see.

'Grab him,' a voice yelled from the window of 204. The men located Usman, still on the ground, and pounced on him.

All three were arrested, and Nadgouda informed Maria of the arrests. After formalities with the local police were completed, they started the drive back to Bombay.

In the two-and-a-half months since the blasts, Maria had been working closely with the crime branch in the police headquarters, and regularly briefing JCP Singh and CP Samra. Eventually, he was made a direct deputy to Singh, as DCP (crime) and shifted to the crime branch offices at the police headquarters.

On 27 May, he had the beginnings of a pounding headache when he reached work. Nadgouda informed him that Sayeed,

Raees and Usman were waiting, he could interrogate them whenever he wanted.

'Who is the most intelligent and easy to talk to?' Maria asked.

'I think interrogating Usman will be better than the others,' Nadgouda said.

'Send him in,' Maria said, rubbing his temple. He took two tablets of aspirin and washed them down with a glass of water. The pain was growing. He raised his head and saw a haggard-looking man standing in front of him. 'This is Usman Man Khan, sir,' Nadgouda said.

'Usman,' Maria began wearily, 'I don't have the time nor energy to wheedle information out of you. Start talking.'

Silence.

'Are you deaf? Can't you hear what I am telling you?'

Usman looked at Maria and then at Nadgouda, but could not find a trace of mercy or sympathy in either pair of eyes. There was no option left.

'Sahab, I was close to Salim Kurla. I used to hang out at his office a lot, and we used to collect hafta money. We made good money. It was a good life. But it all changed after the riots when many Muslims were killed.

'We all were seething with revenge, but we didn't know what to do. Then one day Salim bhai got a call from Anis bhai, who wanted some youths to train to bomb Bombay. Salim bhai told him about the four of us.

'We went to Dubai and from there to Pakistan for training. The training was rigorous: we fired AK-56s and imported pistols, made RDX bombs, threw hand grenades. We were being trained to operate rocket launchers but this stopped after Ibrahim got injured ...'

'What happened?' Maria asked.

'The rocket launcher has a very complicated firing

mechanism. Once when Ibrahim was shooting, it misfired and he was badly injured. He was in hospital in Islamabad for a month, and came back long after us.

'After Ibrahim's accident, we didn't use rocket launchers any more. We returned to Bombay after about ten days of training.'

'Didn't you meet others who were also being trained?' Maria asked.

'No, sahab, it was just the four of us.'

'Don't lie. We know that there were about twenty others,' Maria said threateningly.

Cringing in terror, Usman swore that there had been no one else. Maria thought he was speaking the truth. Then there had been at least two groups being trained. He decided to start on a different line of questioning. 'Did you meet Tiger Memon?'

'No, sahab, I don't know who Tiger Memon is.'

Maria was stunned by this disclosure. All this time, Tiger had been the focal point of the plotting. If Usman was speaking the truth—and Maria was inclined to believe that he was—then were there two separate conspiracies following uncannily similar lines? Maria's headache returned with renewed vigour as he tried to puzzle this out. He decided to re-read the statement of Sultan-e-Room, which had earlier puzzled him, but which now suddenly seemed to fall into place.

■

His father Ali Gul named him Sultan-e-Room, king of Rome, because he dreamt that he would become as wealthy as that mythical monarch was. Young Sultan was religious, wore only traditional pyjamas and grew a long beard. His friends nicknamed him Maulana. Sultan failed to make the expected fortune in Bombay, and wanted to travel to Saudi Arabia and work there.

But the medical test for the visa revealed that he had tuberculosis, and the application was rejected. So Sultan had another passport made in a different name to try again.

Sultan met Ejaz Pathan, who put him in touch with Ehtesham who, Ejaz told him, would take him to Dubai. He was also told he would be given money, clothes and training in handling firearms and explosives in Pakistan. Ehtesham, who had aided Tiger Memon at the two landings, in turn introduced him to Babulal Qasim Shaikh, Shakeel Ahmed, Murad Khan, Aziz Ahmed and Manzoor Qureishi (Manju) who would be his fellow travellers. On 14 February 1993, they met at Sahar Airport and left for Dubai. However, when they reached Dubai they were not allowed to leave the airport as they did not have visas. Murad, Ehtesham and Babulal managed to organize the visas after a couple of hours and a few telephone calls. An unknown escort bundled them into two taxis and took them to an eight-storey building close to the sea. Sultan did not know the name of the building, but he did know that their spacious three-room flat was on the seventh floor. An Indian woman in her fifties was there to cook for them, and she had a male assistant of about thirty-five. But Sultan never found out what their names were.

They stayed at this flat for eleven days during which they met nobody, and no one came to visit them. Their only excursions were to the nearby masjid for namaz. Occasionally Ehtesham, Shakeel, Aziz and Murad would go out to meet their acquaintances. They all waited eagerly for the day when they would leave for Pakistan for their training.

On 25 February, they were told that as their visas were going to expire in two days, they should leave Dubai within that period. They were all intensely disappointed because they all had dreamt of becoming mujahideen and laying down their lives for Islam, especially Sultan with his intensely religious streak.

After the night prayers (isha) on 27 February, their escort took them back to the airport, where they boarded a Cathay Pacific flight back to Bombay. The king of Rome was back in his old kingdom.

■

The biggest change in Rakesh Maria's life since the blasts was that he no longer had fixed working hours, and that in order to pursue his research, he had to read late into the night to keep up with the progress of the case and think about the import of the information gathered.

At first, the case had seemed straightforward, as it appeared that Tiger Memon had masterminded and organized the bombing. With the arrest of the group from Vadodara, Maria could see that another clearly defined group, led by Anis Ibrahim, had been sent for training. Now other individuals who had travelled to Dubai, but then not gone to Pakistan for training seemed to be falling into a third group, which had no leader that the men knew. Abdul Kader (arrested on 21 April), Mohammed Shahid and Nizamuddin Qureishi (both arrested on 31 March), Manzoor Qureishi and Sultan-e-Room (both arrested on 8 April) and Babulal Shaikh (arrested on 10 May) had all gone for training but denied any link to Tiger Memon or Anis Ibrahim.

Maria scoured through his records, trying to work out who else could have belonged to this group. Soon he found some other names: Ehtesham, Mohammed Iqbal, Murad Khan and Shakeel Ahmed. This made a team of ten men.

The case seemed to be growing beyond Maria's ability to comprehend it. Why were there so many different groups floating around? There was something especially sinister about this third group, which had no acknowledged leader who had organized, financed and led the whole operation.

The only link seemed to be Ejaz Pathan, who was known to be a trusted companion of Dawood Ibrahim. Ehtesham and Shahid had also named Ejaz in their statements. Ejaz had been absconding since the blasts. He had links with the Pathan syndicate in Bombay, and there were several extortion cases registered against him.

Maria wondered how Ejaz had put together the team and made the travel arrangements for the group. There had to be a common link within the city itself. Had they booked their tickets together?

His men were sent to check out the tickets, and they reported that eleven tickets had been booked together in the second week of February. The tickets had been booked at the Hans Air office at Nariman Point, and they had been paid for by Abu Travels at Colaba. Abu Travels was solely owned by Abu Asim Azmi, a millionaire who was reputed to own half of Arthur Bunder Road, Colaba, one of Bombay's prime areas. Of the eleven tickets, one—in the name of Ayub Khan—had been cancelled.

It seemed the team had reached a dead end, as Abu Asim Azmi could not be questioned as he was in Saudi Arabia for Umrah, the minor pilgrimage.

Abu Asim Azmi hailed from Azamgarh, UP, and had come to Bombay when he was a teenager. He was known as a man who had built himself an empire through hard work and determination.

However, the intelligence wing of Bombay police, Special Branch II, and the crime branch suspected that Azmi's climb to the top had been facilitated by murders and shady deals. This did not trouble Azmi.

When Azmi heard that the police suspected that he had financed the travels of men to Dubai for training in arms, he cut short his trip and returned to the city in July. The first thing he did on his return was to meet JCP Singh and CP Samra. He stated that Maulana Ziauddin Bukhari, who had been killed on 21 April by people of the Arun Gawli gang, had planned the trip, and he had not been involved.

During the course of several sessions of interrogation at the crime branch, Azmi explained that Bukhari used to have an account in Abu Travels, which he used to book tickets. Azmi had owed Bukhari Rs 1.1 lakh, and the money for the Dubai tickets had been deducted out of his total debt. He argued that no person of average intelligence would have incriminated himself by paying for tickets for a criminal conspiracy by issuing bank drafts as he had. It was not difficult to buy tickets so that purchase could not be traced to him. The very openness and public nature of his dealings indicated that he was not aware of the conspiracy.

Two officers of Samra's special team, S.S. Puri and Gyanchand Verma, were set to probe his financial transactions. There were exhaustive searches at Azmi's residence, offices, hotels and other properties. Many newspapers stated that the police had identified one of the major financiers of Dawood Ibrahim's gang. Allegedly, the police had also released confidential information to the press, which linked Azmi with Dawood Ibrahim.

Azmi claimed that he had submitted his original account books to the police, which they had misplaced. He also stated that he had given several receipts and other documents to substantiate his innocence. After about two months of questioning and raids, Azmi was finally arrested on 20 September and charged under TADA. He had previously been arrested twice in connection with some murders, but the third time was devastating as it formally associated Azmi with Dawood Ibrahim and Tiger Memon and made him out to be a traitor. The police believed they had captured the mysterious leader of the third team. Also, as JCP

Singh told the weekly *Sunday* magazine, this arrest proved that the 'law does not distinguish between rich and poor'.

■

Badshah Khan's story

I think Rakesh Maria is right. It is now August, five months since the blasts and over two weeks now since I met him last, but the more I think about it the more convinced I am by his arguments.

I have read the history of Islam. They say that whenever Allah aided the Muslim army, the believers vanquished their foes and overpowered the infidels. Whenever Allah did not help the Muslims for some reason, the Muslims lost. Maria said that Allah did not help us in our mission to destroy Bombay, and so our mission could not have been right. If Allah had helped us, we would have totally destroyed the BSE and the Air-India building so that nothing of them remained, and killed Bal Thackeray and other Shiv Sena leaders at their Sena Bhavan headquarters. The very fact that we could not succeed despite all our best efforts means that Allah did not help us, that He did not want us to do this.

I see now that Tiger Memon used us in his personal vendetta against Hindus. Tiger bhai was the only one among us who suffered tremendous losses in the riots. Chikna had a bullet wound, but it was minor. But Tiger's Mahim office was burned down; he lost a lot of money. Maybe he thought nothing else could motivate others to join him in his war against the Hindus except the name of Islam. We were all just used ...

Tiger made sure that he escaped, and that everyone in his family had left Bombay by 12 March. He was concerned about his personal safety, but not about ours, though he did leave some money. But he did not make any preparations for us. His family is safe today, while we are suffering. And as a result of what we did so many innocent Muslims have been tortured, women and girls treated horribly. Tiger must have known this would happen, but he did not care about his people, did he?

I have been in prison for weeks now, and I know how bad it gets. Even the food is bad—watery dal, inedible rice and stinking water. And the things I see around me, the torture ... I have heard that they have detained up to twenty people from a family to extract one confession. If Tiger is such a good Muslim, how could he let this happen? He cares only for his family, not for his community.

We were naïve, and he was shrewd; he used us and saved himself. I feel I have to do something so that he can't get away with it. I know all about Tiger Memon and his real designs now. I should be the one to expose him. I will talk to someone—Rakesh Maria, Sharad Pawar, anyone—but I will tell them the truth. Somebody has to speak up.

I heard that last week, on 16 August, M.N. Singh had personally visited the Arthur Road jail, which is where all of us are. He called for many of the men who were with us—Dawood Phanse, Imtiyaz Ghavate, Aziz Ahmed, Raju Kodi, Baba Chauan and Parvez Qureishi. He told them that someone would have to turn approver, be a police witness. He said that they had better stick to their confessions or else he would take it as a gesture of personal enmity and use the entire police machinery to destroy them and all their families. And the way Singh says these things with his expressionless face ... Well, you cannot expect ghazals from cops.

I don't know why none of them spoke up. After hearing this, I decided to speak up. Some of my fellow accused already call me an informer. So be it.

I called out to a passing constable and told him that I wanted to meet Maria sahab. The orderly looked at me and said that if sahab needed me, he would call me. I looked at him pleadingly and told him that I had something very vital to say to Maria sahab. He looked at me strangely and left.

I was not sure whether the constable would convey the message, but apparently he did, for a few days later one of the officers on Maria's team came to fetch me.

I was asked to wait outside Maria's office, and summoned in after about half an hour. Maria was my link to the outside world.

'Sahab, I want to become a police witness. Will I be forgiven and pardoned?' I asked.

Maria looked at me quizzically. 'You have to make an official request for that.'

'I'm ready to do anything,' I said. 'What do I have to do?'

He told me to write a letter to M.N. Singh. He seemed to be appreciative of my offer. I returned to the lock-up and asked for paper to write the letter. Unlike other times, when my requests were unheeded, this time I was provided with pen and paper instantly.

I later heard that when my letter reached M.N. Singh, he forwarded it to ACP Shivajirao Babar, who was designated the chief investigating officer in the case. I also heard that Imtiyaz and some others had also offered to turn informers but their requests had been turned down.

As the days went by and I did not hear anything, my resolve to expose Tiger strengthened. I made an official offer to turn police witness to Babar. I know the police choose only those people as police witnesses whose involvement is minimal and who they think possess the most information.

The news that I was planning to turn informer had spread among the other accused and I was called traitor, who took money from the police. I got accusing glares and veiled threats from others in the lock-up. I knew that from now on life would be difficult for me here. When I joined Tiger, I had undergone extreme hardship for something I believed in. And this time I believed that what I was doing was the right thing.

■

After the blasts, Dawood Ibrahim realized that he would perhaps never have the opportunity to return to his city of birth. The political connections he had built up over the years in the hope that someday they would help him in returning to India were now rendered useless. Soon after 12 March, he had received a call from a woman police inspector in Bombay who had showered him with the choicest expletives, while he had listened in stunned silence. It was clear that he was considered the chief culprit for the deaths of so many people.

In September 1993, Dawood called MP Ram Jethmalani, an eminent lawyer, who was in London at the time. Dawood reportedly told him that he wanted to surrender, and when Jethmalani asked him why, Dawood replied that he was innocent and that his name was being wrongly dragged into the serial blasts case. Jethmalani told him that he should surrender and face trial. Dawood allegedly said that he was willing to surrender but that he had two conditions: the Bombay police should withdraw or close all pending cases against him, except the bomb blasts; and that he should be granted bail and given physical protection. He did not mind being under house arrest for as many years as the trial continued. Jethmalani assured him that he would speak to the concerned authorities and ensure that this offer was conveyed to the government.

Jethmalani called up his son, lawyer Mahesh Jethmalani, in

Bombay and asked him to inform JCP Singh. Singh told Mahesh that this had to be conveyed to the chief minister. A meeting was supposedly held at the chief minister's residence at Varsha, where Samra and Singh were present. It was agreed that the decision had to be taken by the central government as Dawood was wanted not merely by the Bombay police, but by the Indian government.

It has never been established whether Narasimha Rao was informed about Dawood's offer to surrender, though Sharad Pawar maintained in the state assembly that his government would not accept any conditional surrender from Dawood or any of the others accused in the bomb blasts case. 'Nobody will be given any special treatment,' Pawar said at a press conference in Mantralaya. The matter ended there.

Later, Dawood also reportedly tried to negotiate his surrender through some CBI officers. But the negotiators could not assure immunity and protection to Dawood.

Some argue that if the Indian government had accepted Dawood's offer, at least he would have been in custody.

12

The Trial Begins

According to the law, a chargesheet had to be filed within 180 days of the commission of the offence. However, the Bombay police had to seek an extension because the case was too vast to be wrapped up within the stipulated period.

On 15 September, the Bombay police had filed an application at court for declaring forty-four people proclaimed offenders. They had arrested 145 people under the various sections of TADA for their involvement or complicity in the case. Exactly a month later, the specially designated TADA court, presided over by J.N. Patel on the fifth floor of the City Civil and Sessions Court in south Bombay, declared forty-three people as proclaimed offenders. Mobin from Raigad could not be proclaimed an offender as his antecedents were not very clear, though he was named in the chargesheet.

The Bombay police managed to finish all the documentation and make a detailed chargesheet, which was finally submitted on 4 November at the TADA court. The main chargesheet was 9,104 pages long. The preamble was an additional 127 pages, and the list of witnesses another 151 pages.

A total of 189 people were named in the chargesheet, out of whom 145 had been arrested and forty-four were absconding (which included thirteen members of Tiger Memon's family). Twenty-two of those arrested had been given bail, 123 were still in the custody of the police at the time the chargesheet was filed. The total number of witnesses named was 3,741.

About 157 officers from Bombay, Thane and Raigad police and the CID crime unit at Pune had been involved in the investigation. The investigators had travelled to thirteen states and two union territories in the country, and visited seventy-one cities.

At the time of the filing of the chargesheet, Samra requested that Ujwal Nikam from Jalgaon be the chief public prosecutor. Nikam was known for his honesty and his integrity.

A day after the chargesheet was filed, on 5 November, Samra was promoted to DGP, and put in charge of the anti-corruption bureau in Maharashtra. It was a prestigious posting, and ostensibly a reward for his good work, but many realized that Samra was being politely shunted out from the scene. He had been police commissioner for barely eight months. The publicity that Samra had enjoyed throughout the investigation, especially with his daily briefings, had antagonized many. Satish Sahani, an officer with an impressive career record, was made the police commissioner of Bombay.

■

Though it had been announced in May 1993 that the CBI would take charge of the investigation, the actual handover happened on 9 November, five days after the chargesheet was filed, when the state government notified the CBI that the case had been handed over to them for further investigation. The CBI can look into police cases in states only if the court or the home department of that state government passes an order to that effect.

A Special Task Force (STF) of the CBI was constituted, headed by Subhash Chandra Jha, and a makeshift office was arranged in a bungalow near Nariman Point. Coordinating the work in Delhi was the union home secretary, K. Padmanabhaiah. Until then CBI did not have an STF anywhere in the country as all operations were looked after from Delhi. There were, however, specific wing offices elsewhere in Bombay—such as the anti-corruption wing in Tanna House, Colaba, and the economic offences wing in the White House, Malabar Hills.

■

The first hearing in the case opened at 2.45 p.m. on a bleak afternoon, 24 January 1994, in a crowded room, thirty-five feet by fifteen feet, at the Arthur Road jail. It had been chosen out of security considerations as most of the accused were housed in that jail and it was very difficult to move all of them to the City Civil and Sessions Court. The security arrangements at the jail were intensive: the entire central region of the city had been cordoned off, and was crawling with khaki-clad policemen and police wireless vans. To enter the court, everyone had to go undergo a thorough security check. There were policemen everywhere in the compound and in the courtroom itself. The court was presided over by J.N. Patel. The room was packed with the 145 accused, and some eighty lawyers, policemen and court officials, apart from those who had come to attend the trial. The accused were crowded five to a bench and there was not even enough table space to keep the chargesheet

There were several media persons present, Patel having finally allowed the press to cover the court proceedings. Initially, the Bombay High Court and the City Civil and Sessions Court had ruled that the press would not be allowed due to security reasons, and had also suggested that the trial be held in camera. Later this decision was reversed.

The opening of the long-awaited trial was taken up by wrangling about the cramped conditions in the courtroom. Senior counsel S.B. Jaisinghani, who represented Sanjay Dutt and Somnath Thapa, stated that the arrangements were inadequate. The chief public prosecutor, Nikam, defended the government's allocation of space and infrastructure keeping in mind the overwhelming security considerations and need for urgency in progressing with the case. He granted, however, that a public address system should be installed. Patel suggested that the immediate solution would be to ask only those accused who were interested in being present to stay back while the others could go back. The police escorted away about a hundred of the accused who wanted to leave the court premises.

The prosecution then summarized the case, and stated the charges against each of the accused. Nikam submitted a list of over a thousand witnesses, who he said would file affidavits on what they knew about the case. Some of the accused stated that they did not have lawyers; at which Patel offered to provide a state lawyer to all of them. The hearing was adjourned to 2 February.

The issue of the scarcity of space continued in the next two hearings. In the fourth hearing on 23 February, defence lawyers expressed concern over the suggestion made on behalf of the government at the 18 February hearing that the venue of the trial be shifted to Thane or Pune, where there were better facilities. They were indignant that the accused were being encouraged to abstain from attending court merely because the room was not big enough.

The stalemate dragged on until March. In a report to the High Court, Patel had declared that for security reasons the jail premises were the best place to hold the trial. The government stated it was impossible for them to do more, the defence counsel

Ujwal Nikam
(Courtesy Mid-day)

argued that they could not work in such a small space, and Patel supported their contention that the space was inadequate. At the 24 March hearing, Patel declared that he would not proceed with the trial until the issue was satisfactorily resolved. The next hearing was on 12 April at the City Civil and Sessions Court, and Patel stated that the trial would continue there until the jail courtroom was extended and had a public address system.

Justice H.H. Kantharia and Justice Vishnu Sahai, the judges of the divisional bench of the High Court, passed an order that the trial be begun at the Bombay Central Jail premises at Arthur Road and be concluded as quickly as possible. However, on 12 April at the first hearing, the facilities were found to be inadequate. Nikam came under sharp criticism for not making the list of prosecution witnesses available to the defence lawyers. The prosecutor said he was reluctant to do so as there was reasonable apprehension about the threat to their lives. He stated several times that he was ready to open the trial but the defence team said that since it was a historical trial there was need to proceed with caution. Patel declared that the trial would begin from 6 June.

However, even as the courtroom issue was resolved, wrangling broke out over a new issue. On 4 May, six defence lawyers—Jaisinghani, Reshma Ruparel, Usman Wanjara, S.M. Oak, Mahesh Jethmalani and Sonia Sohani—who between them represented over a hundred defendants, stated that their clients had expressed apprehension about getting a fair trial in Patel's court. In their joint application seeking his discharge from the case, the lawyers asserted that they felt that they would not get the requisite relief for their clients. This application roused a storm of controversy. Nikam called the charge a conspiracy to delay the trial, and charged the six complainants with abetting their clients. Jaisinghani refused to enumerate their specific complaints and said these would be recounted before the Supreme Court. Should the Supreme Court find their grievances invalid, they would return to Patel's court in all good faith.

Patel found himself under immense pressure. The trial was scheduled to commence. The matter was finally resolved when Patel summoned all the defendents and asked them whether they had faith in his impartiality. When they declared they did, he took the six lawyers who had filed the application to task and barred them from appearing before him. The trial finally commenced on 30 June.

On 4 July, Sanjay's bail application was heard. The monsoons were in full swing, but journalists had gathered to hear the outcome of this much postponed bail application. Sanjay's lawyer C.B. Wadhwa had warned him that the prosecution would seek cancellation of his bail, but assured him that his chances were good. The tension level in the court, after all the drama of the past few weeks, was high.

Patel broke the silence. 'I hereby order that Sanjay Dutt's interim bail stands cancelled and he be taken into judicial custody immediately.'

Sanjay half rose. Wadhwa protested that the CBI never opposed Sanjay being granted bail and the judge could at least grant him a stay for two weeks so that Sanjay could appeal.

'There is no question of staying the order and also no way

that he can be given few days to file an appeal unless there is a legal provision for that.' Patel also rejected an oral bail application and left the courtroom.

Ashen-faced, Sanjay was taken away in the police van to Thane prison.

■

Short, stockily built, clean-shaven and bespectacled, advocate Niteen Pradhan's thoroughness, meticulous preparation and enthusiasm impressed all. In the brief time that he was involved in the case, he attracted more media attention than any of the other lawyers involved. In February 1992 he had shot to fame for getting an acquittal for the former chief minister of Maharashtra, A.R. Antulay, accused of allotting cement quotas to builders in lieu of funds for a public trust he had created.

Pradhan's association with the blasts case began in May 1994, when builder Mohammed Jindran hired him. Gradually, however, he was asked by other accused to defend them.

In his submissions in the TADA court on 8 August, Pradhan argued that the bomb blast cases could not be considered one consolidated terrorist act. He believed it was constituted of several different cases. The Dighi landing, Sanjay Dutt's alleged purchase of the AK-56, the conspiracy for the blasts in Dubai, Bombay and Pakistan, the actual blasts, the two seizures of the ammunitions and RDX from Nagla Bunder and Mumbra, and other such seizures were all separate cases. He argued that the division of the cases would facilitate the trial, and ensure that the accused were distinguished according to the severity of their crime and the level of their involvement.

Pradhan argued that the bomb blasts should not be interpreted as an act against the government, but against the Hindu community; that they were not a terrorist attack but were an outcome of communal strife. This line of argument earned Pradhan the ire of some fundamentalist Hindu organizations. The Patit Pawan Sanghatana, a Pune-based organization, threatened to humiliate him publicly by blackening his face, making him sit facing backwards on a donkey and parading him through the city!

Niteen Pradhan
(Courtesy Mid-day)

His dedication also won him followers, among whom was the Milli Council, then the only Muslim organization which was trying to help Muslims involved in the case. The Council asked him to take up the case of some more of the accused. Although severely pressed for time, Pradhan agreed. Later, there were more such requests. By 8 August 1994, he was officially representing forty-eight of the accused, the largest number represented by a single lawyer.

Pradhan argued that the Muslims among the accused could not be charged with waging a war against the country as the prosecution alleged. Before the demolition of the Babri Masjid, none of the accused had been involved in activities that could be construed as anti-national, and even after the demolition, they had never demanded it to be rebuilt. Their ire had been directed towards the community that destroyed it, not the government. Had they demanded that the mosque be rebuilt, they could have been charged under TADA for trying to overawe the government. Pradhan argued that the accused in this case could not be likened to militant organizations like the JKLF, the Khalistanis or ULFA, because their actions had been different. If the Sikh militants in the Golden Temple who had fired on the Indian army during Operation Bluestar had not been accused of waging a war against the country, then how could these people be? Thus Pradhan managed to transform the way in which the accused were being viewed—from people trying to overthrow the state to those attacking a community.

As a result of this line of argument, in January 1995, J.N. Patel ruled that the accused were no longer charged with sedition and waging war against the country but that they could be tried only under TADA. This was the first major victory for the accused, and for the community. It was even more gratifying that someone outside the community had supported them so strongly.

Pradhan had been ill, and soon after this he had to be hospitalized. This compelled him to withdraw from the case, a decision perhaps reinforced by attacks from some other lawyers. In the brief time he had been associated with the case, he had changed it fundamentally.

13

Yaqub Memon

By the time Yaqub Abdul Razak Memon, the third of the Memon brothers, was in his early thirties, he had already acquired the reputation of being the best read and smartest criminal that the Bombay police had ever known.

But Yaqub's story was unusual. Educated in English-medium schools and college, he graduated with a degree in commerce. He became a chartered accountant in 1990. His accountancy firm was quickly successful, and in 1992 he won an award for the best chartered accountant in the Memon community.

In 1991, he launched an accounting firm called Mehta and Memon Associates, with his childhood friend Chetan Mehta. Later there was a third partner: a fellow accountancy student Ghulam Bhoira. When this firm closed down in 1992 Yaqub started another called AR & Sons. He also set up an export firm, Tejareth International, with its office at Samrat Cooperative Society, Mahim, to export meat to the Middle East. So great was Yaqub's financial success that he bought six flats in the Al-Hussaini building, Mahim, where Tiger owned two duplex flats. In the same year, he married Raheen in a lavish ceremony at the Islam Gymkhana, and many people from the film world attended the wedding. He and Tiger were dimetrically opposed to each other in nature. One had no compunctions about making money by illegal means; the other was suave, educated and successful through legitimate means.

It was inevitable that there should be friction between the two most successful Memon brothers. Another source of friction was that Tiger allegedly ill-treated his wife Shabana, and had an extramarital relationship. After one particularly vicious dispute, Abdul Razak turned Tiger and Shabana out of the family flat. Shabana and her children were soon allowed to return, and Tiger too returned to the family home about a year before the blasts.

It was Yaqub's well-known financial acumen that made the investigators suspect his involvement in the blasts case. During the investigations, it was found that complex financial transactions had taken place through several of Tiger's accounts, and the police assumed that Yaqub must have organized these.

The crime branch alleged that Yaqub had remitted Rs 21,90,000 to Samir Hingora and Hanif Kadawala on 13 March 1993 to distribute to the other accused. The payment was supposedly arranged over the phone so that there were no records. During their search of the Memon flats in Al-Hussaini, the police had come across documents that showed that the family had four NRI accounts at the Turner Road, Bandra, branch of the Hong Kong and Shanghai Banking Corporation (HSBC). The accounts were in the names of Tiger's brother Ayub Memon (account number 11679297-07), his wife Reshma Memon (account number 11679813-07), Tiger's brother Suleiman's wife Rubina Memon (account number 11979321-07) and Tiger's wife Shabana Memon (account number 11679305-07). The police said that $61,700 was deposited in cash in the British Bank of Middle East, Dubai, from there it was transferred to Marine Midland Bank in New York, USA, and then to these accounts in HSBC. They suspected that this was an attempt to conceal the source of the money. Yaqub had the authority to handle the accounts of the entire family and they suspected that he had used this money to pay various people, including his own company. Since the entire amount was tendered at the British Bank of the Middle East in Dubai, the police thought that somebody had financed the operation, fully or at least partly, from abroad.

The police also discovered that between December 1992 and March 1993, various accounts at the Mahim branch of the Development Cooperative Bank in the names of Tejareth International and Al-Taj Exports as well as the personal accounts of the Memon family showed heavy cash transactions. The balance in all these accounts on 12 March stood at meagre amounts. Clearly the accounts had been emptied prior to the blasts.

All this careful financial planning made the investigators conclude that Yaqub Memon must have been involved. Accordingly, in December 1993, a reward of Rs 5 lakh was offered for anyone who had information about his whereabouts.

On the morning of 21 July 1994, a well-dressed businessman carrying a Pakistani passport in the name of Yusuf Mohammed Ahmed sauntered through Tribhuvan International Airport, Kathmandu. He had just got off the PIA 250 flight from Karachi. Though he looked serene, Yaqub Memon's mind was in turmoil. For the last seventeen months, he and his family had been on the run, and the life of a fugitive was wearing him down.

Yaqub took a taxi to Karnoli Hotel, accompanied by his cousin, Usman, who had come to receive him. They stayed at the hotel for three days. It was a time for introspection.

The Memon family had been in Dubai on 12 March 1993. The Indian government had been putting pressure on the UAE government to repatriate them. Initially, the UAE denied the Memons were there, but eventually requested them to leave. In early April, an ISI agent escorted the family to Karachi. Each person was supplied with a Pakistani passport and a national identity card.

Meanwhile, the Indian government had received information that the Memons were in Karachi and asked the United Nations, the US and various European countries to support their request to Pakistan that the Memons be handed over. Therefore, on 15 April the Memons, escorted by four ISI commandos, took a Thai Airways flight to Bangkok, where they were accommodated in a spacious bungalow on Pattaya Road. It was virtually house arrest, as they were not allowed to leave the bungalow and were under constant surveillance. After twelve days, the protests by the Memon family grew so intense that they were brought back to Karachi again. They were housed in the Karachi Development Scheme area, popularly known as the Defence Colony and predominantly inhabited by army officials and personnel. This was a high-security zone and meant that the Memons were virtually untraceable.

Since then things had been better. Yaqub had gone to Dubai for a week on his Pakistani passport, though always trailed by ISI men. He realized that for his family, there would never be true freedom again. There were two choices before him: he could live with this polite imprisonment by Pakistan, or he could go back to India, face a trial and try to clear his name. These were the options he had come to Kathmandu to try and think about. He decided that the best option for him was to try to make a deal with the Indian government and convince them that the rest of the Memon family was innocent. It was better to try to go back to their old lives rather than live at the mercy of the Pakistan authorities, as tales of the intelligence services killing off those who had outlived their usefulness were legion. He was especially concerned about his parents, who were now old and deserved better, and for his wife Raheen who was due to deliver their child soon. He did not want his child to live his whole life under the shadow of fear.

On 24 July, Yaqub was back at the airport at 8.15 a.m., checking in for the 10.45 a.m. Lufthansa flight LH 765 from Kathmandu to Karachi. At about 9.15 a.m., after he had cleared immigration formalities, he went in for the security check. On opening his briefcase, the officer found two passports belonging to him—Indian and Pakistani—as well as passports of all the other members of his family, a Pakistani national identity card, and a large amount of Pakistani and US currency. The Nepal police informed Interpol and later New Delhi. The interrogation began at Kathmandu itself, and continued for three days, with both Indian and Nepali police participating, though the latter's involvement was minimal.

On 28 July, a blindfolded Yaqub was reportedly dropped off at Sunoli, on the border of UP, at 3 a.m. He was hungry and totally drained of energy. He was taken to Gorakhpur, about two hours by road from Sunoli, and then flown to Delhi in a special plane. On the plane, Yaqub met Union Home Secretary K. Padmanabhaiah who headed the CBI investigation in Delhi. Until now events had been more or less as Yaqub had scripted them when he placed his two passports in his briefcase.

At 4.30 a.m., 5 August, Yaqub Memon approached New Delhi railway station. He was carrying a briefcase and a suitcase, containing various incriminating documents. There are no trains that arrived or departed at that hour, so it was a somewhat odd time to be there.

Four CBI officers along with armed commandos were waiting. They had allegedly been tipped off that a member of the D-Company was out on the prowl. They descended upon Yaqub and whisked him away to the CBI headquarters at Lodi Road.

Eight hours later, Union Home Minister S.B. Chavan announced the sensational arrest of one of the kingpins of the blasts in Lok Sabha: 'We had given up hope of arresting the Memons, we thought that we had reached a dead end but now we are lucky to have arrested Yaqub Memon in Delhi.' Later he told a crowded press conference that Yaqub had been caught with Pakistani documents including a passport, a national identity card, a driving licence and high school certificates, all in the name of Yusuf Mohammed Ahmed. He was also carrying an Indian passport. 'This proves that there was Pakistani complicity in the bomb blasts. Its role in sponsoring terrorist activities in India has been concretely established,' said Chavan.

Yaqub Memon was driven to Patiala House in a CBI van, preceded and followed by armed commando vans. He was produced in front of magistrate V.K. Jain, to whom he stated that apart from Tiger Memon, no other member of the Memon family was involved in the blasts. He denied the CBI account of his arrest. He stated he had been arrested on 24 July, and had been in Delhi since 28 July, where the CBI had interrogated him. The CBI counsel C.S. Sharma and SP Harishchandra Singh however stuck to their story. The proceedings lasted an hour. Yaqub was remanded to CBI custody for thirty days.

Yaqub Memon's arrest spread a wave of elation in Bombay. Speaking to the press on 6 August, Sharad Pawar declared that Memon's arrest proved what he had always known: that Pakistan was involved in the conspiracy. Everyone involved in the investigation was elated, as there had been little development in the case since the filing of the chargesheet. JCP Singh too believed that the documents recovered from Yaqub established Pakistani complicity. With Memon's evidence, it would now be possible to arrest more people involved.

The CBI stated that they had recovered a video cassette from Yaqub, which had footage of the wedding of Taufiq Jaliawala's daughter Rabia at Karachi, where Dawood Ibrahim and members of the ISI were honoured guests. Yaqub was also carrying three audio cassettes on which he had allegedly secretly recorded important conversations that the CBI was now transcribing and analysing.

The media too found renewed interest in the blasts case. All newspapers reported the CBI version, but many carried Yaqub's denial as well. There was also much investigation and speculation about Yaqub's real role.

Two countries reacted immediately to the media reports. The G.P. Koirala government in Nepal, facing general elections and wary of charges of yielding to pressure from India, quickly issued a denial. On 5 August, a spokesman of the Nepali home ministry stated that no one called Yaqub Memon had been taken into custody by the officials at the airport on 24 July. The wording of the denial was ambiguous as Yaqub had been travelling under the name of Yusuf Ahmed.

The second, and sharper, denial came from Pakistan. The Pakistani high commissioner to India stated in a press release on 7 August that the arrest of the Indian citizen Yaqub Memon did not surprise Pakistan as it had always maintained that the Memon family was not in Pakistan. Prime Minister Benazir Bhutto described Chavan's statements as 'a pack of lies'. She added that India was wrongly implicating Pakistan to divert attention from its own problems, especially the human rights abuse in Kashmir. Relations between the two countries were already tense as at the end of July Pakistan had virtually given notice at a UN press conference that they planned to raise the Kashmir issue before the General Assembly the following month.

Soon after the blasts, Pakistan had said that it was willing to help to bring to book the people behind the blasts. Officially there was a task force set up for this purpose, though subsequently there was no report of its activities. When Indian intelligence sources said that the Memons were in Karachi, Pakistan had denied this.

With the fresh evidence unearthed with Yaqub Memon's arrest it was widely felt that Delhi would make renewed attempts to have Pakistan declared a terrorist state. For months Pakistan had been on the US watch list of countries likely to be declared terrorist states. Memon's arrest could prove to be a major blow to Pakistan's international image.

There was considerable public and media speculation about how Yaqub, despite being under constant ISI surveillance, could fly out of Karachi, carrying incriminating documents. According to one theory, RAW agents had wooed him away; according to another, Benazir Bhutto was behind it as she was seeking to expose the security establishment which was loyal to her arch rival, the previous prime minister Nawaz Sharif.

A third theory was that Dawood Ibrahim had persuaded Yaqub to return to India to delink his name from the conspiracy. The CBI had announced a Rs 15 lakh reward for information about him. In an interview to *India Today* (31 July 1994) Dawood had said: 'I am in a desperate situation. The Indian government has reduced me to a mouse, one who is trapped and cannot move around freely.'

Dawood's link with the blasts, so far mentioned only in Dawood Phanse's confession, had been reinforced when one of his close aides Usman Gani Mohammed Memon, a hawala operator, had been arrested on 20 July by the anti-terrorist squad of Gujarat police. During interrogation, Usman stated that Dawood had wanted to avenge the killings of innocent Muslims and so acquired and arranged for the shipment of RDX, arms and other explosives from Pakistan to India. The three hundred pages of Usman's diary contained the names of top businessmen and builders who sought Dawood's help to launder money. This arrest considerably bolstered the CBI's theory that Dawood Ibrahim had masterminded the blasts.

During interrogation, Yaqub Memon stubbornly maintained that he had never met Dawood, and named Tiger Memon and Taufiq Jaliawala as the prime movers of the conspiracy.

The fourth theory about the arrest was that Yaqub had actually been on a business trip to Kathmandu and was apprehended while returning to Karachi. Off the record, CBI officials accepted this version. It was also speculated that the CBI had struck a deal with him, which all officials unanimously denied.

Yaqub sat in the darkened room and gazed at the ceiling. There was hardly any sound around him, and he felt cut off from the world. He thought about how his life had changed, of Raheen, who was due to have their first child in the first week of August. It was now 9 August, and he did not know if he was a father yet. He wished passionately that he had not left Bombay on 9 March. They would have undoubtedly faced a lot of trouble, but they would not have been branded traitors.

He had now spent twelve days with CBI officers, patiently answering their questions for hours every day. He had celebrated a mournful thirty-second birthday on 30 July.

A CBI officer came to him and told him that he was to give an interview on television.

Yaqub looked at him blankly. 'What interview?'

The officer grinned broadly. 'You're about to become a celebrity. It will be on the national TV—Doordarshan—and the whole of India is going to watch you.'

Yaqub was in half a mind to refuse, when it struck him that

he could use this opportunity to let ninety crore of his countrymen know that apart from Tiger Memon, the other Memons were decent, law-abiding citizens. He asked the officer, 'When am I supposed to be on television?'

'We have to go in for a recording now, it will be aired later tonight.'

He was escorted to the Doordarshan studio. The programme on which he was being interviewed was *Newstrack*, a half-hour news analysis show. In response to the questions, he narrated the tale of his journey to Kathmandu, his interception at the airport, and his handing over to the CBI. He stated that it was Tiger Memon and Taufiq Jaliawala who had been the kingpins, and explained how Tiger had been used by the ISI in the plot.

Yaqub spoke at length about the role played by Taufiq Jaliawala. It was Jaliawala who had coordinated with Dubai and Bombay on behalf of the Pakistani authorities, and played a major role in selecting the blast sites. Jaliawala's construction business, automobile shop and sari emporium in Karachi were merely fronts for his more lucrative illegal businesses. He was a close associate of Dawood Ibrahim, and of Tiger Memon. When the Memons moved to Karachi, Jaliawala had initially given them shelter in his own bungalow, and aided them in securing new identity cards and passports. He had also given shelter to about ten of the men directly involved in the blasts—including Javed Chikna and Anwar Theba, Tiger's two most senior aides—when they had arrived in Karachi. Yaqub also described the wedding of Jaliawala's daughter Rabia to Farooq, son of Feroze Dadi of Crawford Market, Bombay, on 30 April 1994. Many prominent citizens of Bombay, and underworld leaders from Bombay and Dubai had been invited and Jaliawala had indicated that he would rather the Memons did not attend as it would cause embarrassment if anyone from Bombay recognized them.

Apart from Jaliawala, there was another smuggler, Sayed Arif, also working from Dubai, who had aided Tiger Memon. With the money lent by Jaliawala and Arif, the Memon family had built a lavish bungalow called Ahmed House, which had cost Pakistani Rs 1.16 crore, in the Karachi Development Scheme area. However, despite material comforts, the Memon family was not happy exiled from their native land. From Yaqub's account, the family came across as good Indians, only circumstantially connected to the blasts and now in danger.

During June and July 1994, copies of the chargesheet in the blasts case had reached Karachi. Yaqub had talked to lawyers who studied it and said that based on the evidence detailed, only Tiger could be convicted. The other members of the family would, at worse, receive light sentences. It was this assurance which had prompted Yaqub's return. He had prepared for the homecoming carefully. He had driven around Karachi, photographing the homes of Jaliawala, Dawood and Tiger's lieutenants who had executed the bomb blasts. He had recorded conversations between Jaliawala, Tiger and others on microcassettes, secured a video of Rabia's wedding, and gathered documents which showed how the Memons had all been given new identities. His cousin Usman had been his confidant.

Finally, Yaqub was asked whether he had met Dawood Ibrahim. He denied meeting him, but said that he knew his name.

The interview was aired on Doordarshan at 9 p.m. It created a huge sensation, as such an interview was unprecedented in the annals of Indian television. The government's aim had been fulfilled: the world had heard how Pakistan had been involved in the blasts and even now was sheltering its perpetrators. Many viewers were impressed with Yaqub's courage and intelligence, and intrigued by the discrepancies between the CBI account and Yaqub's.

There were eight armed commandos waiting at the arrivals terminal at Indira Gandhi International Airport, New Delhi. Several CBI officers also prowled around, keeping their eyes glued to the main arrival gate. It was 24 August 1994.

Air-India flight 736 from Dubai had already arrived. Soon they saw a group of six adults whose faces looked familiar and who had an uncertain air about them. Suleiman Memon and Isa Memon supported sixty-six-year-old Abdul Razak and sixty-year-old Hanifa. Immediately behind them walked a youth in his twenties, whom they assumed to be Yusuf. Following him was Suleiman's wife Rubina and their two children, seven-year-old Iliyas and five-year-old Aliyah. Each of the adult male Memons carried a price of Rs 1 lakh, and each of the adult women carried a price of Rs 25,000. Only five adult members of the family were still missing—Tiger and his wife Shabana, Ayub and his wife Reshma, and Yaqub's wife Raheen who had recently delivered.

The Memons had travelled to Dubai, where they had contacted the Indian embassy, filed their affidavits and informed the embassy of their intention to return. The embassy had in turn informed the CBI, and escorted the group to the airport and on to the plane.

As the group reached the CBI officers, one of them came forward, introduced himself and told them that they were under arrest. They were taken to a safe house in a central government police colony in south Delhi, guarded by eight ferocious-looking and fully armed commandos. Metropolitan magistrate V.K. Jain remanded them to CBI custody for fourteen days under TADA. The children were allowed to stay with the family. The media had no inkling about these arrests at that time.

On 11 September the clan was joined by Raheen and her month-old baby. Raheen too arrived from Dubai, was arrested at the airport and remanded into custody.

Many believed that this mass surrender by the Memon family meant that a deal had been struck. The Indian government and the CBI, embarrassed that none of the important people in the conspiracy had been captured, had probably offered the Memons lighter punishment or an acquittal if they returned to India. However, the CBI maintained that there was no deal and the Memons were not planning to turn approvers. Its director, K. Vijay Rama Rao, said that the Memons had surrendered because they had had no other option.

■

The evidence provided by Yaqub and Usman proved useful in tracing the RDX back into Pakistan. They had also supplied information which indicated Dawood's closeness to powerful people in Pakistan. Yaqub revealed that after the communal riots in Bombay, Raza Ashfaq Sarvar, then a minister in the Muslim League government of Punjab, Pakistan, frequently met Dawood in Dubai. He also stated that Dawood was close to several men in the Pakistani army, as well as to Taufiq Jaliawala, who Yaqub alleged had organized the RDX supply for the ISI. Usman furnished details of a meeting in Dawood's Dubai house on 10 January, where the plan for the blasts was reportedly discussed.

Earlier, there had been some other small pieces of evidence which showed Pakistani involvement. For example, Rakesh Maria's team had seized twenty-seven cartons from the Memons' garage and compound space in Al-Hussaini—twenty-five on 21 March 1993 and two on 24 March. The cartons were covered with black stains which made it difficult to read the labels. On a couple however the words 'Packstile Packages Ltd., Lahore. Consignee: Wah Noble' could be read. The police laboratory at Kalina declared after examining the boxes that they had been used to carry plastic explosives. Investigation revealed that Wah Noble was a private limited company whose official address was 12/92 GT Road, Wah, Pakistan. The company dealt with the manufacture of dynamite, emulsion and powdered high explosives like black powder and PETN, safety fuses, detonators and blasting equipment. Thus the explosives used seemed to have been manufactured and sent from Pakistan.

The government of every country monitors the sale of explosives, especially their import and export. It could be inferred that the government of Pakistan or at least some central government agency there had given its tacit consent for the smuggling of these deadly explosives. They had also entered India illegally. When the CBI checked with the Indian Director General of Foreign Trade, it was discovered that five companies in India had a licence to import explosives. For each consignment, approval had to be obtained from the Controller of Explosives at Nagpur. These five companies were Hutti Gold Mines Company, Raichore; HLS Geeta Ltd., Jaisalmer; Hindustan Petroleum Corporation Ltd., Vishakapatnam; Hindustan Petroleum Corporation Ltd., Bombay; and HLS India Ltd., New Delhi. As none of these firms had imported the explosives, it was clear that they had been smuggled illegally to the country from Pakistan.

The hand grenades used also seemed to be sourced from Pakistan. The markings on them read 'Arges 69', and weapons experts said this was an Austrian company. A sample was sent to the Federal Ministry for Interior in Austria for investigation. They sent a report to the Indian government dated 28 April 1993. It reported that the grenades were manufactured by two firms—Ulbrichts-Witwe and Arges-Armaturen in Schwanenstadt. The two firms were owned by the same person and were located about a hundred metres from each other. Ulbrichts processed metals and synthetics, while Arges manufactured hand grenades and helmets.

In 1968, both firms had received an enquiry from Akhtar and Hoffman from Islamabad, regarding the licensing of machinery for the production of hand grenades of model HG 69. A deal was struck, and from 1968 to 1971, the requisite machinery was licensed to them. After 1971, this was replaced by machinery for model HG 72.

There were plans for setting up a company called Ulbrichts Pakistan in collaboration with Akhtar and Hoffman but there was a dispute regarding payment of licensing fees and no official agreement could be reached. However, during 1972–75, there was a firm called Ulbrichts Pakistan, which described itself as a joint-venture partner of Ulbrichts Austria and produced and sold HG 69 hand grenades in Pakistan. There were still three cases pending in the courts in Pakistan regarding this firm.

The Austrian report stated that the samples sent indicated that the grenades had been made with the machines sold to Pakistan in 1968. The markings on the detonators of the grenades and the serial numbers showed they were manufactured by Ulbrichts Pakistan in 1983. HG 69 grenades had not been produced in Austria since 1971. The grenades sent for examination differed from those produced in Austria in two ways: the steel pellets in the casing were different, and the explosive substance used was not nitropenta which the Austrian company used.

Besides the explosives and the grenades, the Star brand pistols which had been recovered were also of Pakistan manufacture. These were very popular with the Bombay underworld.

But the most clinching evidence of Pakistani collusion was the fact that they had harboured the Memon family and given them false passports, even after they had denied that the Memons were in Pakistan when India had requested their deportation. The passports of the Memons which Yaqub had been carrying showed that all members of the family had been issued Thai visas from the embassy of Thailand in Islamabad on 15 April 1993, valid until 14 July 1993.

Real name	Name in Pakistani ID papers	Pakistani passport number	Thai visa number
Suleiman Abdul Razak Memon	Aftaab Ahmed	AA 763651	749/2536
Rubina Suleiman Memon	Mehtaab Aftaab Ahmed	AA 763653	750/2536
Yaqub Abdul Razak Memon	Yusuf Ahmed	AA 763242	744/2536
Raheen Yaqub Memon	Zeba Yusuf Ahmed	AA 763646	745/2336
Yusuf Abdul Razak Memon	Imran, son of Ibrahim	AA 763654	743/2536
Isa Abdul Razak Memon	Akhtar, son of Siddique	AA 763650	751/2536
Tiger Memon	Ahmed Jamaal, son of Mohammed Jamaal	AA 762402	752/2536
Shabana Ibrahim Memon	Fatima Ahmed Jamaal	AA 763652	746/2536
Ayub Abdul Razak Memon	Qayyum Mohammed Ahmed	AA 763648	741/2536
Reshma Ayub Memon	Taranum Qayyum Ahmed	AA 763647	742/2536
Haneefa Razak Memon	Zainab Ahmed Mohammed	AA 763645	747/2536
Abdul Razak Memon	Ahmed Mohammed	AA 763649	748/2536

All these details added up to significant confirmation of Pakistan's involvement. Yaqub Memon's return had paid rich dividends for the CBI.

14

The Helping Hand

It was a typical neta reception room on the sixth floor of Mantralaya. On this day in December 1994, orderlies rushed in and out purposefully, and hangers-on milled around. Sharad Pawar was very busy in his office, so the crowd in the reception room grew.

Among the people waiting was a sixty-year-old whose face was familiar to most of his countrymen, and many beyond its shores. Sunil Dutt had been waiting for over three hours. Dutt was used to waiting: he had spent many hours here or in the reception of Pawar's bungalow Varsha since Sanjay had first been arrested in April. The chief minister was very busy nowadays.

Dutt and his wife had been close friends with Indira Gandhi and her family, and had received the friendliest of treatment from them. In Delhi, as an MP, he had access to people in power, though all Narasimha Rao would give were half promises. Bombay however, though his party was in power, was proving to be a different experience. Pawar, when he finally granted Dutt an audience, said that the matters were in the hands of the judiciary so he was helpless.

Dutt had had a lifetime of coping with crises—the early death of his father, being a refugee from Pakistan, his early struggles as an actor, the commercial failure of his first directorial venture *Yaadein*, his wife's long illness and death, and his son's battles with drugs. He had taken over Nargis's work as an activist after her death. He had marched for peace in ravaged Punjab in 1987, and for nuclear disarmament in Japan in 1984. He had worked with the riot-affected in Bhagalpur in 1984. He had dealt with all of these, and he resolved not to be defeated by the latest crisis.

During the communal riots, Dutt had spoken out stridently about the Shiv Sena, and Thackeray too had criticized Dutt vehemently. In the constituency of northwest Bombay, Thackeray's candidate Madhukar Sarpotdar had repeatedly lost to Dutt. But now Thackeray seemed to be the only man who could help him, and Dutt resolved to approach him.

Thackeray's bungalow Matoshree, Kala Nagar, was heavily guarded with policemen swarming all over the fortress-like building. The hall was crowded with shakha pramukhs, the chiefs of the area branches, and politicians from the villages of Maharashtra, Delhi and UP. Dutt was the only Congressman present, and a buzz went up when he was finally escorted in after going through several security checks.

Thackeray was busy in a high-level meeting with Sena stalwarts, as the assembly elections were around the corner. But informed of Dutt's arrival, he immediately adjourned the meeting, something leaders who had worked with him for decades had never seen him do. He asked that Dutt be escorted to a special visitor's room.

Thackeray entered in his usual saffron silk kurta-lungi with a rudraksha necklace around his neck. The beginning was cordial but slightly awkward.

'I have come to you, not as a representative of a party, but as a helpless father ...' Dutt began.

Thackeray heard him out patiently. It took a while, and the Sena leaders waiting in the conference room got restive. At the end, Thackeray assured him that he and his party would do everything they could to help. Dutt could detect a note of sincerity in his voice.

When he left, it was with a strange feeling of reassurance that good things would happen soon.

Bal Thackeray began by calling up the prime minister and asking him to help the Dutt family. He issued an edict to the Shiv Sena that they were not to hold dharnas or criticize Sanjay any more and threw the support of the Shiv Sena mounthpiece *Saamna*, of which he was the editor, behind Sanjay. *Saamna*, though not taken as a serious paper, was read by everyone in Bombay to keep abreast of Sena activities. Hitherto, the paper had portrayed Sanjay Dutt as a villain. Now in a rapid volte face, they turned their venom onto another favourite, Sharad Pawar, while Sanjay was portrayed as a helpless victim.

Jolted by the turn of events, some Congress leaders, who sympathized with Sunil Dutt but had kept silent, began advocating leniency for Sanjay. Cutting across the party lines, the stalwarts from within the film industry began rallying to Sanjay's support once again. Dilip Kumar, Raj Babbar and Shatrughan Sinha had made several trips to Delhi and met the prime minister and President S.D. Sharma to reiterate that Sanjay's punishment exceeded his crime. Sanjay acquired an unlikely supporter in Maneka Gandhi, a former schoolmate who was now actively involved in politics. She launched a Sanjay Bacchao Manch to demand the immediate release of Sanjay and other TADA detainees who were 'unjustly' languishing in jail. She met leaders in Bombay to rally support to the forum at both state and national levels in early 1995.

After the Maharashtra assembly elections in February 1995, for the first time a stridently fundamentalist alliance—the BJP and Shiv Sena—came to power. The Congress defeat was humiliating. In the 1990 elections, out of the total 288 seats, Congress had secured 141 whereas the Shiv Sena won fifty-two. In the 1995 elections, the Congress won only eighty, while the Shiv Sena won seventy-two. Once in power, the Shiv Sena clamoured for Sanjay's release.

'It is because of that adamant judge that poor Sanjay Dutt is still languishing in the prison,' Bal Thackeray thundered to the resounding applause of thousands of his supporters who had gathered for the inauguration of the Bandra flyover on 8 July 1995, named after his father, the late Prabhodhan Thackeray. During his one-hour diatribe, he referred to Judge Patel as 'halkat' (bullheaded) and biased, and claimed credit for all the moves to get Sanjay out of jail. Conspicuous at the opening was Sunil Dutt, whose name on the plaque on the new flyover was also prominent.

During Sanjay's second period of incarceration, a constant source of support was Rhea Pillai. They had known each other since September 1994. Like other wives and lovers, she would wait for hours outside the Arthur Road jail to ensure Sanjay's meals reached him. When he was hospitalized at JJ Hospital in early 1995 for depression and blood pressure problems, she visited him regularly, along with his immediate family. Their relationship became the talk of the town. Despite the tension of the trial and the pains of imprisonment, Sanjay was happy again.

However in July 1995 Rhea herself was hospitalized. Sanjay was beside himself with desolation and wanted to go and see her. He asked his lawyer Kajal Anand, who tried to dissuade him. However, Sanjay put in an application and the judge J.N. Patel, to everyone's astonishment, granted it.

On 22 July 1995, Sanjay went to visit Rhea at home after

she had returned from hospital. He was mobbed by photographers as he left in a police van, with a police escort blaring sirens. There were consequently traffic jams in the morning rush-hour traffic, but for once no one minded. At the Mayfair building, Churchgate, there was another group of photographers. Sanjay looked clearly delighted at the prospect of spending a day with his girlfriend, family and friends.

After this, Sanjay's recovery from his various health problems was amazing. He exuded grit and determination to endure courageously. After Dilip Kumar visited him on 29 July, his thirty-sixth birthday, at JJ Hospital, he commented, 'I adore and admire Sanjay Dutt for courageously standing up against all odds.'

A state review committee instituted by the Pawar government in 1994 had recommended that the conspiracy charges against five of the defendants—Sanjay Dutt and the four who had helped him to destroy the guns: Ajay Marwah, Russi Mulla, Kersi Adajenia and Yusuf Nulwala—be dropped.

In August 1995, the CBI filed an application in the TADA court stating that the prosecution had no objection to the release of twelve of the defendants, including Sanjay on bail. It was speculated that the highest authorities had instructed them to facilitate Sanjay's bail. The advocate general of Maharashtra, C.J. Sawant, submitted in the TADA court in September 1995 that the charges against Sanjay and the others should be changed. They should be charged only under Section 3.5 of TADA (which pertains to unauthorized possession of a weapon in a notified area), and not under Section 3.3 (which pertains to aiding and abetting a terrorist act). This was in direct contravention of the stand taken by the prosecution. The CBI by this time was willing to relent if Sanjay asked for bail on grounds of ill health, but was furious at the volte face by the state government, as sixty other defendants could now ask for similar concessions and weaken their whole case. The date for the hearing was fixed for 11 September.

On 11 September, there was bedlam outside the TADA court. Milling crowds extended to almost two blocks around the court, making it impossible for vehicles to move. Vandana Hotel, at the corner of the lane, was doing brisk business. There were many persons from the media, though they were prohibited from taking photographs within a fifteen-foot radius of the courtroom. Only one representative from each newspaper had been allowed into the court. Two wireless battalions of the SRP and dozens of policemen from the NM Joshi Marg police station tried to keep the crowds under control. The courtroom was bursting at the seams.

The babble ceased suddenly when the judge began to speak: 'Granting bail is the prerogative of the court irrespective of the no objection of the prosecution. The learned public prosecutor has come with reasons and justifications which are contrary to the law. Public prosecutors were supposed to assist the court in dispensing justice and not dispensing with justice. The prosecution's no objection to the accused persons has been made for extraneous reasons.' He concluded that there had been no change in fact, situation and circumstances of the applicants which would enable them to seek bail on fresh grounds.

With the last statement, pandemonium broke out.

Sunil Dutt instructed his lawyer, Kapil Sibal, to file an appeal in the Supreme Court. This was done within ten days to the three-judge division bench of Justices J.N. Ray, N.P. Singh and B.L. Hansaria. Sibal, a lawyer with impressive credentials, spoke eloquently before the bench on behalf of Sanjay. The judges said they would give their decision on 16 October.

Sanjay Dutt leaving the TADA court (Courtesy Mid-day)

It was a pleasant morning. The huge grandfather clock at the TADA court showed it was 10.40 a.m., twenty minutes before proceedings usually began. The defendants usually started coming in from 10.30, or even earlier, to confer with their lawyers. Reporters thronged the courtroom and canteen.

Sanjay Dutt was visibly tense. He was flanked by his lawyers Satish Maneshinde and Kajal Anand, who carried their cell phones. The three-judge bench in the Supreme Court was supposed to deliver judgement on his case that day.

Meanwhile in Delhi, Court 7 of the Supreme Court was also packed. Two of the country's most famous lawyers, Kapil Sibal and Lalit Bhasin, were representing Sanjay. They had presented their arguments at the previous hearing and the verdict was to be delivered today.

Reading out the unanimous judgement, which set aside Judge Patel's order, Justice Ray observed that judge J.N. Patel had failed to understand the CBI's no-objection plea in the proper perspective. Sanjay was to be granted bail, on a surety of Rs 5 lakh and on surrendering his passport to the court. He was also not to hamper the investigations or tamper with the evidence.

Halfway across the country, Maneshinde's cell phone trilled. It was from Delhi. He yelled in joy.

The entire courtroom broke out in celebration. Sanjay alone did not react. He seemed shell-shocked as people came forward to congratulate him.

It was 11 a.m. The court proceedings were about to begin. Maneshinde sought permission from the judge to take Sanjay to the canteen. Overjoyed, Sanjay was in tears. Many reporters wanted his reactions but he was too stunned to speak. The long battle was over.

The eight-page Supreme Court order did not reach Bombay till the following evening. It was only on 18 October that Sanjay could finally leave.

He did so in style, in a convoy of cars with friends and family. He bade an effusive farewell to the jail staff. Many well-wishers gathered to see him off.

The cavalcade left for Prabhadevi, for Sanjay wanted to pray at the Siddhi Vinayak temple before going home. Unable to find words, he did the parikrama. After about an hour, the men in the group left for Thackeray's house.

At Matoshree, Thackeray came to the door to welcome them and embraced Sanjay. After that, they finally went home.

15

The Case Continues

Apart from the detention of Yaqub Memon and other members of his family, there were few dramatic developments in the investigation after the CBI took over in November 1993, thought within the first month itself there was a ripple of excitement.

On 6 December, the first anniversary of the Babri Masjid demolition, five bombs left in bags and briefcases went off in five long-distance trains: on the Bombay–New Delhi Rajdhani Express, which exploded near Kota; the Surat–Bombay Flying Queen Express, which went off near Surat; on the Howrah–New Delhi Rajdhani Express; on the New Delhi–Howrah Rajdhani Express, which exploded near Kanpur; and on the Hyderabad–New Delhi AP Express which went off soon after the train left Hyderabad. A sixth bomb had been placed in the Bangalore–Kurla Express, but an alert passenger had thrown the unclaimed bag out. The bombs were of low-intensity, and killed two people and injured twenty-three.

There were chilling similarities with the serial blasts, and many suspected that this was a follow-up to that. The CBI was asked to look into the case, and finally the mastermind behind the blasts was identified as Dr Mohammed Jalees Ansari, a doctor practising in Madanpura, south Bombay, who was arrested by the CBI STF on 13 January 1994. Ansari was accused of involvement in the serial blasts, produced in the TADA court and remanded into custody.

Ansari confessed that he was a member of the fanatical Ahle Hadees sect, and claimed to have organized fifty-four bombings all over the country, including many it was clearly impossible for him to have committed. His modus operandi was like that used in the three hotel bombings on 12 March 1993, where bags filled with explosives were left at key spots. However, the explosives he used were of low-intensity. At least one of his associates had been trained in Pakistan, and Ansari himself trained others in bomb making.

Ansari remained in the custody of the CBI for over six weeks, after which he was discharged in the blasts case in February 1994. He was subsequently convicted in other cases, and sentenced to ten years' imprisonment.

■

It was January 1995. In the drab office of the CBI STF, Raman Tyagi was now an integral part of the team investigating the bomb blasts case. When the phone rang, interrupting his work, he picked it up with some annoyance.

'Sahab, Salim Kurla *ke bare mein*,' the caller had recognized his voice.

'What about him?' Tyagi asked.

'He is in Hyderabad, I know his landlord's telephone number.'

'Give me the number,' Tyagi ordered. He wrote it down and asked some more questions, which his informant answered.

Tyagi called the telephone number he had been given and the gentleman at the other end confirmed that he did have a tenant, who called himself Ahmed Pasha, who matched the description that Tyagi gave him. A special team of officers was formed to travel to Hyderabad immediately. Plane tickets were booked, and other preparations made. The team left the same day, a record by CBI standards.

However, it was not going to be that simple. The caller who had called Tyagi also tipped off Anis Ibrahim, Salim Kurla's boss, that a police party was on its way. Anis in turn alerted Kurla.

Kurla had been on the run since May 1993. He had first fled to Bangalore and lived there for a year. Then he had spotted a police team from Bombay and, frightened that they were looking for him, moved to Pune. But he had not felt secure there and had later shifted to Hyderabad, where he lived in a rented flat in Vijayshri Apartments near Chikoti Gardens. He had also married and had a one-year-old son.

When Salim Kurla heard of the police party's plans, he immediately shifted to a hotel and moved all his belongings from the flat.

When the CBI team reached Vijayshri Apartments, Salim Kurla's first-floor flat was locked and empty. They settled down to wait, not suspecting that he had been warned about their arrival. As the hours passed, they started discussing whether they should break the lock and enter the flat. However, eventually, they decided to continue their vigil.

They might have waited indefinitely had there not been a flaw in Kurla's planning: he had left his scooter behind. In the evening, Kurla hired an autorickshaw to come to his old flat and collect the scooter.

As the rickshaw turned into the narrow lane and came up the building, two things happened at the same time. Kurla saw the waiting officers, who had made no efforts at concealment, and frantically asked the driver to turn back. The next moment, Raman Tyagi noticed that a rickshaw was turning back and dashed towards it. He had been a javelin thrower in college and his coach had commended his broad shoulders, but his athletic days were now firmly in the past. However, undeterred, he ran on.

As the rickshaw and Tyagi raced, the machine had a clear advantage over the man though it could not move at full speed on the rough gravel. Tyagi was getting out of breath, but carried on resolutely. He noticed that the rickshaw had to take a narrow turn to reach the main road. He realized the rickshaw would slow down to make the turn, and made one last desperate effort.

The rickshaw beat him to the turn by a split second. Tyagi suddenly remembered his coach's words and decided to use his shoulders. He gripped the middle rod of the rickshaw and heaved with full force, yelling, 'Ya Ali madad,' a traditional Muslim battle cry. To his surprise, the speeding rickshaw crashed on the pavement on its side, Kurla inside screaming in agony and fear. Tyagi too fell but was promptly up to grab Kurla as he struggled to get out of the rickshaw.

By this time, the other CBI officers had joined Tyagi.

■

In August 1995, the CBI got a lead through Gujarat's Anti-Terrorist Squad (ATS). Bombay hoodlums traditionally seek refuge in neighbouring Gujarat when their home state becomes too dangerous. The Gujarat police were also involved in the investigation of the landing of RDX, weapons and other contraband on the coast of Porbunder, Gujarat.

One of the people named as an absconder in the blasts case whom the ATS picked up was Mohammed Salim Mira Moiuddin Sheikh, better known as Salim Kutta as he hailed from Kottanellur, Tamil Nadu. He was arrested from a village in Bijnor, UP. On interrogation, they realized that he was an accused in the blasts case. He was handed over to the CBI STF in Bombay on 20 August 1995.

Salim Kutta's confession read like a Bollywood potboiler. His father Mira Moiuddin Sheikh was a special Mukadam at the Bombay Port Trust (BPT). Salim had been educated at St Ignatius School, Bombay, and the Khoja Khan Mohammed Habib High School, Dongri. However, he had abandoned school and joined a bunch of delinquent children. By his teens, he was involved in several cases of rioting and was wanted at several police stations—Pydhonie, MRA Marg, Byculla and Colaba. In the late 1980s, he and some friends started the Arjun gang, inspired by the film of the same name where Sunny Deol and other unemployed youths, fundamentally honest and yearning to make sense of their lives, are unwittingly drawn to crime when they fight injustice.

In 1990, his mother had to be hospitalized and Salim needed money desperately. The police were also after him. At this point he met Mustafa Majnun, Mohammed Dossa's brother. Mustafa offered him membership of his gang, assured him of protection, and promised to pay his mother's bills, for which he gave him Rs 5,000 on the spot. Mustafa and Mohammed Dossa had good contacts in the police department. Salim Kutta was released on bail and his mother discharged from the hospital. This act of kindness won Mustafa and Mohammed his complete loyalty, and Salim became their bodyguard. He was third in the hierarchy of their gang, after Tiger Memon and Mechanic Chacha.

The Arjun gang still remained in existence, but Salim took up additional responsibilities such as delivering gold biscuits and silver ingots on behalf of Dossa. The gold and silver would be landed in Raigad and delivered to Dossa's office in Nakhuda Mohallah, Pydhonie. Buyers would come there to haggle over prices.

When Tiger Memon moved to Dubai, Salim Kutta moved into his place in the gang. According to him, what caused the rift was not Tiger's ambition but a woman whom both Tiger and Dossa were besotted with. In the same year Dossa offered Salim Kutta a partnership in the smuggling ring. The other partners, apart from Dossa and his brother, were Mechanic Chacha and Feroze Abdul Rafiq. These three partners were to get a five per cent share each in the total amount of gold smuggled.

Salim Kutta had participated in at least eight landings of silver at Mhasla and Dighi. He had also participated in several landings on the Mangalore coast, and was introduced to landing agents there. He also reportedly carried out killings at Mustafa's behest.

During the riots of January 1993, Kutta was with Dossa when the latter received a call from Mustafa in Dubai. Salim could make out that Mustafa was desperate to send an arms consignment to Bombay through Mhasla. Dossa was reluctant for logistical reasons, but eventually agreed. Dossa's landing agents Shabbir Qadri and Uttam Poddar were asked to organize the landing on 9 January, and Salim Kutta was deputed to supervise. In the dark of the night, they offloaded 300 silver ingots, about thirty wooden crates and a similar number of canvas bags. Salim surmised that the boxes contained AK-56s and magazines, while the canvas bags held RDX. The cargo was divided. Most of it was sent to Gujarat in trucks while the rest was deposited at the landing agent Qadri's house at Raigad. Salim returned to Bombay. He later realized that Mustafa had not only sent arms and explosives to Mhasla and Dighi, but there had been other landings in Porbunder, Gujarat, organized by his landing agents Punju Mia and Farookh Lotta.

Towards the end of January, Mohammed Dossa bought tickets to Dubai for Kutta and five others of the Arjun gang—

Qayyum Sajni, Yusuf Batla, Shoaib Baba, Syed Qureishi and Ahmed Lambu. Mustafa organized the visas. In Dubai, they stayed at Mustafa's office in Dera Towers for a couple of weeks. On one occasion, Mustafa took Salim to Dawood Ibrahim's palatial bungalow. In his confession, Salim gave elaborate descriptions of the lavish house.

He also described a meeting in Dawood's house, attended by Chhota Shakeel, Salim Talwar, Ejaz Pathan, Haji Ahmed, Munna Abdullah, Mustafa and the five others of the Arjun gang. Dawood had spoken provocatively for about an hour about Hindus and their role in the demolition of the Babri Masjid and in the riots. He exhorted his listeners to rise and rebel against the tyrannical rule. He instructed Mustafa to collect the passports of those who wanted to participate in the action so that arrangements could be made to take them to Pakistan for training.

Kutta was unwilling to go. However, the other members of the Arjun gang were enthusiastic. The five of them went to Islamabad for a week, and on their return, described how Pakistani officers had escorted them out of the airport without any formalities, how they were taken for training in one of several camps on a hillside, and how they were taken sightseeing after their training. They had met several other youths from Bombay in the training camps. They had been trained in handling AK-56s, hand grenades and making bombs. They told Salim that they had seen other camps at a distance where Bosnian Muslims were being prepared for the fight against the Serbs.

The five men of the Arjun gang returned to Bombay, while Salim Kutta stayed on in Dubai. A few days later, on instructions from Mohammed Dossa, he went to Kathmandu to meet gold smugglers and then returned to Bombay. On the day of the blasts, he had been in Bombay but he had not participated in them.

After the blasts, Salim realized that some of Dossa's men

who had been arrested had mentioned his name, and that the police were looking for him. He fled to Delhi, and from there to UP. He heard that he carried a prize of Rs 1 lakh on his head.

He remained in touch with Dossa throughout, and continued to participate in his smuggling activities. Dossa would instruct him on where to go, and what to deliver. He also remained in touch with the Arjun gang, all members of which were still at large and working with Dossa. This last revelation was startling.

Trained in modern warfare, skilled at staying in hiding for over five years, and led by an affluent man like Mustafa, the Arjun gang is capable of perpetrating another crime like the one that tore Bombay apart.

Salim Kutta's was only the third statement that linked Dawood Ibrahim to the blasts. The earlier two had been by Dawood Phanse and Usman Gani.

■

Mohammed Kasam Lajpuria, better known as Mechanic Chacha, had been on the run for more than six-and-a-half years. He had been in Kathmandu for a while, and then in Dubai where Mohammed Dossa had ensured he was well looked after.

Mechanic Chacha was on the list of proclaimed offenders in the blasts case. The list had now shrunk to thirty-three people, and their details were with the Interpol.

In the early 1980s, when Dossa was serving his time at Bombay Central Prison, his cellmate had been Mechanic Chacha, who had also been arrested for smuggling. His boss then was Yusuf Patel. Dossa proposed that Chacha join him. Gradually, Chacha assumed more and more responsibility, supervising Dossa's landing operations. When Dossa asked him to take delivery of arms and explosives, Chacha did not demur.

The first landing of arms and RDX was on 9 January at Dighi. It was sent by Mustafa Majnun. Over a walkie-talkie, Chacha had coordinated the activities of Kutta and the Arjun gang. A part of the consignment was sent to Porbunder and Jamnagar. Mustafa had sent strict instructions. The Kalashnikov guns and RDX were neatly divided up. Some cartons were sent to Surat and Raipur, and the rest was concealed in safe houses in Bombay and Raigad. When the blasts happened on 12 March, Mechanic Chacha realized that some other don had upstaged his boss.

The four years in Dubai had been good. Initially he had looked after Dossa's business. Later he had started his own. Yet the fear of stalkers never left him. He was sure the Indian agencies knew all about him; it was just because he was in Dubai that they could not do anything about it. He knew that the bigger dons—Dawood Ibrahim, Tiger Memon and Mohammed Dossa— were beyond the arm of the law, but he knew that lesser people were always expendable.

When Dossa asked him on 1 November 1999 to make a trip to Kathmandu, he felt a knot in his stomach. Kathmandu was no longer a haven for people like him. But then no place was truly safe. Taufiq Jaliawala had died on his way to perform Umrah in Saudi Arabia in June 1995 as his car was nearing Riyadh. It was allegedly an accident, but Chacha was not convinced.

As he took the flight to Kathmandu on 4 November, he felt relieved to note that he had not been followed. The relief was shortlived. After the plane landed at Tribhuvan International Airport, and he cleared immigration, he found the CBI waiting for him. The IB had already called ahead of him and tipped off the necessary people. DSP A.K. Singh of the CBI had done the groundwork for Chacha's welcome.

Police records showed that Chacha was arrested in Raxaul,

an entry-exit point on the porous Indo-Nepal border. He was flown to Delhi, and from there to Bombay where he was handed over to the STF officers. During the course of interrogation, Chacha confirmed what the investigators already knew, and added some new details. For example, when Memon's consignment of explosives was to land at Shekhadi on 3 February, Dossa was supposed to have personally tipped off customs officials, while Chacha had alerted the then collector Bhardwaj about Memon's 9 February Shekhadi consignment.

16
Retaliation

The simmering rivalry between Chhota Rajan and Chhota Shakeel and its outcome for the city of Bombay is the stuff of gang lore. It was said that Rajan had got into Dawood's disfavour for overspending on new recruits and other things. Gradually, the landing areas near Bombay over which he had influence were not used by Dawood. Also, Rajan received little booty for the killings he organized. Yet Rajan continued to remain loyal to Dawood, to the extent of defending him when Bal Thackeray chided the police for taking action against Hindu dons like Arun Gawli and Amar Naik. In an open letter carried in a city tabloid after the blasts, Rajan claimed that there were no communal divides in the D Company.

The serial bombings with their communal bias had undermined Chhota Rajan's belief. He saw this as an opportunity to establish himself as the patriotic don of the city, and reportedly vowed in 1997 to take on the traitor.

Salim Kurla was recuperating in the special ward of Bellevue Nursing Home, Andheri, Bombay, on 21 April 1998. His friend Arif Cablewala had come to visit him.

Two men entered the hospital. Their purposeful gait indicated that they knew where they wanted to go. They entered Kurla's ward and pulled out their revolvers. Kurla and Cablewala died in the volley of the bullets.

Builder Mohammed Jindran delighted in the fact that he had shared the same cell in jail as film star Sanjay Dutt. Since he had been released on bail on 16 November 1995, he had told this story many times.

At 9.30 a.m. on 29 June 1998, Jindran was about to get into his car in front of his house in Khar, when he saw his neighbour Kiran Pandey walking towards him and paused to greet him. Before Pandey could reach him, two men who had been loitering nearby walked up to him and shot him at point-blank range. Jindran sustained four bullet injuries and slumped to the ground.

As the gunmen turned to escape, they saw Kiran Pandey standing close to them, shocked into immobility. Pandey turned and ran for his life. The gunmen followed him into a garage, where Pandey slipped on the monsoon slush, and shot him.

The proprietor of MK Builders, Majid Khan, was released on bail on 3 April 1995. He had heard about the murder of Kurla and Jindran and of attempts on the life of others accused in the blasts case. Khan had asked Shakeel Ahmed, another accused, to be his bodyguard.

Around 12.30 p.m. on 1 March 1999, Khan was standing at the Nagpada Road junction outside Pahelvi Hotel, Bandra, when a motorcycle emerged from the bumper-to-bumper traffic and whizzed towards him. The pillion rider began spraying bullets indiscriminately. The target was Khan but also mown down were Ahmed, Khan's business partner Nizam Khan, and an ice vendor Akram Rafi. The hail of bullets also injured a bystander, Mohammed Rafi, and a seven-year-old schoolgirl Sadika, returning home from coaching classes.

The police were baffled at such indiscriminate gunfire; they could not even ascertain the exact number of bullets fired.

It was alleged that it was Chhota Rajan who had managed

to finish off two of the blasts accused—Khan and Ahmed—in one hit. The bloodstains on Bombay's streets congealed into a definite pattern, spelling out a sinister message for the accused in the blasts case.

Among those who narrowly escaped death were Ayub Patel—two unidentified men at Oshiwara fired five rounds at Patel but he managed to escape—and Salim Durrani, whose stalkers mistakenly killed another man, Shaikh Shabbir, in May 1998, who had been driving a car Durrani also drove. Sixteen bullets were pumped into Shaikh. Former Addl. CC Somnath Thapa walked into a trap when he responded to a telephone call at Hotel Rang Sharada, Bandra, on 18 August 1999. Two men opened fire at him at point-blank range. Thapa was critically injured but survived.

Chhota Shakeel was furious with rage. If Dawood's men failed to respond, it would mean loss of honour.

Shakeel planned a daring operation. He, along with Rajan's trusted aide Rohit Verma, kept tabs on Rajan's movements in South-East Asia. On 15 September 2000 Rajan, using the alias Vijay Daman, moved to Bangkok from Kuala Lumpur. Shakeel's men zeroed in on him at an apartment at 21 Sukhumvit Soi. The plan was to kidnap Rajan and get him to Karachi alive.

When Shakeel's men barged into the first-floor apartment and opened fire, Rajan jumped into the bedroom and closed the door, while Verma was hit by some forty bullets. Rajan had been hit by three bullets in his back, leg and hand, but he managed to jump from the first floor and escape.

The operation put Rajan on the defensive. He spent time recuperating in Smitivej Hospital, Bangkok, and on 24 November, escaped to Europe.

Film producer Hanif Kadawala had realized long ago that he could be a target. After the initial killings, Kadawala had turned his house into a veritable fortress, and his office too had extensive security. But after he had allegedly paid Rajan Rs 2 crore to spare him, this had changed. On 7 February 2001, Kadawala could sit relaxed in his plush air-conditioned office at Bandra, and talk to the three unknown men who had come to talk about a business deal. Even the closed circuit television in his office was not in operation any more.

An office boy stepped in and served tea. As the boy left and Kadawala picked up his teacup, one of the men abruptly rose and whipped out a revolver. Before Kadawala could utter a word, five bullets were pumped in him. The impact of the bullets threw his chair back. Tea splashed across the table and blood gushed out from several wounds. His eyes had remained opened with incredulity.

The trio walked out of the office hastily. Soon they melted into the crowds on the streets of Bandra.

It is said that Rajan had decided that he could not ignore Kadawala any more as any leniency to him diluted his claims of patriotism. Moreover, Kadawala was easy to get because the other blasts accused had become cautious.

Within two months, Rajan allegedly ordered another hit from an undisclosed hideout in Europe. On 3 April 2001, Akbar Abu Sama Khan was killed at Dongri. The remaining accused were petrified. Police commissioner M.N. Singh refused to grant protection to them. Salim Kurla's visitor Cablewala; Jindran's friend Pandey; the ice vendor Rafi; Durrani's lookalike Shaikh— none had been involved in the case at all but they had died. When two giants fight, the expendables are always the common people—like the people butchered in the riots or killed in the blasts, none of whom perhaps shared a fraction of the religious and political zeal of their so-called leaders.

The common man will keep paying the price for the ambitions of his leaders.

17

Life after Death

One of the most enduring images of the blast for many was the photograph in the *Indian Express* on 13 March: an injured man stumbling through the wreckage of the Air-India building, fear frozen on his dust- and blood-caked face.

The man in the photograph was Brigadier G. Natarajan. Since his retirement from the Indian army in 1991—he had been an engineer in the Corps of Signals—he had been working at Tata Consultancy Services, one of India's leading information technology companies. Five years earlier, in 1988, this clean-shaven, slightly built officer, now fifty-five years old, had seen the war from up close in the Indian Peacekeeping Force Operations in Sri Lanka, when he had set up a communications data-link there. He had seen suspected informers 'necklaced' with burning tyres by fanatical Tamil Tigers and hung from trees to die. He thought he would never forget the stench from the smouldering bodies.

On 12 March, he left his office at the eleventh floor of the building to attend a post-lunch meeting. As he was walking past the elevators, he saw a wall of flame shooting towards him. 'I felt an intense searing sensation and thought I had been thrust into the burning trunk of a car.' In his delirium, he saw himself surrounded by monsters, who were leading him towards Yama, the god of death. 'I fell at Yama's feet and told him I needed six months more to complete my duties in this world.'

After this, he vaguely remembers hearing voices identifying him. Before passing out he recalls mumbling his blood group, home phone numbers, and the medicines he was allergic to. Bleeding from the stomach, he was rushed to the Bombay Hospital some two kilometres away. Hospital records show that he was attended to at around 2.52 p.m. He stayed in the Intensive Care Unit (ICU) of the hospital for the next week and has absolutely no recollection of what happened during those days.

His wife Vasantha was informed of his plight at around 6 p.m. She was driven from their residence at Ghatkopar in Bombay's eastern suburbs by a Muslim taxi driver, who first calmly drank a bottle of water to break his Ramazan fast and then drove her at record speed through the dense traffic. The ICU was stretched beyond capacity with twenty-three critically injured patients. Only four of them were to survive.

Over the next few days, every few hours, the nurses would come out of the ICU and call out the names of the patients, Vasantha recalls. 'We never knew whether it was for buying medicines or whether it was to tell us that they were dead.'

A splinter had pierced Natarajan's stomach and ruptured his intestine, over ten inches of which had to be cut out. His ears and face were filled with glass powder, and his eardrum was ruptured. Occasional splinters surface in his body even today. In 1996, he needed to have an MRI scan but could not because the magnetic shrapnel embedded in his skull would damage the machine. In 1998, he found that he couldn't bend his left index finger. A tiny embedded metal piece was found to be the cause.

Natarajan's memory has diminished considerably. He believes he owes his survival to his army training, and the generous help his firm gave him. After the blasts his personality changed and he became pessimistic and reclusive. But now he believes that the experience has made him stronger.

The couple think of leaving the city, but never have. 'The city is so indifferent at times but so helpful in a crisis,' Vasantha says.

For thirty-three-year-old Suryakant Parshuram Patil of the housekeeping department in the government-run Centaur Hotel near the domestic airport, 12 March had been like any other day.

Towards the end of his shift, he was mopping a patch of oil fifteen feet from the lobby door, when there was a huge noise and some force propelled him face down on the marble floor. The last thing he remembered was a sensation of intense pain and of being surrounded by red.

He woke up in the Nanavati Hospital the following morning. Flying glass had gouged a tennis-ball-sized hole in his right leg, exposing the bone beneath. There was a six-inch-long gash on his left shoulder blade and injuries on his head. It took a fortnight of painful treatment, stitches and skin grafts to put him together again. Over the years, the countless scars on his body, his inability to sleep on his left side and the weakness in his left arm have remained constant reminders of the blast. But what has been worse is the mental agony: loud noises, thunder and lightning turn him into a cowering wreck. He is now a fervent believer in God. There are huge portraits of Sai Baba and Ganapati in his home. 'We light lamps every 12 March to thank Him for saving my husband's life,' says his wife Sudha.

Suryakant still works at the Centaur, in the same lobby and corridors. 'I have to,' he says. 'This is the best job I ever had.' But he could not manage to go to work on 12 March until 1998. That, he felt, was the biggest step he had taken.

Suryakant's neighbour at the Gulmohar Society, a row of

single-storeyed tenements behind the Tata Power Station at Magathane, Borivli, and his colleague in the housekeeping department at the Centaur is Sukhdev Laxman Zende, forty-eight. On the afternoon of 12 March 1993, he was on the first floor of the hotel, discussing the blasts that had ripped through southern Bombay, when he heard a loud noise from the end of the corridor and saw thick black smoke.

'The noise was unlike any other I had ever heard,' says Zende. He scrambled towards the exit, like hundreds of others streaming out of the hotel, ignoring the searing pain in his ear. It was only after he saw the patches of blood on his pillow the following morning that he realized something was amiss. A visit to the doctor confirmed that his eardrum had been ruptured by the blast. The blast turned Zende into a pill-popping high-blood pressure patient. He has been visiting the doctor nearly every week since then. Loud noises terrify him and he spends every Diwali indoors.

There's no time to cry in Ashalata Phatak's one-room first-floor tenement in the Kranti Sadan chawl in Prabhadevi, central Bombay. Losing her husband Prakash Phatak in the blasts seems almost as long ago as her wedding, twenty-five years ago. This frail and diminutive forty-year-old is too busy grappling with the more immediate problems of educating and fending for her three children: Sarita (twenty-two), Santosh (nineteen) and Sandesh (seventeen).

On 12 March 1993, Ashalata had just gone to sleep after lunch. Prakash was away at work in the Saraswat Bank near the passport office at Worli, where he had been a peon for twenty years. She remembers waking up with a start at around 2.30 p.m. after hearing a loud noise which shook the entire building. She rushed out to the gallery of her house where dozens of residents had gathered to see what had happened. Thick black smoke billowed skywards from the direction of Dadar. Ten minutes later, there was another sound from the opposite direction, from Worli. As she was to find out later, this was the blast that killed Prakash as he was going to a nearby restaurant for lunch. She began worrying about Prakash, but friends advised her not to leave the house.

She huddled at home with her children, waiting for news. This was to come only on the following morning when she got a call from the KEM Hospital at Parel. 'I could identify him only from his clothes. The rest of his body was covered by deep wounds and was burned black, almost like it had been roasted in a fire.'

Ashalata didn't know how it happened and didn't bother to find out. After the seemingly endless days spent grieving over his death, she started lobbying for her husband's job at the bank to support her children. 'I discovered there was no use crying. It doesn't help for very long. And then there were the children to look after,' she says resolutely. She got the job with help from the bank union after a year of wrangling. She now works as a peon in the Dadar branch.

'Why my husband? What wrong had he done?' she asks plaintively, echoing the feelings of hundreds of families across the city. 'So many buildings destroyed, so many people killed. The people who did this will never rest in peace.'

Radheshayam Potdar, a cloth merchant in Bombay's densely populated Kalbadevi business district, was at his shop that afternoon when news of the blasts reached him. Shutters were downed within minutes and the market cleared out. Potdar himself reached home at around 4 p.m.

A little while later there was a phone call. His second son, twenty-one-year-old Prashant, had been injured. Radheshayam was asked to come to GT Hospital. The police had got the phone number through a railway pass they found on Prashant. 'I reached there nearly an hour later. There were scores of bodies piled there, my son's amongst them.'

Prashant was studying to become a chartered accountant like his elder brother Pradeep and had been working with a firm of accountants in Flora Fountain for three years. He and seven friends had gone for lunch near the BSE that afternoon. All of them were injured, two died.

The Potdar family is still trying to cope with the loss of the bright and cricket-crazy Prashant. On 12 March each year they perform the ritual of feeding five Brahmins.

The thought of revenge has long left Radheshayam, though he thinks he would have been able to give the trial judge quite an earful. The patriarch believes the policies of political parties and the demolition of the Babri Masjid were directly responsible for the bomb blasts. As for punishing the accused, that seems so far away. 'Even the murderers of Rajiv Gandhi are yet to be punished eight years after they killed him,' he says. 'And Prashant was just an ordinary person.'

It was a quirk of fate that brought Shakuntala and Tukaram Sorte to the Air-India building that Friday. They were to meet Ashok Chaturvedi, an old family friend who always met up with them when he was in Bombay.

When the bomb exploded, all three were seriously injured, and Chaturvedi died soon after. Some time later, a passer-by, Clifford, who worked for the Oberoi hotel adjacent to the Air-India building, was asked by the driver of an Ambassador where he should take the injured couple dumped in his car by some anxious members of the public. Clifford hopped in and directed him to the Bombay Hospital.

He helped to get Shakuntala and Tukaram admitted and

stayed on to take his home phone numbers from Tukaram. The couple was admitted in separate wards so neither knew about the other's condition.

Their daughter Namrata, twenty, heard about a bomb blast at VT around 4 p.m. Namrata went to a neighbour's house to call her mother's office to check that she had not been anywhere near VT at that time as she knew about the lunch appointment with Chaturvedi. Shakuntala Sorte was the head clerk in the government salt department. Her office was at Ballard Pier. Namrata was told that her mother had not come back. She left a message, asking her mother to call her back.

The phone rang again only between 5.30 and 6 p.m. It was Clifford. 'He told me that my father had been injured in the bomb explosion and was at the Bombay Hospital ... I thought he must have just got hurt while passing by, a few bruises ...' Her neighbours rushed to the hospital, but told her and her two teenaged siblings to stay behind. At 8 p.m., they called to say that her mother had also been injured. 'I did not worry too much. Aai and Baba were together, so he would take care of her. He was very capable and efficient.' Fifty-seven-year-old Tukaram Sorte worked for the BMC.

When Namrata went to the hospital the following morning, her father had died. She could not meet her mother either. 'I was afraid to meet her. I didn't want to tell her about Baba.'

Shakuntala kept asking the nurse in her ward about her husband. On the night of 14 March, the day her husband was cremated, she dreamt of him. 'He came in my dream and told me that they had cremated him and wanted to know whether I was planning to stay back or go with him,' she told the nurse accusingly for they had not told her of his death. She feared that she too would not survive, and handed over all the jewellery she was wearing—she had dressed in her best for the luncheon—to the nurse, requesting that it be given to Namrata. After that she lapsed into unconsciousness.

On 15 March, Namrata finally decided to visit her mother. It was her parents' wedding anniversary, and her sister Yogeeta's nineteenth birthday. 'I was shocked to see the state she was in. In the ICU, I passed by her but didn't recognize her. Her scarred, swollen face seemed familiar. Her eyes were closed and there were small tubes running through her mouth. The nurse asked me if I wanted the tubes removed so that she could speak to me. I thought that would disturb her. Later I wished I had grabbed that last chance.'

Outside the ICU, she met Clifford. As they were speaking, her mother died. But her aunt and uncle did not tell her. The following morning, she wanted to see her mother again. Her aunt forced her to eat breakfast and they drove to the hospital. It was only when they were in the hospital that she realized what had happened.

She had to tell her brother Vinod and sister Yogeeta. Yogeeta, the youngest and her mother's pet, took it very badly. Later she attempted suicide several times.

Yogeeta is still trying to come to terms with the tragedy. She taught for a while in a college, and is now doing computer courses. Namrata works with her father's old employers, the BMC, and has married a childhood friend. She hopes to have a baby soon. Vinod got his mother's job in the salt department. He too is married, and has a baby. They are still in touch with Clifford, who always comes over on 12 March.

Shyam Sundar Shroff of the RBI was well known in certain circles because he had busted a soiled notes recycling racket in Bangalore in 1992, which involved crores of rupees and the patronage of the political masters of Karnataka at the time. As a result, there was even an attempt on his life. After he was stabbed, the newspapers publicized his story, and many praised his work, including the Governor of Karnataka. As reward, his request for a transfer to Bombay was granted.

On 12 March, he was asked by an officer to do an unscheduled inspection at the Bank of Oman at the Air-India building. That was his last assignment.

For his widow Savithri, his death was only the beginning of a nightmare. The RBI had told her that she could retain their huge RBI flat for another seven years. However, she then turned down an RBI job as a clerk. She was a teacher at the Sacred Heart High School, Worli, and loved children and teaching. The RBI asked her to move out of the flat. She had to share a small chawl with a friend who offered her space. Her possessions were all locked away in a godown. One son, a student at Stanford University, had to discontinue his studies because there was no money. Another son was studying marine engineering in Calcutta. Finally, she packed her bags and moved to Calcutta to be with him.

Epilogue

The mammoth trial in the serial blasts case, which started on 30 June 1995, still drones on.

The CBI formally closed its case in 2001 after examining 684 witnesses. The last witness to depose was the chief investigating officer, CBI's O.P. Chatwal. The document transcribing the evidence runs into over 13,000 pages, in answer to 38,070 questions put to the accused. There are an additional 2,500 documents produced as exhibits.

The defence closed its case on 9 August 2002. After the prosecution rebuttal, it will be time for the verdict. It is believed that this will be in late 2002 or early 2003.

When the trial had started, there had been 195 charge sheeted, of whom forty-four were then absconding. Today there are 124 accused, of whom thirty-four are still in custody, while the rest, including Sanjay Dutt, are on bail. Tiger Memon, his brother Ayub, and their wives are among those who are still absconding. Abu Asim Azmi and Amjad Mehr Baksh were discharged by the Supreme Court while co-accused Riaz Khatri jumped bail. Judge Patel had discharged twenty-six of the accused, who had been charged for unloading the RDX, due to lack of evidence. Judge Kode, who took over the trial in 1996, discharged Syed Javed Hussain. Two others, Hamid Dafedar and Harba Hari Khopatkar, passed away. Seven accused—Salim Kurla, Majeed Khan, Shakil

Ahmed, Mohammed Jindran, Hanif Kadawala, Akbar Abu Sama Khan, Mohammed Latif—were killed either by rival gangsters or in police encounters. Two of the accused—Badshah Khan and Mohammed Umar Khatlab—turned approvers. They stepped into the witness box in June 1995 and unfolded the prosecution story that Dawood Ibrahim and Tiger Memon had masterminded the blasts in the aftermath of the demolition of the mosque in Ayodhya.

Of the investigating officers in the case, Samra retired as DG, Maharashtra police; M.N. Singh is now the Bombay police commissioner, and Maria was promoted to DIG, and is currently the commissioner of railway police. Judge J.N. Patel became a High Court judge and was transferred to Nagpur in 1996.

Sanjay Dutt has gone on to do many successful roles in Bollywood. In December 2001, at a TADA court hearing, he disowned the confessional statement made by him to the police while he was in custody, and said he was forced to sign a document following an assurance given by them. He has denied that he ever owned an AK-56.

Dawood Ibrahim now lives in Karachi, where he has a palatial house spread over 6,000 square yards, with a pool, tennis courts, a snooker room and a gym with the most sophisticated equipment. He wears designer clothes and a Rs 50-lakh Patek Phillipe wristwatch, drives a top-of-the-line Mercedes and luxurious four-wheel drives, and showers money on his many women. He does not shirk his obligations: a former Bollywood actress, with whom he had a child, is reportedly still being supported by him.

His daily regimen is kingly: his day begins in the afternoon with a swim and leisurely breakfast after which he gives his employees an audience. There may be cricket or snooker later;

the evening is for drinks, mujras and gambling. He and his men have made huge investments in property, and are major players on the bourse and hundi, the parallel credit system. His other businesses include smuggling gold and drugs and allegedly match-fixing. Businessmen approach him to settle disputes. His connection with the blasts was never actually proved.

Tiger Memon too today lives in Karachi. But, according to Usman Majid, formerly of the Jammu and Kashmir Students Liberation Front, he is no longer happy there. Usman met Tiger in Muzaffarabad, in Pakistan-occupied Kashmir, when he was working for the Ikhwan-ul-Muslimeen, to raise funds. He first met Tiger in late 1993. At the end of that year, to counteract the growing pressure on Pakistan to send him back to India, Tiger allegedly returned to Muzaffarabad to videotape a mock press conference to prove that he was still in India. Usman became close to Tiger, who told him stories of his lavish house in Karachi, the Rs 1.5 crore he had received to start a business, and the three cars he owned, including a Toyota. However, after his brother Yaqub returned to India, the ISI believed that Tiger had a hand in facilitating Yaqub's return. As a result, his cars were withdrawn and his cash inflow stopped. He tried to move to Peshawar and Dubai, but security concerns compelled him to return to Pakistan where, according to Usman, he is today a slave of the ISI. Usman believes that Tiger's decision to carry the serial bombings was impulsive, and that he did not realize that he would spend the rest of his life a hunted man.

The last time Usman met Tiger was in January 1995. Tiger was back in business by then, but Usman sensed that he was unhappy with the way things had gone. He was then negotiating to set up the Jammu and Kashmir Islamic Front (JKIF). He was to provide the JKIF with safehouses and guides in Nepal and Gujarat through his network, enabling them to operate securely northern and western India. However, this plan did not work out.

Usman also adds that when the initial plan to bomb Bombay was formulated, it was suggested that seven other cities—including New Delhi, Calcutta, Bangalore, Chennai and Ahmedabad—be bombed as well. However, due to logistical problems, this did not work out.

Sources

This is a work of non-fiction based on four years of research and investigation. Nowhere have the facts been tampered with. Some of the dialogues have been restructured and the precise sequence of events reconstructed, but nowhere do they deviate from recorded fact. I have briefly outlined the principal sources below.

The primary sources of information are the chargesheet filed in court by the Bombay police, the supplementary chargesheets filed by the CBI, the records of court proceedings in the case, the confessional statements of the accused, and the many FIRs filed in the case. I have read the confessional statements of all 145 of the accused, though some have been more useful than others.

I have also made extensive use of newspaper and magazine reports covering the blasts and their aftermath, especially the *Times of India*, the *Indian Express*, *Mid-day*, the *Afternoon Despatch & Courier*, the Gujarati newspaper *Janmabhoomi*, and the weeklies *India Today* and *Sunday*. Also, I have been a crime reporter for several years, and there is much information that I have gathered over the years while covering stories about the Bombay underworld.

Other important texts I referred to were the report of the Srikrishna Commission, constituted to look into the riots in Bombay in 1992-93, and the booklet *Voices* issued by the All India Milli Council.

The details of most of the incidents have been collected from the confessional statements of the accused, or information recorded during their depositions in the court. This relates to all the matter attributed to Badshah Khan, Hanif Kadawala, Nasir Dhakla, Asgar Mukadam, Firoz Malik, Sultan-e-Room, Dawood Phanse and the other landing agents, Baba Chauhan, Samir Hingora, Hanif Kadawala, Sanjay Dutt, Jalees Ansari, Salim Kurla, Mechanic Chacha, Usman Gani Memon and Yusuf Nulwala. In the case of Badshah Khan, there were also long and intensive interviews with him. Some of the accused however later retracted their statements. The information on the landings was gathered from the statements of the landing agents Dawood Phanse, Dadabhai Parkar, Raju Kodi and others who were involved in the smuggling activities of Tiger Memon.

It was widely reported in the media and by certain NGOs that the police had unleashed brutalities on those detained under TADA, as well as their relatives. Affidavits were filed in this regard. I have mentioned only those episodes for which there is documentary evidence. The experiences of the people arrested are gathered from the affidavits they filed in court and from newspaper reports. Khurana's story has been verified by his former cell-mates.

The story of the Memons was difficult to reconstruct as there were no confessions and they were unwilling to talk to the press. The background information on Tiger Memon was gathered from the police chargesheet, the supplementary chargesheets, CBI dossiers on him, confessional statements, and interviews with his relatives and friends who want to remain anonymous. The information on the meeting in Dubai was gathered from various confessional statements, and interviews with customs officer Farooq Batatawala and some police informers. At least one person who was present at the meeting spoke to me on the condition of anonymity. The report of the conversation with Aziz Ahmed came from Ahmed himself. I have used three sources of information to reconstruct Yaqub Memon's story. The first was the CBI report. The second was his statements in a Delhi court, on the Doordarshan interview *Newstrack*, and his few statements to newspapers and magazines. The third was the information given by his lawyer Majeed Memon and some CBI officials.

The information on Dawood Ibrahim comes from police and CBI dossiers on him, as well as interviews with a close confidant and others who have worked with him. The information on Dawood's background and criminal record was gathered from CBI dossiers, police records, various FIRs filed against him and his associates, and court documents. The sources for the conversation between Dawood Ibrahim and Chhota Shakeel in Dubai are interviews with CBI officers, some of Dawood Ibrahim's aides and some of the accused who do not want to be identified. The information about his willingness to surrender comes from interviews with Mahesh Jethmalani, A.S. Samra and some of Dawood's aides.

My main source of information about Sanjay Dutt was his own confessional statement. This has been reinforced by information from the statements of some of the other accused, like Hanif Kadawala and Samir Hingora, as well as CBI documents. I have also used material from newspapers and magazines covering his story, and information from an interview with Sunil Dutt.

Thapa's story is culled from CBI documents, and from interviews with Ulhas Joshi, Raman Tyagi and Thapa himself.

The details of the police investigations into the case were reconstructed after prolonged discussions with the officers involved with the case, including A.S. Samra, Y.C. Pawar, Rakesh Maria, Arup Patnaik, Bhaskar Dangle, Nand Kumar Chougule, Ulhas

Joshi and Srirang Nadgouda, among others. I have tried to verify each detail with at least two officers. Several officers of junior rank also spoke to me on the condition of anonymity. I have also heavily relied on the police records, and the dossiers prepared by the CBI. The details of the customs operations came from customs records and interviews with various officers.

The police officers were also of help in reconstructing the events of 12 March 1993. The former chief of the fire department, Durgadas Kulkarni, the head of the BDDS, Chougule, and paramedics at various hospitals also gave me valuable information, as did some stockbrokers who were trapped in the BSE after the blast.

The late Rajesh Pilot gave me time to discuss the political ramifications of the case.

With regard to details of legal proceedings, I was helped by the presiding judge Pramod Kode, and advocates Niteen Pradhan, Abbas Kazmi, Majeed Memon and Farhana Shah. I was also assisted by members of the CBI STF, especially Raman Tyagi, and media reports, especially those by Sunil Shivdasani of the Press Trust of India, Shubha Sharma of *Mid-day* and Pranati Mehta of the *Indian Express*. Former additional collector of customs, S.N. Thapa, helped me to understand several details of the story.

For the different theories regarding Yaqub Memon's return, my information came from interviews with lawyers Shyam Keswani and Majeed Memon, CBI and police officers, and customs officer Farooq Batatawala.

The information on the explosives recovered from Tiger Memon's compound and the hand grenades, as well as on Wah Explosives and on Ulbrichts Austria and Pakistan comes from CBI dossiers, the supplementary chargesheet filed by the CBI and the document sent by the Federal Ministry of Austria to the Indian government which has been cited in the text.

The information about the Pakistani passports and Thai visas of the Memons was taken from the supplementary chargesheet filed by the CBI and other CBI documents.

The stories of the victims and their families were garnered from newspaper reports and interviews by Sandeep Unnithan of *India Today* and Velly Thevar.

Appendix

The Srikrishna Commission

The Srikrishna Commission, headed by Justice B.N. Srikrishna, was set up in 1993 to look into the riots in Bombay in December 1992 and January 1993. Its brief was to identify the people responsible and also to look into the role of the police during this period. Later this was expanded to look into the possible connections between the riots and the serial blasts of 12 March 1993. The Commission delivered its report on 16 February 1998.

One significant part of the Commission's report dealt with the failure of the police to control the riot and the role played by some policemen in actively participating in the riots or using excessive force. On the subject of the link between the riots and the bomb blasts, the Commission concluded that 'the former appear to have been a causative factor for the latter'. Three or four of the accused who were involved in substantive riot-related offences were also accused in the bomb blasts case. Tiger Memon and Javed Chikna had both suffered during the riots, and therefore would have had a motive for revenge. However, the Commission also stated that there was no material placed before it that suggested that the riots and the serial blasts were part of a common design. Their conclusion was that the bomb blasts were a reaction to the totality of events at Ayodhya and Bombay in December 1992 and January 1993.

TADA

The Terrorist and Disruptive Activities (Prevention) Act came into force on 23 May 1985. It gave sweeping powers to law enforcement machinery to deal with 'terrorist' and 'disruptive activities'. The most important features of the law were wide definition of terrorist and disruptive activities with enhanced punishments and separate trial procedures through designated courts. TADA also altered the normal criminal trial procedure in many ways. The police were not obliged to produce a detainee before a judicial magistrate within twenty-four hours, and the accused could be remanded up to one year in police custody (whereas otherwise the maximum is ninety days). Confessions made to police officers was admissible in court as evidence and the onus of proof was on the accused, and trials could be held in camera with the identity of witnesses being kept secret. TADA had to be extended every two years by an act of Parliament.

As of 30 June 1994, the number of people arrested under TADA had crossed 76,000. The police dropped twenty-five per cent of these cases without any charges being framed. Trials were completed in thirty-five per cent of the cases that were actually brought to trial, of which ninety-five per cent of the trials ended in acquittals. Thus, less than two per cent of those arrested were ultimately convicted.

There were complaints from various concerned groups, human rights organizations and political parties regarding the alleged abuses and ineffectiveness of TADA, and it was allowed to lapse in 1997.